THE PUNK ROCK OF BUSINESS

APPLYING A <u>PUNK ROCK ATTITUDE</u>

IN THE MODERN BUSINESS ERA

JEREMY DALE

GREENLEAF
BOOK GROUP PRESS

Published by Greenleaf Book Group Press
Austin, Texas
www.gbgpress.com

Distributed by Greenleaf Book Group

For ordering information or special discounts for bulk purchases, please contact Greenleaf Book Group at PO Box 91869, Austin, TX 78709, 512.891.6100.

Design and composition by Greenleaf Book Group
Cover design by Benji Roebuck

Cataloging-in-Publication data is available.

Print ISBN: 978-1-62634-453-2

eBook ISBN: 978-1-62634-454-9

Part of the Tree Neutral® program, which offsets the number of trees consumed in the production and printing of this book by taking proactive steps, such as planting trees in direct proportion to the number of trees used: www.treeneutral.com

TreeNeutral®

Printed in the United States of America on acid-free paper

18 19 20 21 22 23   10 9 8 7 6 5 4 3 2 1

First Edition

To all those who have been with me on my journey so far, thank you for the experiences we enjoyed, the lessons you taught me, and—most of all—the friendship we have shared.

To my family, Gerry, Alex, Maddie, and Francesca, thank you for your support, your love, and keeping me grounded—you mean the world to me.

———

This book is also dedicated to Andy Biddle. "Bids" was the best friend anyone could ever wish for. So many memories, so many laughs, so very special, so badly missed. Love you, Bids.

CONTENTS

FOREWORD

For far too long, companies have been hamstrung by endless meetings, bureaucratic processes, and corporate politics. Like the music scene of the 1970s, when punk rock burst onto the scene and pressed the reset button, many businesses today need the same dose of punk attitude.

What we need today is some pure, stripped down, no bullshit business leadership. *The Punk Rock of Business* is about adopting an attitude that echoes many of the attributes of punk.

The punk rock businessperson says, "I am not okay with the current status quo," and vows to do something about it. "I detest mediocrity, as I want to do amazing things. I loathe playing things safe, because it's dull and there is no such thing as job security anymore." *The Punk Rock of Business* is a call to arms for businesspeople who despise the constraining bullshit that is far too prevalent in the business world. Applying a punk rock attitude in business is for those who want to make a difference, who love to dare greatly, who strive for excellence—characteristics that are far too rare.

This is a change that is long overdue in many organizations.

Welcome to the revolution!

ACKNOWLEDGMENTS

I have been privileged to work at many great companies; thank you for the opportunity.

I have been fortunate to work alongside many amazing people at those companies or in our business partners; thank you for all that I learned from you and the success we shared.

I have been blessed to share my working life with people who became firm friends, where a laugh and a smile were never far away; thank you for the experiences we shared and the bond that will forever exist.

—

To all those who contributed to creating the stories in this book, thank you for your inspiration. I have documented these stories as faithfully as I remember them, and I've checked my recollection with others, but forgive me if some minor details differ from yours.

Thank you to the team at Greenleaf for your patience and humanity as you navigated me through my first book.

INTRODUCTION

I n 2006 Motorola joined the Product (RED) campaign. Bono and Bobby Shriver (the nephew of John F. Kennedy) had founded (RED) with a simple mission—to make it easy for people and businesses to join the fight against the deadly AIDS virus. Companies would make (RED) versions of their products, and consumers would choose to buy them because a portion of the profits would go to help eliminate AIDS in Africa. As Motorola's Retail Global Marketing leader, I was leading the (RED) initiative for Motorola.

The (RED) campaign was to be launched in Chicago on *The Oprah Winfrey Show*. Bono was to explain the concept to Oprah on air, and then the two of them would go shopping down the Magnificent Mile of North Michigan Avenue. They would buy a (RED) watch in the Armani store, (RED) clothes in the Gap store, and then they'd close their trip by buying a (RED) RAZR phone from Motorola.

Twelve days before the show my phone rang. It was Motorola's Chairman and CEO, Ed Zander. "I've just had Bono on the phone, Jeremy. He told me all about the PR launch plans and the Oprah show."

"Yes, it's really cool, Ed. It'll be great," I assured him.

"But Jeremy, where are they going to buy our phone from? Because we don't have our own stores," he pressed.

"Don't worry, Ed," I said reassuringly, "The Gap has given us some space in their store, and we're building a shop-in-shop. It will look just like we're in our own store on television."

"That's not good enough! We need our own store!" he barked.

"I know, Ed. It would be great if we had a store, but we don't have one yet."

"Well, we need to get one," Ed demanded.

"I know, Ed. But the show is in twelve days' time, and it takes twelve months to build a store, so this is all I can give you."

At that time, we were actively working on a plan to build a Motorola retail store in Chicago. We had been on it for about three months trying to find a suitable location, with the prospect of us opening one in about nine months. I am sure Ed knew of this concept and the sort of timescale we were talking about, so I was stunned by the absurdity of his demand.

"Well that's not good enough! You're going to build me a store." <Click>. Ed hung up on me.

I rushed around to Ron Garriques' office (Ron was President of the Mobile Phone business and worked directly for Ed) to try to get him to talk some sense into Ed. Ron headed up the mobile devices business. He was on the phone and shooed me out of his office doorway. A couple of minutes later he called me in.

"I've just had Ed on the phone, Ron," I started.

"I know, that was him."

"Good, did you tell him?" I asked hopefully, meaning *Ron did you tell him he is insane and there is no way on this planet he can have a store in twelve days?*

"Yes, I told him."

"Good," I said, relieved.

"I told him you would build him a store," Ron clarified the matter.

"Ron, I can't build a store in twelve days," I pleaded.

No response.

"Ron, I can't build a store in twelve days. Ron, it's impossible! Ron?"

No answer. Ron was back typing away on his PC. He looked up and said in a very perplexed tone, "Are you still here? Haven't you got a store to build?"

———

So, I found Guto Andrade (my head designer) and quickly explained to him my sudden predicament. Minutes later, we were driving down North Michigan Avenue looking for an empty storefront. On the best and busiest shopping street in America's Midwest, they just don't exist. I would rather have been looking for a unicorn or the abominable snowman.

As expected, there were no empty stores—nor unicorns nor abominable snowmen, for that matter. We did, however, find a museum, opposite the Nike and Apple stores and just down the road from the Gap store, that was closed for refurbishment. After a few hasty phone calls, we found out that the refurbishment work was limited to the second and third floors, and the street level floor was not affected. We managed to secure a temporary lease of the ground floor for the next four months so that we could build a pop-up store for the duration of the key holiday selling season.

Somehow, miracle of miracles, we now had a location. But how were we going to turn a museum lobby into a retail store in twelve days?

This is where Guto's genius came in. The (RED) logo is a pair of parentheses. Guto's idea was to build false walls by stretching printed cloth over a curved wooden frame, so the walls would literally mirror the shape of the logo. With these curved walls, the concept was that people entering the store would literally be walking into the brand.

Suddenly there was an air of excitement, a glimpse that the impossible could actually be possible. But the question now was: How do we make this space great? How could we use it to inspire Chicagoans to act in the fight against AIDS? In the following few hours, my team came up with great idea after great idea.

Most tellingly, the entrance needed to explain the extent of the grim reality of the AIDS crisis, the magnitude of which I had been blissfully unaware of until two months earlier. The entrance would be a plain red background displaying nothing more than the statistics telling the horrific story of the pandemic unfolding in Africa. One read, "Every day in Africa 5,500 people die from a preventable treatable disease." That was the equivalent of two 9/11s every single day. We all know how traumatizing that day was for us, witnessing that loss of life. Well, the equivalent of two of those tragedies was happening every single day in Africa, and we were oblivious to it. Another read, "Today in Africa 1,200 babies will be born with HIV." Every single day over one thousand babies' lives were destined to be cut short before they were even born. The entranceway stated the problem in cold hard facts.

Once inside the store we would unveil how we all could be part of the solution.

We created a glass underfloor space where we would display all (RED) products from all (RED) partners. Beautiful images of Africa were hung on the canvas walls together with an explanation of the (RED) concept. We created a hall-of-fame wall where we would celebrate those who joined our cause, and people who bought a (RED) product would be asked to sign their name.

Workers started appearing, and building work was soon under way. Eleven days later, on the evening before the show, I walked into the store and was blown away by the transformation and the beauty of the space. In the store was Kanye West. He was going to be the store sales representative who would sell the RAZR phones to Bono and Oprah the next day, and my team was busy briefing him on the product. But I hardly noticed Kanye (I know that sounds insane, but it is true). I was mesmerized by the transformation of this museum lobby into not just a retail store but a work of art that told a story that needed telling. Where had all these pieces of furniture been manufactured? How did they get produced? Who did all this? It was incomprehensible how this had been achieved in such a short span of time. I was feeling a mixture of pride in my team, confusion at how it could be so, and a sense that a little bit of magic dust must have been sprinkled by someone. As I have often found in my career, there is that special power in the universe that makes all things work together for good. Crazy ideas do cause crazy coincidences.

I couldn't wait to see people's reaction the following day. It was going to blow their minds. I hadn't shown anyone the store, I hadn't even shown anyone the designs (I think they were nothing more than hand-drawn scribbles anyway), and I don't think anyone had even told Bobby or Bono of our change of plan, mostly because we hadn't been sure we could pull it off.

Filming started around eight a.m. the next day in Oprah's studio. About an hour and a half later, Oprah, Bono, and their entourage arrived at Motorola's brand new store—their very last stop having already purchased a (RED) Armani watch and a collection of (RED) t-shirts—and they bought ten phones from Kanye to give to their friends. Filming stopped, and everyone buzzed around excitedly on the shop floor—a space that hadn't even been an idea two weeks earlier. When Bono saw me from across the store, he hurried over, hugged me, and whispered in my ear, "twelve *******
days, twelve ******* days." That was all he said—and it was all I needed to hear.

Over the next four months, the store attracted tens of thousands of visitors, and we sold thousands of phones. Remarkably (and a great testimony to Guto and his team), it was nominated for and won several North American Retail Store of the Year awards. Unbelievable.

At the end of a very long day and an even longer week, I arrived home, and my wife Gerry, who had been at the filming of the Oprah show and seen it all unfold, was buzzing. It had been a very special day for everyone. She said, "I assume you heard what Bono said about you on *Oprah*?"

"What are you on about? What did he say?"

She was surprised I hadn't heard, but all our people had been in the store, so we had no idea what had gone on in the studio.

She said, "Oprah asked him why they were launching in Chicago and he said something like, 'Because it's the home of Motorola. We love all our partners, but Motorola are special; they put on concerts in Trafalgar Square in weeks and they've built a (RED) store in just twelve days. They are the punk rock of business: no long introductions, three beats and you're in. They say they are going to do something, and then it just gets done.'"[1]

I liked that, *The Punk Rock of Business*. Hence the title for this book.

THE ESSENCE OF THE STORY

This story tells the origin of the phrase *The Punk Rock of Business*, but in many ways, it also contextualizes the whole book and is a great example of Punk Rock Business put into practice. That experience was a defining moment in my career. I'd already embraced many of the elements of punk rock attitude in my work life, but this experience unveiled for me the full power of that attitude and the thrill of living like that. A little bit like taking the red pill in the movie *The Matrix*. In that movie, Morpheus says, "You take the red pill, you stay in Wonderland, and I show you how deep the rabbit hole goes." I had experienced wonderland and wanted to go deeper, and I was never the same again.

The specific lessons I took away from those fraught, grueling, anxious but magical twelve days were:

- Don't settle: Good enough is never good enough. Guto and the design team wanted to deliver excellence. They didn't start with the constraint

---

1 Bono, statement made during filming of *The Oprah Winfrey Show* (October 13, 2006), not in final cut of the show.

of time in mind; they started with what they were excited to deliver and then explored possible ways to overcome the time problem.

- When you expect great efforts, you need to call upon the power of a compelling vision. There were many workers involved, who slaved away around the clock to deliver this showcase experience of (RED). They understood the concept and were inspired by the idea and realized how their work would help change people's lives.

- Anything is possible. Thank you, Ed and Ron, for your utter unreasonableness. If either of you had shown any common sense or understanding, we wouldn't have achieved or learned what we did.

So, how often do we settle for adequate because we don't push talented teams to reach for the stars and trust in the power of human ingenuity to overcome problems that may arise? Do we know the full potential of our teams? Do we push them to achieve excellence, strive for greatness, and be the best they can be?

I accepted so much of the credit for the amazing store that took just twelve days to move from idea to reality, yet I was only part of the team. Ed had the idea, Ron ordered me to do it, Guto and his team created a beautiful store design, and the workers labored valiantly, spurred on by Bono's vision for (RED). I have asked myself what contribution did I make? I think my contribution was that, after my initial five minutes of objection, I was open-minded enough to drive to Chicago to look for something that we knew didn't exist, and then Guto and I inspired the team to explore our ability to deliver the impossible. I could have walked out of Ron's office with a mentality of "let me get the facts to prove to him why you just cannot do this sort of thing in twelve days." But while I did walk out thinking Ed and Ron were insane and didn't understand this type of stuff, I allowed myself to explore the impossibility of the instructions, and when we saw the crack of an opportunity that the museum represented, we seized upon it with childlike enthusiasm. Our team already had a kind of never-say-never attitude and a fearlessness to give anything a go. We had a naïveté and enthusiasm for trying anything, as long as it would deliver something remarkable.

I concluded there and then that I will forever believe in the impossible,

(continued)

> go for it, and trust in the power of human ingenuity to overcome the challenges that inevitably arise.
>
> Punk Rock Business became my shorthand for this attitude.

Intimately Know Who You Are

If the Product (RED) story created the concept of Punk Rock Business, this next story is essential for understanding how it guided my career.

As I just wrote at the end of the previous story, I decided to forever believe in the impossible, go for it, and trust in the power of human ingenuity to overcome the challenges that inevitably arise. I committed to embracing this punk attitude, and it became a core part of who I was and how I operated. This was crystallized for me in 2015.

Pete Carroll joined the NFL's Seattle Seahawks as Head Coach in 2010, and he began to ingrain his philosophy into the players from day one. Shortly afterward, he was introduced to Dr. Michael Gervais,[2] a leading sports psychologist who is fascinated by the psychology of high performance. Mike was working with a bunch of amazing people (including Olympians, NBA players, pro-golfers, and world record holders from the world of extreme sports) helping them to uncover the many paths towards what Mike calls "Finding Mastery." As the story goes, Pete and Mike clicked, and Mike joined the Seahawks soon after. In subsequent years, it was clear that the culture Pete and Mike were building with the Seahawks and the

---

2 Dr. Michael Gervais is the co-founder of Compete to Create, a licensed psychologist, and an industry visionary. Dr. Gervais focuses most of his time on people at the top of their game, from the NFL's Seattle Seahawks and NBA players, to Olympians, extreme athletes, and corporate leaders. Spending years in the trenches of high-stakes circumstances, Gervais has developed clarity for the tools that allow people to thrive under pressure. Gervais is a published, peer-reviewed author, and a nationally recognized speaker on issues related to high performance for those who excel on the largest stages in the world. Visit www.findingmastery.net for more information about Mike.

team's mental strength were having a huge impact on team performance. In 2013, the Seattle Seahawks won the Super Bowl with a group of players who had a unique and powerful team spirit. They reached the Super Bowl the following year as well.

One day in 2014 Pete said to Mike, "I think we are onto something here, do you think anyone outside of sports would be interested?" So they went and met with some of the local companies, including Boeing and Microsoft. Satya Nadella, our CEO at Microsoft, was very interested in developing a growth mindset culture and began to involve Mike with our company at the most senior level. Indeed, in Satya's book *Hit Refresh: The Quest to Rediscover Microsoft's Soul and Imagine a Better Future for Everyone* (New York: HarperBusiness, 2017), he mentions Mike's engagement with his senior leadership team in the first few pages. It wasn't long before word of the impact of the training sessions with Mike reached me; everyone was speaking about them with such glowing praise, so I arranged for Mike to spend the first of many days working with my team at my house in late 2015.

Mike fundamentally believes in the power of a personal philosophy, and our pre-work was to build out our own. We were told to write our personal philosophies in twenty-five words or less.

Mike told us that a personal philosophy is a statement of our most basic beliefs, values, and guiding principles that impacts our thoughts and actions. In essence, our philosophy governs the daily choices that we make and how we come to those decisions.

He told us that it takes time to craft and clearly articulate a personal philosophy and that our philosophy will grow and evolve as we grow and evolve.

To stimulate our thinking, he suggested we look at other personal philosophies from people we admired, but remain true to who we were. Once we had a draft of our philosophy, we were to share it with others who were close to us: our family, friends, and trusted work colleagues. We were to refine it by listening to how it sounded as we articulated it out loud and by taking feedback from those we shared it with and who knew us well. This undoubtedly produced greater clarity, and I was amazed at the insights brought by my colleagues. I understood what they valued in me.

The evening before our training session, I met Mike for dinner. I wanted to brief him on our group and explain some of the things I wanted to achieve the following day. Mike asked me to recite my personal philosophy. I knew it by heart, so I rolled it off . . . "Be authentic, act justly, care deeply—believe in the impossible by embracing punk rock attitudes—make the most of every day, surrounded by great people, loving life's game."

Mike asked about the punk rock phrase, and I told him the story that I recounted a few pages ago. Mike loved the story and asked more about that mindset, so I gave him some other examples from my career. As I was leaving, Mike told me he would analyze my philosophy tomorrow during the training, but he needed me to make it shorter, crisper—it was too long.

So the next day when I was asked to recite my philosophy, I recited it as follows . . . "Be authentic, act justly, care deeply—believe in the impossible, loving life's game."

Mike verbally came at me . . . "What happened to punk rock?"

"You told me to shorten it," I replied.

"I didn't tell you to take out the good bit," Mike fired back at me. "Why did you do that?"

"Well, I took it out because that bit . . . er . . . takes a bit of explaining."

"Bullshit. Everyone's philosophy has an understory that needs explaining. Why did you take it out?"

"Well, probably because it sounds a little weird."

"I don't buy it."

"Why?" I asked.

He explained, "Look—I listen for the passion in people's voice when they tell me their philosophy. That's how I know what really matters to them. Last night, punk was where your passion was, and now it's gone. Really?"

Mike was definitely not letting this go. This had been going on for about ten minutes now and was taking place in front of my team, which was fine, because we were close.

I then made an admission that was in my unconscious. "Well, I suppose I cut it because I am not sure that I am living up to it like I used to."

One of my team spoke up and said, "No, Jeremy is punk."

I had to admit, ". . . but not like I used to be."

Mike's face lit up; he had got to the heart of the issue. "So how do you feel about that?"

"Well, I feel that I am not being true to myself, and I need to be more punk. And I want these guys to hold me accountable to that."

"Good," Mike said. "Anything else?"

"Yes, I wonder whether I can be true to who I am at Microsoft. It was so much easier to be punk at Motorola—we didn't have the complexity of Microsoft's organizational matrix. At Microsoft, you need about four people to agree to any decision." It's much more collaborative, and you progress by getting consensus, which is fine, but I had toned down the punk in me as a result.

I continued, "I need to see if I can be more punk, and I'm going to give it a go, but I'll soon know if I can be true to who I am at Microsoft."

That was a deep and intense discussion. It wasn't one where I felt entirely comfortable throughout, but it was a vitally important one for me. I felt like my inner mind was being picked apart and analyzed by a psychologist. And then I realized that was exactly what had happened. I came away with a great sense of calm. I knew myself better, and I definitely knew what I had to do. In the months that followed, I did regain more of my punk, but I also knew my time at Microsoft needed to come to an end.

The beauty of the personal philosophy process is that you go on a journey of self-discovery. You start off alone and then bring in some close friends, family, and colleagues. If you are lucky, you get to share the philosophy with someone who can listen to the passion in your voice as much as your words and identify what you are really trying to say. They can help you refine your philosophy and "crisp it up," but it is you who needs to feel the hairs on the back of your neck stand on end as you say it. If it doesn't resonate emotionally, then you haven't nailed it yet.

I would argue vehemently now that you must have a personal philosophy. Others call it their personal brand, but whatever you call it, self-awareness is vital, and you have to know who you are and what you stand for and be able to articulate it crisply. It is for you, first and foremost, but if you share it, people understand you more and gain great benefit from their extra insight into you.

Now let me state clearly that the purpose of a philosophy is to help guide you through every day. I believe you can only be truly happy if you are being yourself and are true to who you are. So your personal philosophy should be in front of you every day reminding you exactly that—who you are and what you want to be.

KEY LESSONS

A personal philosophy brings clarity; it helps you understand who you are. When our actions in any and every environment are aligned with our principles and beliefs, we can be authentic to our true self. A personal philosophy that is in tune with your true self enables you to live a life of conviction. It encourages you to be the real you.

Everyone needs a personal philosophy. Have you got one? Can you recite it now? Many people have a bunch of principles they tend to follow, but for most people they're not written down. And if they're not written down, they don't direct your daily decision-making process as strongly as they should.

As Dr. Michael Gervais would say to us, there are only three things you can train: your body, your craft, and your mind. No one had ever tried to train my mind before. I am not sure I even knew you could. It was a revelation. Mike taught me more about myself and how to achieve mastery and high performance in my field than any other trainer, and he did that by focusing on the training of the mind. Invest time in this area—once you've finished this book!

SO WHAT ARE YOU GOING TO DO ABOUT IT?

Read this book, and then return here to write your personal philosophy. You need one. You really need to know who you are, and if you cannot recite one immediately, then you don't have one.

Once you have it, pin it on your wall, and use it to guide your life. That is who you say you truly are, and if you don't live up to it, then you aren't being who you want to be—so then you have to change what you are doing and stop being a fraud.

Ask your team to create their personal philosophies. Then share them with each other, and you will get a much deeper appreciation for who everyone is.

Use them to understand how to get the most out of your team members. Personal philosophies hold the most powerful insights for how to inspire your team to greatness.

So, What Is Punk Rock Business All About?

You've read how Bono coined the phrase "Punk Rock of Business," and you've seen how Mike helped me understand its importance to me. Now let me explain how it can be of value to you too.

Many businesses these days are clogged up by bureaucracy that thwarts innovation, slows down creativity, and encourages mediocrity. I hate mediocrity. I'd much rather have spectacular success or fantastic failure. I believe mediocrity occurs far too often because too many people in business, particularly those in middle-management roles, are far too cautious, pessimistic, and more concerned about protecting their jobs rather than striving for greatness and being everything they could be. They are fearful of putting their heads above the parapet, so they take a play-it-safe attitude and come up with the conservative, tame, and expected proposals. Too many businesses create an environment and a culture that encourages averageness and behavior that is destined to deliver results that, at best, can only ever be lukewarm. This is a huge problem as lukewarm is no good to anyone

I originally took *The Punk Rock of Business* to be only about the speed and bias to action that Bono had referenced . . . "three beats and you're in, no long introductions." But as I thought about the influences of punk, I realized how much more inspiration modern businesses and businesspeople could and should take from punk rock culture and a punk rock attitude. Let me explain.

The Ramones were key influencers in the American punk movement . . . Joey Ramone, the band's front man, once stated, "We decided to start our own group because we were bored with everything we heard. In 1974 everything was tenth-generation Led Zeppelin, tenth-generation Elton John, or overproduced, or just junk. Everything was long jams, long guitar solos . . . We missed music like it used to be."[3] Drummer Tommy Ramone slated rock music at that time; he said it was dominated by "endless solos that

3 Andrew J. Edelstein and Kevin McDonough, *The Seventies: From Hot Pants to Hot Tubs* (New York: Dutton, 1990), 178.

went nowhere. By 1973, I knew that what was needed was some pure, stripped down, no bullshit rock 'n' roll."[4]

This is the perfect expression for what many businesses need today. In today's market, everything is tenth-generation product versions, overprocessed, and just plain boring. For far too long, companies have been hamstrung by endless meetings that go nowhere. Like the music scene in 1973, what we need today is some pure, stripped down, no bullshit business leadership.

Pure, stripped down, no bullshit—beautiful! You will come to see that Punk Rock Business is all about adopting an attitude that echoes the attributes of punk. The punk rock businessperson says, "I am not okay with the current status quo," and vows to do something about it. I detest mediocrity, as I want to do amazing things. I see no sense in playing things safe, because there is no such thing as job security anymore. I am not going to stick to some conservative, cautious game plan, because life is precious, and life is about creating something amazing with the people you choose to share your life with.

In an article entitled "Don't look over your shoulder but the Sex Pistols are coming," Steve Jones (the Sex Pistols' guitarist) famously said, "We're not into music, we're into chaos."[5] I'd love to be able to say that Punk Rock Business is into chaos, but people would take that word out of context. So instead let me say, "We're into disruption." Disruption that is positive. Disruption that eradicates the futile and pointless activities, the destruction of processes that curtail speed with minimal benefit, and the removal of those people who block progress in the name of caution.

Do you endure inefficient, ineffective, cumbersome processes at your workplace? Are you frustrated beyond belief at the conservatism and cautiousness that prevail in too many business leaders? Does it make you angry? It should. As Tim McIlrath said,

---

4 Tommy Ramone, "Fight Club," *Uncut* (January 2007).

5 Neil Spencer, "Don't Look Over Your Shoulder but the Sex Pistols Are Coming," *NME* (February 21, 1976).

"If you're not angry, you're not paying attention." So, open your eyes and see the reality.

Punk has an anger associated with it. Punks were angry; they were pissed at something, pissed at the dull music and the hopelessness they saw for their futures. I'm pissed too. I'm mad at the corporate bullshit, the play-it-safe middle managers who don't want to rock the boat, but all the time they moan and whine in the corridors. All they want to do is plod along, work acceptable hours, take a decent paycheck home, and enjoy corporate job security while they live in suburbia with 2.4 children, a Volvo, and a hypoallergenic dog that was chosen because it would not get hairs on their new Pottery Barn sofa.[6]

John Lydon defined these people perfectly in his book *Anger Is an Energy: My Life Uncensored*, "All those kinds of people, the complacent ones that don't contribute, that just sit by and moan and don't actually do anything to better themselves or the situation for others. The nonparticipating moral majority."[7] This nonparticipating moral majority is the cause of so many of the problems I mention. They are the conservative, cautious, ineffective, bureaucratic safe managers that I loathe.

We don't need safe managers; we need entrepreneurs, or at least business leaders with entrepreneurship flowing through their veins. Moreover, the people who work with and alongside us are crying out for a leader who can inspire and chart a journey that brings vibrancy to the lives of those who share the journey.

Punk Rock Business is a call to arms for businesspeople who can relate to this desire to dare greatly and strive for excellence and who loathe the constraining sludge that prevents progress in so many businesses these days.

———

6 Now let me admit that I have a hypoallergenic dog and live in the suburbs with my family. But, I have none of the other traits and—more importantly—nothing of the attitude I mentioned so disdainfully here.

7 John Lydon, *Anger Is an Energy: My Life Uncensored* (New York: HarperCollins Publishers, 2014), 106.

Punk threatens the norm and changes the status quo. It is non-conformist, it is rebellious, and it pushes the boundaries in every way possible. It's about one person saying, "It doesn't have to be this way," and finding a group of like-minded people who agree it's time to rebel and change things . . . for the better.

"The rebellious part of it is very important because people get too complacent. The fight against that complacency is punk rock . . . At this point and on the planet it seems like eighty percent of the people are ******** asleep you know . . . You know you only need five percent or less to embrace ideas and change it, change the way people think all over again," said Jim Jarmusch (Film Director, Actor, Writer) in an interview from the film *Punk: Attitude.*

I agree, eighty percent of people are asleep in this world, not literally but metaphorically. They walk around in a daze, they accept the norm, and they don't even realize how bad things are. And even if they did, they don't have the desire or the fight to make things better . . . whereas punks do, and so should you! This is where you come in.

A key part of punk rock is about getting straight to the point, so let's not waste any time and let me state why I am writing this book:

1. **I want to see bureaucracy stripped away.** I am mad (mad as hell, to be truthful) at the bureaucracy that clogs up busi-nesses—and there is, sadly, far more of it around today than when I started out. All too often I have seen companies who worship at the shrine of process and pay scant regard to cre-ativity and the power of ideas. If this book can help shift that balance, then it will have served its purpose.

2. **I want to see talented businesspeople realize their full potential.** I see too many highly talented people achieving good results and enjoying reasonable success without ever becoming everything they could be. Various things hold them back and most (if not all) could be overcome if they

just went for it more often—all guns blazing. Adopting a punk attitude could be the catalyst they need.

3. **I want people to enjoy business.** Ninety-nine percent of the time during my career I have woken up each day, excited for the day ahead. This is because I have found that a punk attitude has allowed me to be true to who I am, and that has enabled me to enjoy work so much more than I ever would have imagined.

4. **I want to help accelerate people's careers.** I figured out loads of things along the way in my career so far, but they took me far too long to learn. Why didn't anyone tell me so much of this stuff when I was starting out? Those lessons could have helped fast-track my career. Some things you will only learn by experiencing them for yourself, but hopefully some of what I will say will shorten your journey of understanding. This book contains so many of the lessons I wish someone had told me thirty years ago.

5. **It's the only way to succeed in the future.** We need to be far more punk if we are to succeed in the world of rampant technology we see exploding around us. The world is experiencing exponential change, and the old adage—the only sustainable competitive advantage is the ability to innovate more quickly than your competitors—has never been truer. If I were in the middle of my career, the digital revolution would, quite frankly, scare the crap out of me and hugely excite me, at the same time.

6. **I am a storyteller.** There is also one selfish motivation: I am a storyteller; telling stories has been at the heart of my career. If you are a storyteller, then it seems natural to want to write it all down at some point in your life and share your stories broadly.

If I can achieve the first five for you, I hope you won't mind indulging me with the sixth reason.

Who is this book for? First, this book is primarily for people of action, passionate people who aren't prepared to accept the status quo, who want to change the world—or at least their world.

But let's try to identify them in more traditional and obvious ways. I think there are a few key groups of people who can benefit from this book:

- Young men and women who have recently entered the business world or are about to—you are my real hope. Young people have the beauty of naïveté that makes them immune to some of the negativity that constrains others. If we can really inspire this generation and they can become empowered, then maybe they can drive the broad change so desperately needed in our corporations.

- Like-minded businesspeople who believe in the power of ideas and speed, who fight against being suffocated (or at the very least being shackled) every day by the policies and procedures and the more-than-my-job's-worth co-workers who continually say why something couldn't or shouldn't be done or why it wouldn't work—avoid people who associate with the three words *couldn't, shouldn't*, and *wouldn't*. The *'ouldn't* triplets are poisonous.

- Senior business leaders who have the power and author-ity to make the changes so desperately needed—they preside over all the pointless and futile actions that waste time, effort, and money and which, in turn, frus-trate everyone along the way. Often, they do this in blissful ignorance. So wake up and realize what is going on and then change it; make the world better for all your stakeholders. You have the power.

Now, this book is not about reliving the past: It's all about creating a better future. My goal/ambition is that the content will not only prove valuable to you, it will drive you to action. That is why I have structured the book as I have. In true punk spirit, there won't be long introductions to each section—we will get straight to the point. The entire book contains more than eighty stories, mainly from my career or ones I heard along the way, that are generally fast and to the point and imbued with the lessons I have learned.

This is not a book to be just read. I don't even like calling it a book; I prefer if you would think of it as your Action Plan to complete along the way.

The most important part of the book should not be any of the words I have written but rather what you will write at the end of each story. I want you to stop after each story and write down what you learned on top of what I have identified and—even more importantly—what you are going to do as a result. Now I am absolutely fine with you writing *no action*, but let it be a conscious statement of no action.

Psychology says that if you do not act within fifteen minutes on something you learn, then the likelihood is that you never will. Learning something is almost pointless if it doesn't drive an action. Punk was never passive; it was active, and if you don't act, then what's the point? That is why there is space at the end of every story; so, don't you dare read this book without a pen within arm's reach.

I _____ [insert name] agree to use this book as an action plan for change. _____[signed] _____[date]

THE GOALS OF THIS BOOK

To motivate like-minded businesspeople to be more punk; to accelerate their careers; to help them find the freedom to be true to who they are and what they believe in; and to erode some of the bureaucratic crap that constrains so many businesses, so that punk rock businesspeople not only enjoy the rewards of having a successful career but also (more importantly) enjoy their journeys and experiences more. Life is too precious to waste a single day.

I have learned lessons from each of the stories I will tell here, lessons that I have since tried to embrace and apply in my career. They enabled me to progress from working as a Trainee Management Accountant for a construction company in the industrial Black Country of the UK to leading the worldwide retail business for Microsoft. I say this with humility, because I didn't ever have a plan to do that. It just seemed to evolve along the way, and I was fortunate (or rather blessed) at almost every step. The achievements, quite honestly, are almost irrelevant to me; what are far more important are the experiences I have enjoyed with a host of amazing people, as these ensured the most exciting and enriching journey possible . . . and, God willing, there are plenty more to come.

The Eight Elements of Punk Rock Business

Now that we all understand where the idea of Punk Rock Business came from and the essence of it, I'll dive in and explain the eight elements of Punk Rock Business that I believe we can all learn from. This will help you understand the journey we will be going on together.

I see eight elements in the attitude of punk rock music and the punk rock movement that I love when it comes to business today. Let's look at each of these elements, and you will see how these are so applicable for Punk Rock Business.

ELEMENT 1: HAVE A CAUSE

Punk came out of an era where people didn't like what they saw. They didn't like it and weren't prepared to accept it—whatever *it* was for each of them. Punk was all about wanting something better, being clear about what that was, and making that their cause. They then seized responsibility for driving the required change. Punk is where passion for the cause, whatever that may be, intersects with a refusal to accept the status quo, and the inevitable result is an explosion that drives change. But it all starts with the cause and the desire to make things better.

ELEMENT 2: BUILD A MOVEMENT

Punk was attractive to like-minded people, and it galvanized that segment of the youth. Until punk came along, they were directionless and confused—but they knew something wasn't right. Punk gave them a cause and provided an alternative to the dull music and hopelessness they saw in society at that time, and in return, their passionate acceptance of this new alternative created the movement that swept their generation. Any cause, however worthy, will fail if it doesn't translate into a movement that originates from a committed band of believers.

ELEMENT 3: CREATE NEW AND RADICALLY DIFFERENT IDEAS

Punk was completely different—never seen before. John Holmstrom (*Punk* magazine) said in the movie *Punk: Attitude*, "We wanted Punk to wipe out the hippies, blow up the whole of rock and roll, and start all over again." Punk wasn't some tiny iteration, small evolution, or incremental improvement. No—punk was a never-seen-before jaw-dropping creation that exploded into our consciousness. No one was ambivalent to punk; you loved it or hated it.

ELEMENT 4: DRIVE SPEED AND ACTION

Punk was three beats and you're in. It upped the tempo, and the music grabbed you by the throat and forced your body to pogo along as it was shaken like a rag doll in the jet stream of sound vibrations from the speaker system that was cranked to maximum. There was never the option to stand still on the sidelines when punk was playing loud. Punk didn't wait for permission from anyone; it didn't ask for permission. The do-it-yourself mentality may have meant things were less polished, but things undoubtedly happened fast.

ELEMENT 5: SAY IT AS IT IS

John Lennon said, "Say what you mean, mean what you say and put a beat to it. Go!" That was very much the punk attitude, and punks embraced it to the fullest. Punk lyrics came with a contagious honesty. As the music critic Lester Bangs stated, "Punk's essential claim to worth, to durability, to cultural importance, was—*is*—honesty."[8] Punks said exactly what they felt. They didn't care if they offended someone as long as they said the truth, or at least their truth.

---

8 Phil Strongman, *Pretty Vacant: A Story of UK Punk* (Chicago: Chicago Review Press, 2008), 15.

ELEMENT 6: BE AUTHENTIC

Punk gave people permission to be themselves: true to who they were. No one had to put on a false front just so they could be accepted; quite simply they didn't care. It was more important to be who you were, rather than who someone else wanted you to be. That's not being selfish, just self-aware, self-confident, and comfortable with yourself.

ELEMENT 7: PUT YOURSELF OUT THERE

To be punk you had to make a very visible and belligerent statement; it required you to put yourself out there, say "this is me," and invite criticism. Punk's do-it-yourself mentality amplified this attitude of putting yourself out there. It was far more important to just give it a go, rather than get it perfect. You couldn't get it perfect without giving it a go first.

ELEMENT 8: REJECT CONFORMITY

Billy Idol called it when he said, "The punk credo was to stand up for your own beliefs and tastes, not bow down to yet another new set of rules. Meet the new boss, same as the old boss, indeed."[9] Punk paid total disregard to everything that had gone before. It didn't evolve; it burst on the scene destroying so many of the accepted practices that had sterilized music and sanitized the whole music scene. Punk pressed the reset button. The whole safety pin dress code thing was just an anti-fashion statement that ironically became a fashion statement.

These eight elements were at the heart of punk rock music, movement, attitude, fashion, and culture. As I hope you can already start to see, these elements are highly attractive for businesses and businesspeople too.

---

9 Billy Idol, *Dancing with Myself* (New York: Simon & Schuster, 2014), 07.

The Bottom Line

Just as punks burst onto the scene, were immediately noticed, and instantly made an impression, so, too, can those businesses and businesspeople who embrace a punk rock attitude. That is because the current state of many companies is a depressing statement about the commercial world today. But rather than be depressed, you should be shouting for joy and screaming from the rooftops . . . because it means that those rare exceptions (and yes, they are rare) of bright, vibrant, energetic, and fast people shine through like a beacon on a foggy night. That is true at a company level, a team level, and an individual level. The establishment, the incumbents, are fat, happy, and ripe for the taking by some fast, agile, spirited (but charming) young punk upstart or start-up.

Punk Rock Business is my articulation of the antidote to the cumbersome and soulless way of doing business that we see far too often. Not only have I found it to deliver far better results, I have learned that embracing the punk mentality allows you to become the best you can be in every aspect of your life and, just as importantly, love every step of the journey.

Welcome to the revolution . . .

THE EIGHT ELEMENTS OF PUNK ROCK BUSINESS

Element 1:

HAVE A CAUSE

"The only way to do great work is to love what you do. If you haven't found it yet, keep looking. Don't settle. As with all matters of the heart, you'll know when you find it."

STEVE JOBS

"For me, punk is about real feelings. It's not about, 'Yeah, I am a punk and I'm angry.' That's a lot of crap. It's about loving the things that really matter: Passion, heart and soul."

JOEY RAMONE

Punk rock is rebellious, and the rebellious element is critically important. Punk rebelled against several things. Their first target was the soulless, overproduced music of the early '70s with its endless guitar riffs. Bands such as The Ramones were sick of the happy-clappy hippy music, the repetitive rock of that time, and the sugar-coated disco tracks. Punk set out to drive all of these into oblivion and replace them with authentic rock music—and they did that by playing loud and fast.

The second target for punks' rebellion was the politics of that day. The youth of the day saw nothing but hopelessness and a dead-end future. The Clash used their music to make political statements, and Joe Strummer's songwriting at the time of their *London Calling* album was particularly politically motivated.

Other bands just rebelled for the sake of it. They rebelled against everything and nothing; they liked the anarchy of it all. But real punk rock was focused on rebelling against the sterile music of the time and the bleakness the youth saw in their future.

Those two were the real mission or cause of punk rock: to restore rock music that had heart and to revive the hopes for the future of the young.

Punk has always been anarchic and has always had an anger associated with it, but at its soul, punk is optimistic. It is about seeing what's wrong, having a passion to change it, and then having the guts to stand up and do something to make a difference. The Ramones wanted rock music back, so they created it. Strummer wanted political change, so he screamed about it through his lyrics.

Punk attitude in business is exactly the same, and the starting point has always been the same. Have a cause that you care passionately about. Finding your cause may be the hard part—but start with your passions. Choose to work for companies who are doing something you care deeply about. Look at the instances where you are outraged by the status quo that we have all come to accept as normal, but we know is wrong. Then be prepared to be the voice that says, "This isn't how it should be, I am going to stand up and drive the change we so desperately need." That's the only way you will make things better for yourself and those around you.

So you have to start by asking yourself: Do you care about what your organization does? Again. Consider this question very carefully. Do you care about what your organization does? Do you really care? If you don't, then let me suggest that you are never going to have the passion within yourself to dare greatly, deliver some amazing work, and reach your full potential. Instead, you will be destined to do a mundane job that you don't really care about. If you allow that to happen, you will be settling, and the inevitable consequence is that you will be allowing a level of apathy to creep into your life, and if apathy is present, then I fear you will only ever deliver what you know to be mediocrity. That surely cannot be an alternative you can live with. What a waste that would be! If you are going to be the best you can be, you have to align yourself with an organization whose cause you care greatly about.

APATHY = CONFORMITY

Wikihow's article on "How to Become a Punk Rocker" calls out one key criteria of being punk: "Care about something. Apathy is conformity. Find something you're passionate about and take back your desire to change the world. Get head over heels into veganism, feeding the homeless, or whatever else."

I haven't always worked in an organization where I truly believed in the cause; I can admit this now. It took me nearly twenty years of my career to work out what I really wanted to do. It took me that amount of time because I never thought about it. It took me far too long to be able to articulate what I was passionate about. The worst thing about this sad state of affairs is that I never really worked it out for myself—I just got lucky, stumbling upon it by chance, rather than by any clear, well-thought-out process.

I used to think I was passionate about ready mixed concrete and overnight parcel distribution (the first two industries I worked in)—and I was, really, I was! The reason was because I didn't know any better. What excited me then was the fun and competition of business, and when I was young that was enough motivation. Let me say there is nothing wrong with those two industries if they are your passion, but I now know they weren't mine. Having now stumbled into world-changing technological products and services, I found my passion, my eyes were opened, my horizons were broadened, and—most importantly—my purpose was defined.

If you don't want to rely on luck like I did, then build a plan and be intentional about what role, what company, and what industry you want to be in. This is one of the biggest things I wish I had been told when I was embarking on my working life. Reread that Jobs quote from the start of this section: "The only way to do great work is to love what you do. If you haven't found it yet, keep looking. Don't settle. As with all matters of the heart, you'll know when you find it."

Finding it will probably not come instantly, but I certainly hope it will come far more quickly for you than it did for me. It took me twenty years, not because I was settling, but rather because I wasn't looking. Let me spell this out very clearly: If you are not genuinely excited about your job, do something about it, and realize that your number one job is to start to search for a new one immediately, today! You have an honor-bound obligation to yourself to do so. Get on with it. If you are supposed to go to work tomorrow, don't—call in sick and start working out what you want to do and get on with it, NOW!

In this section, "Have a Cause," I share some of the stories that helped me get to the point of knowing that the things I work on are worth my energy and enable me to energize my teams behind the organization's mission.

HAVING A CAUSE IS AN ESSENTIAL PART OF PUNK ROCK BUSINESS

You should understand very early on that adopting a punk rock attitude isn't easy. It will require at times blood, sweat, and tears; it's the challenging, difficult, and energy-sapping path. Recognize that it isn't easy to rebel against the accepted norms. It's challenging to always say it as it is, because doing so doesn't always make you popular. It takes guts to put yourself out there when others will snipe. It takes real conviction to make the key calls, knowing that sometimes you will get them wrong and receive criticism from life's bystanders and spectators. It requires great energy to move at speed, and it is tiring to constantly be driving people along. IT IS NOT EASY! Believe me it isn't, but to me, there is no alternative. The antidote to all these challenges and difficulties is an unwavering commitment to the cause, combined with a belief in the value you are contributing. To become the best that you can be, you need to be a passionate person of conviction—someone who believes in what they are doing and who is energized by the cause, whatever that may be.

There are two aspects to this element, and finding an organization whose cause aligns with your passion is one part. Once you have done that, then the second part is for you as a leader to use that cause to inspire your teams to pursue the organization's purpose and deliver it.

Together we will investigate how certain organizations (big and small) make the world a better place and how they state their causes through great mission statements and manifestos that set the right direction. Then we will move on to how your group needs to deliver on your cause through substantive plans that excite your customers. Then we will conclude with examples that prove that you must tirelessly communicate your cause, passionately articulate it, deliver on it, and never deviate from it. It starts and finishes with the cause. Everything is about the cause, and so it should be.

The Cause Is Vitally Important for Four Key Reasons

1. **It inspires effort and fortitude.** If the cause is compelling and is passionately communicated, it will inspire great effort and grit from those who chose to participate in driving it forward. Now, Ralph Waldo Emerson (poet and lecturer) wasn't exactly punk, but I have always bought into his belief that, "Nothing great was ever achieved without enthusiasm."

2. **It guides action.** A clearly articulated cause, goal, or vision defines where we are going. Without that, we are just thrashing around in the dark.

3. **It unites a team.** A cause inspires a movement; a movement requires followers who share a group mentality, and the subsequent togetherness provides the support and reassurance that remove both doubt and uncertainty when they raise their ugly heads.

4. **It attracts talent and builds loyalty.** People want to be part of something bigger than themselves. A mission attracts people, and a great mission attracts great people. Then, once on board, a commitment to the cause means there is something fundamental to give up, if there was ever the thought of switching jobs.

So, the key questions to ask are: Does your organization or group have a cause? Do you believe in it? Does it justify fifty percent of your waking hours? Now, there are only three answers . . .

1. **Yes, it does.** One of the hardest parts of Punk Rock Business is finding something you are passionate about, so if this is you, stand up and shout "Hell yeah!" You are one of the lucky ones.

2. **I think it could.** Clearly there is something that you are doing that is great, inspirational, or excites you. So take some time to work out what it really is. Why does this world really need what you are doing? Create the *why* for your organization, and get it solidified and articulated fast. Ensure it is inspiring, worthy, has clarity, and that it is passionately communicated. Get your team to discuss it, ensure people believe in it, and then start to use it to define your decision-making together. Then you get to #1.

3. **No, I will never have any passion for what my organization does.** If your company or organization is incapable of having a cause that you are passionate about, then quit. Find a job you really believe in. Or if you need to be a little more circumspect, reverse the order. But if you want your working life to be truly fulfilling, then you have no option other than to accept that you need to find a new job—end of debate. I don't know what that job is for you, only you can answer that. But start by looking at your passions and explore from there.

So either celebrate that your work is something you truly believe in or get looking.

Are you pursuing your cause? Are you taking on the challenges that really matter to you? Ask yourself that challenging question and remember, as Marianne Williamson said, "There is no passion to be found playing life small—in settling for a life that is less than the one you are capable of living."

Are you doing something that will inspire you to live your life big and allow you to have the fullest life you are capable of? Jobs and Williamson both said not to settle, and that is a great question to ask yourself: Are you settling? Stop reading for at least a minute and really think about it. If you're settling, you'll know. This next minute is very important . . . so, THINK HARD!

Make the World a Better Place . . . In a Big Way

The best place to start when trying to understand if your company can fulfill your desire for a cause is its mission statement. Look at your company's mission statement and consider the impact your company is having in the world; does it make you proud? I have worked for (and with) some great companies whose inspiring mission statements changed the world.

Microsoft: "Our mission is to empower every person and every organization on the planet to achieve more."

When I worked at Motorola, we always said ours was: "To connect people through communications."

When I worked on Product (RED), its purpose was "To help eliminate AIDS in Africa."

I wish I could tell you I had handpicked these brands with care and attention and a careful review of their mission statements, but that would be an absolute lie. I didn't. I wanted or sometimes needed these jobs. But, wow, was I lucky to end up at companies with great mission statements who were changing the world. However, you don't have to be a huge, super company to have a great mission statement and a higher purpose—and you don't have to make high-tech, never-seen-before products that change the world, either. A t-shirt manufacturing company can do the same. Here are some of my other favorite companies with a cause:

- Google: "To organize the world's information and make it universally accessible and useful." Isn't that beautiful! Isn't it daring! The entire world's information. Universally accessible and useful. Isn't it worthy!

- Life is Good: A t-shirt company whose mission is "To

spread the power of optimism." WOW! T-shirts can have that power? Hell, yeah!!

- Starbucks: "To inspire and nurture the human spirit—one person, one cup and one neighborhood at a time." I love this statement "one cup at a time." Starbucks isn't about selling coffee. It isn't about becoming the world's most prominent coffee shop. It is to nurture and inspire the human spirit. WOW! If you are a coffee barista at Starbucks, I hope you go to work every day with that message running through your head. And when you shout, "Dale—small black Americano with one cube of ice" and hand me the cup, fleetingly catching my eye, I hope you know you are sending me on my way having nurtured and inspired my human spirit!

. . . Okay, time out. I am now sounding full of crap, and sarcasm has crept into our conversation. But this is the real crux of the issue. Starbucks has changed the way we consume coffee, and it has changed our daily ritual. It has made life more pleasant, and I find myself looking out for the mermaid logo as a familiar and welcoming harbor in a storm. Let's admit it: It has nurtured the human spirit. Even if you are unconvinced about the "inspire" part, the world is better for Starbucks, in my humble opinion.

Let's move on to Airbnb. I really love this. At one time, their statement was "To create a world where you can belong anywhere. Where people can live in a place instead of just traveling there." This is my favorite mission statement from the perspective of nailing the reason why they exist.

Tesla isn't about cars. "Tesla's mission is to accelerate the world's transition to sustainable energy." Elon Musk, their CEO and co-founder, seems hell-bent on protecting the environment, and his other ventures are focused on creating intergalactic travel and colonizing Mars. How audacious of him is that? I'd love to be part of that.

Let's look at the mission statements of football clubs. So many of them will say "To be the world's most <insert superlative here> football club." Insert your choice of word, like powerful, successful, popular, etc. Do you know who is different? Barcelona. Their slogan, "Més que un club," which translates to "More than a club," sums them up. Their mission, "Sport as a focal point promoting Catalonia via Barça, children and young people as the main beneficiaries, promoting values and education." Brilliant! It is! This is the club that didn't carry a shirt sponsor until 2004 when it started to have UNICEF's name appear on it in a deal worth €1.5 million per year. The only shirt sponsorship deal where the club paid the sponsor. Yes, Barcelona paid UNICEF the money rather than the other way around.

DON'T SETTLE!

Life is short, we get one go around, so for goodness' sake, do something you love doing! Do something that adds great value and creates a legacy. Remember, "DON'T SETTLE." If you are good—why settle?

KEY LESSONS

You are giving nearly fifty percent of your waking hours to your company. Your company must have a cause that deserves that level of your personal investment. It must have a cause that you can use to inspire your teams and stimulate their energy and commitment.

SO WHAT ARE YOU GOING TO DO ABOUT IT?

My suggestion: Review your organization's mission statement, your division's mission statement, and your team's mission statement, and ask yourself: Does it inspire me? If not, change it or the place where you go each day.

Write your thoughts here:

Make the World a Better Place . . . In Your Own Small Way

Not many companies change the whole world, but there are lots of companies that make the world of their customers better. Let me give you an example. Michael's Fine Dry Cleaning in Bellevue (near Seattle) is in many ways your normal run-of-the-mill laundry, but I wouldn't go anywhere else while I lived there. And the reason why has nothing to do with how well they clean my clothes.

My wife, Gerry, had gone to visit family in England for about three weeks, and so I was largely left to fend for myself, which wasn't something I was used to. Just before she left, she gave me a dry-cleaning ticket, as she hadn't been able to pick up my shirts before heading off to the airport. I popped in to collect them; I gave my name, the woman fetched my shirts, we exchanged a few pleasantries, I paid and left. All pretty routine. Two weeks later I went back to drop my dirty shirts off. I walked in. "Hello, Mr. Dale," the woman greeted me. I was a little stunned and checked my person to make sure I didn't have a name badge anywhere. She told me I could collect the shirts tomorrow, and I left a little bit speechless.

Later that day on our family's Facebook chat group, I jokingly mentioned that I had reached a new level of domesticity as I was now recognized and known by name in our dry cleaners. My wife replied to that post saying, "Yes that's normal. When I walk in, they already have my things hanging on the hanger at the front of the store and the cost rung up on the cash register. They recognize my car and get everything ready before I have even walked in the door."

This dry cleaners brightens my day by being superefficient, making the mundane chore of collecting my shirts easy, simple, even enjoyable, and as personable as possible. They add the personal touch of calling me by name, and let's admit it—most of us like to be recognized. Nobody would argue that Michael's Fine Dry Cleaning has a mission statement like Tesla's or Airbnb's. But while they may not be changing the whole world, they're certainly making the world they interact with a better place.

Michael's Fine Dry Cleaning's mission is so clear I barely need a second to define it: "To put a smile on our customers' faces, for the fleeting moments they are in our store."

KEY LESSONS

If a small laundry service can have a compelling vision and make the world better in a unique and differentiated way, then surely you and your company can too. The mundane can be made interesting with amazing customer service.

SO WHAT ARE YOU GOING TO DO ABOUT IT?

Write your thoughts here:

Define Your Cause and Then Let It Define Everything About You

It is standard for a company to articulate its cause through its mission statement, and in my mind, Microsoft has the greatest mission statement that could ever exist "Our mission is to empower every person and every organization on the planet to achieve more." The mission statement has served the company well as a north star that gives a true higher purpose to the one-hundred-thousand-plus employees who go to work there every day. Microsoft is all about empowerment and helping people fulfill their full potential through the power of technology. I joined Microsoft because of its mission statement and because I thought it was probably the company on the planet that had most changed the way people lived their lives—and changed it for the better. "A computer on every desk and in every home" had been a rallying cry that changed the way we worked and lived.

For a number of years, people could argue that Microsoft had lost its mojo, that spark, that magic, that elusive quality that set us apart from everyone else for so long. During that time, Clay Christensen (author of the bestselling *The Innovator's Dilemma*) came to speak to the Sales and Marketing leaders at Microsoft. He talked about the greatness of the company's mission statement and said, "The world needs a strong Microsoft. There are plenty of companies that this world could manage just fine without. Microsoft isn't one of them." That struck a chord with me.

Microsoft never lost its focus on its cause; it just had a period where perhaps it wasn't innovating or executing as well as it had previously.

Throughout my time at Microsoft, I saw this sense of purpose clearly. Microsoft is all about empowering every person to achieve more. Satya Nadella, Microsoft's current CEO and only the third CEO in its history, speaks regularly to the company's group of corporate vice presidents, and I cannot remember a single talk where he hasn't started the session with the mission statement. Everything he says relates back to this statement in some way.

The mission statement has always been a guiding star at Microsoft. There was one famous meeting on our work in education that involved Bill Gates. He was alleged to have berated some managers and made the point that he didn't understand why we were charging people in education for our software. He didn't think it was right to put a cost barrier in the way of someone who was trying to better themselves. That was his humanity speaking. His business logic was that when they graduate from their school, college, or university, they will move into the workforce, and they will be familiar with Microsoft products, so they will want to continue to use them and then we would get paid that way. That was the catalyst for the $1 Windows licenses for education establishments. That decision helped empower millions of students.

Microsoft also works with the Special Olympics to enhance its systems capabilities. At the 2015 World Economic Forum (the annual meeting of business and political leaders), Microsoft announced a plan to donate $1 billion over three years in cloud services to nonprofits and university researchers, in addition to the $750 million per annum it gives away in traditional software. Those donations helped empower other organizations that were working for the good of others in need.

Microsoft also tries to instill that same sense of helping others get to a better spot with its charitable donations. It has a generous Giving Campaign where every employee can donate up to $15,000 to a charity of their choice, and the company will match that donation. That scheme empowered its employees to give back in a hugely impactful way. That generosity demonstrates the mission statement in a broader way.

I have always thought that Microsoft was a great company, but during my time there, I realized that it was also (and probably more importantly) a *good* company. Everything the company does comes back to that mission statement of empowering people.

Microsoft does walk the talk. It is as evident as night or day.

Throughout the whole of my eight years at Microsoft, I felt honored to work there, to work for a company with such a finely calibrated moral compass.

WOULD THE WORLD MISS YOUR ORGANIZATION?

If I were only allowed to ask one question in a job interview it would be this: "Why would the world miss this company if it weren't here?" If you are going to want to jump out of bed in the morning and bound into work, it better be for a damn good purpose and something more than earning a paycheck. Otherwise, I fear that you are destined to be with the masses that drag themselves out of bed, slouch into work, and feel unfulfilled for much of their waking day. Now, clearly, those are two extremes, but don't settle for anything less than something meaningful.

KEY LESSONS

The mission statement isn't to be produced to meet some business school requirement, nor is it to be filed away until the next strategy day, but rather it must be your north star, your compass directing every single decision. We must always use it like that.

SO WHAT ARE YOU GOING TO DO ABOUT IT?

Write your thoughts here:

When a Mission Statement Is Insufficient, Create a Manifesto

Product (RED) was born out of an idea from Bobby Shriver and Bono. They conceived of a way to make fighting AIDS a commercially viable and sustainable idea, where consumerism could fulfill a useful humanitarian role. The end result was that a group of the world's leading consumer brands would make (RED) versions of their products, and when a consumer chose a (RED) product, a portion of the profits would go to the Global Fund, to help eliminate AIDS in Africa. The concept served a dual purpose: (RED) was a brand that allowed both the consumer and brands to make bold statements about themselves, where they stood on this issue, and how they were going to make the world better for people who desperately needed a better world.

(RED) had a compelling mission statement—to help eliminate AIDS in Africa—but it developed a compelling point of view on the issue. It borrowed from the political arena, and its founders created a manifesto. The words of its manifesto have evolved slightly over the past decade, but the essence is undoubtedly the same.

Every Generation is known for something.

Let's be the one to deliver an AIDS free Generation.

We all have tremendous power. What we choose to do or even buy, can affect someone's life on the other side of the world. In 2005, more than 1,200 babies were born every day with HIV. Today that number is 400. We must act now to get that close to zero.

(RED) can't accomplish this alone. It will take all of us to get there—governments, health organizations, companies, and you. When you BUY (RED), a (RED) partner will give up some of its profits to fight AIDS.

It's as simple as that.

Be (RED). Start the end of AIDS now.[1]

They (Bobby Shriver and Bono) founded (RED) with a simple mission: to make it easy for people and businesses to join the fight against the deadly virus. Consider the prospect of an AIDS-free generation. How great would that be?

KEY LESSONS

A manifesto adds substance to the mission statement. It allows it to be expanded to a more complete story or statement of intent. It states the company's position clearly, and no one is left in any doubt as to where it stands.

If the mission statement is the thinking part of defining what you do, the manifesto is more the feeling part. The manifesto is what you say when you roll up and plant your flag and state what you are all about—the emotional articulation of your mission—your statement of intent.

SO WHAT ARE YOU GOING TO DO ABOUT IT?

My suggestion: Write a passion-filled manifesto for your company, your group, your family-run café, even your family, or whatever else you like. What does your business, organization, or team stand for?

Write your thoughts here:

---

1 Stan Phelps, "How U2's Bono and the Color Red Elevated Purpose in Business," *Forbes* (February 9, 2017), https://www.forbes.com/sites/stanphelps/2017/02/09/how-u2s-bono-and-the-color-red-elevated-purpose-in-business/#28b2fcfb64fa.

Work on Stuff That Genuinely Excites Your Customers, so That They Join You Rather Than Just Buy from You

We have just established that every action must be driven by your mission statement. Now my hope is that your mission statement has something about making things better for your customers—if it doesn't then I am worried for you. But if indeed your mission statement is about making things better for your customers, then the things you are working on should be all about making your customers' lives better, and your time should be focused on what they most care about.

As an example, in the days before mobile phone ownership was mainstream, the telecommunications company Orange painted a picture of a world of easier and more natural communications. The company launched in the UK in 1994 with a compelling vision: "Creating a wire-free world." The launch of a new mobile operator was a big deal, and Orange had three elements to their proposition that resonated with the British public and set them apart as the consumer champion. These three elements were per-second billing, free insurance, and inclusive minutes. All offered more value to consumers than the incumbents did. Per-second billing was a master stroke. All the other mobile phone companies charged by the minute, so if you spoke for 4 minutes and 1 second, you would be charged for 5 minutes; however, on Orange you would be charged for 4 minutes and 1 second. In the 1990s, mobile phone calls were still very expensive, and people would be very conscious of keeping their calls short. Thus, only charging people for what they used, rather than rounding every call up, resonated greatly.

It would have been very easy to come across as the low-cost option, but Orange did two things beautifully. Each benefit was positioned not as a discount, but as something that was fair for the consumer. You shouldn't be charged for the parts of the minutes that you don't use. If you bought an expensive handset from us, we should give you the peace of mind that insurance gives you. If you bought a call plan or rate plan and you were forking out £25 per month for an airtime contract, you should at least get some inclusive minutes for that base payment.

Orange packaged up these consumer benefits in some amazing advertising. They were beautifully artistic, but they also packed a punch.

"Time is money, so how can Orange help you save it? We charge one second at a time for your calls with no rounding up. We include in your twenty-five-pound monthly subscription sixty minutes of calls, one of five monthly price plans with minutes included. The future's bright, the future's Orange."

It was so well written. "How can Orange help you save it?" made a statement about how their focus was on you, the customer. Then they backed up that statement with not one, but two clear demonstrations of it.

They ended every advert with the famous tagline, "The future's bright, the future's Orange," and everyone came to know that Orange had optimism running through its veins and was changing the status quo for the better.

Orange came out and hit everyone with benefit after benefit, time after time. They stated their position and then delivered on it.

One of my colleagues who had been in the industry for years said that retailers saw a key difference in how consumers would talk about Orange. Consumers would go into a mobile phone store and say either, "I want to buy a mobile phone" or "I want to join Orange." Join is a very powerful word, and it embodied the movement that Orange had created; it would help accelerate Orange's growth, and they would become the largest mobile phone operator in the UK.

When I joined Orange as Vice President of Brand Marketing in 2002, it was broadly recognized that we had lost our mojo. The advertising agency we used wasn't particularly highly thought of as recent campaigns hadn't had the impact everyone desired. But it wasn't the agency's fault. What became obvious very quickly to me was that the issue was not the creative execution of our adverts or how we were communicating the message, but rather that the message itself was either confusing or didn't have a real consumer benefit. The style was still aesthetically beautiful, but what we were saying had very little substance. The agency was taking the stick internally for not making impactful ads, but that was unwarranted. We needed to look in the mirror since we were the ones creating lackluster initiatives and giving lackluster briefs. We had become fixated on style over substance, beautiful artistic ads rather than strong propositions. It literally was art for art's sake.

We'd lost sight of the customer, and that is always a bad place to find yourself. I should have known. I remember when I first joined, I sat in a few meetings with our agencies who were presenting various marketing concepts to our team. I wasn't that impressed, but our team kept saying, "This can work once we put Olaf on it," or "Olaf will make these work." I wondered who Olaf was. I presumed he was a Scandinavian who worked somewhere in our team. After the third Olaf reference, I asked when I could meet him. Everyone laughed. Olaf wasn't a person; Olaf was an acronym for Orange Look And Feel. That's why I should have been worried. Olaf could make things look beautiful, but he couldn't fix the lack of substance in the initiative. It proved my point. It is never style or substance; it always has to be both.

So we committed to embracing a renewed focus on creating strong consumer benefits and regaining the company-wide conviction that our initiatives needed to offer our customers benefits that had *hard-centers*—something of substance. That phrase was the acid test. Was it a hard-center benefit that gave the consumer something substantive, or was it just a soft-center that tasted nice for a fleeting moment? We called this renewed determination to be differentiated and be the consumer champion, *Bright Orange*. This was a conscious throwback to early communications where the message really did justify the tagline, "The future's bright, the future's Orange." While

Bright Orange was just an internal name, it set a bar for our product marketing teams to live up to and for the communications teams to hold them to.

KEY LESSONS

A beautifully articulated and compelling cause is pointless if your organization isn't living up to it. A cause doesn't exist by words alone but by the actions that demonstrate the organization's purpose. People should be able to work out what your cause is, just by looking at your actions.

Getting customers to use words like *join* rather than *buy* demonstrates when you are really onto something. Actually, you don't really want customers; you want fans, and we'll come back to that later.

SO WHAT ARE YOU GOING TO DO ABOUT IT?

My suggestion: List the compelling product or service initiatives that your organization is actively working on to deliver the stated cause or purpose. Look at that list tomorrow and assess how many you are genuinely excited about seeing come to fruition. Or, more importantly, how many would your customers be genuinely excited about? Then determine if your list needs more work.

Write your thoughts here:

The Consumer Benefit: Being of Value Always Trumps Being New

When we were seeking to rediscover our mojo at Orange by focusing on the Bright Orange benefits I mentioned in my previous story, we looked at all the initiatives that we could implement quickly, but they were rarely simple and always took time.

However, there was one little-known feature that I loved that had existed for years, and it said a lot about who Orange was. Orange gave all their pay-as-you-go customers (many of whom were teenagers) a one-minute reserve call. This was designed for the type of situation where a teenager who'd missed their last bus home and had run out of credit on their phone (both of which shouldn't happen, but we know they do, far too often) could ring home and ask a parent to come and pick them up. I loved the caring nature of the reserve call concept.

I wanted this to be a key element of our new marketing campaign that we called "Fair," but I met with resistance from our Product Management group.

"That's not very new, we've had that for years," I was repeatedly told.

"But it's cool and no one knows about it," I replied.

"But it's not new." That same old argument.

"But as no one knows about it, it will be new to them!" I pushed, and eventually we included it alongside some other new features, all of which showed how we valued and embraced "fairness" in a sector where consumers perceived there to be many inherently unfair practices.

KEY LESSONS

The most important thing when looking for a consumer benefit is whether it provides real value to your customers. The second important thing is whether it helps differentiate you from your competitors.

Finally, the third important thing is whether it is new. Being of value and being differentiated are the two most important things, and they always trump new. We get too fixated on just talking about new stuff.

SO WHAT ARE YOU GOING TO DO ABOUT IT?

Write your thoughts here:

Never Deviate from Your Cause

For a very long time, Sky Television had been the dominant pay-TV provider in the UK. ONdigital had been created as a challenger brand to Sky, and they provided pay television to the British public without having to have a satellite dish on the side of your house. The extra channels were all accessible through your normal television aerial. Sky was not a well-liked or trusted brand, nor was its owner, Rupert Murdoch, so ONdigital fashioned itself as the consumer champion, the one you could trust and the antidote to all the brashness of Sky.

During my first week at ONdigital as Sales and Marketing Director, there was a directors meeting. Towards the end, there was a proposal to increase the cost of the customer monthly magazine, which was collected by direct debit from their bank account. The customers were going to be notified in a mailing that had been crafted in such a way that the price increase was buried in paragraph three with the hope that the customer would stop reading before they got to that piece of news. This was all designed to reduce the number of customers who would unsubscribe from the magazine.

The proposal was made, and then our CEO Stuart Prebble went around the room and asked everyone individually if they were okay with the proposal. Customer Services approved it, Broadcasting said yes, IT did too, and so did every other department head. With ten yeses from around the table, I was asked that question. Given that everyone else had said yes, I went along with it too. That, in itself, is never a good reason. On top of that, I had a slightly uncomfortable feeling about the whole discussion, but I still said yes. Pathetic. I must have breached at least four of my punk principles in uttering that chicken-livered, follow-the-herd yes.

That evening travelling home on the train, I was thinking of our brand positioning. If we wanted to come across as the consumer champion, we had to act in that way too. I started feeling sick to the pit of my stomach about how we had approved the price increase communication and felt even madder with myself for not speaking up, as I was the brand custodian. Honestly, I had been pathetic in my first big meeting; I had let myself down, let the company down, and—most importantly—let the customers down. I knew Stuart Prebble was always in the office early in the morning to read his emails before the day got started. I set my alarm for five thirty a.m., so I could catch the six a.m. train and be in the office by seven forty a.m. I went straight to Stuart's office and walked in and asked if he had a minute. He nodded.

I said something along the lines of . . . "Stuart, I want to apologize for my performance yesterday in the directors meeting." He looked confused.

"We agreed to bury a price increase communication in the third paragraph of a letter. Trying to hide things from our customers isn't being true to who we set out to be.

"You went around the room and asked every director if their group agreed with the communication. They all said yes, but there was one group we didn't ask . . . our customers! What would they have said?"

Stuart immediately agreed to stop the communication, and I took the action to get the letter rewritten and ensure that the price increase was very clearly explained in the first paragraph.

I went on to suggest something slightly less ordinary: "We should have a physical representation of our customers in every board or directors meeting, to remind us of them and ensure that we never forget the most important group of people again. And anyone at any time must be free to speak up on their behalf. I want a mannequin sitting at the board room table in every meeting, to be that physical representation of our customers." Again, he agreed.

The following week I had smuggled a mannequin into Stuart's office, which was near the boardroom. I arrived at work early again and started trying to build the female mannequin, connecting all her limbs to her torso and dressing her. Stuart stood by and watched as I struggled to dress this female mannequin. I was kneeling on the floor trying to button up her blouse and pull up her trousers. She was proving to be very uncooperative, and I was getting more and more embarrassed as I fumbled around on the floor like some teenager. Stuart announced that we should give her a name—"Clarissa," he offered. Fifteen minutes before our meeting was due to start, I carried Clarissa into the boardroom and sat her in a seat at the center of the table. People wandered in. Some looked inquisitively at Clarissa, everyone was confused, but nobody said anything.

Stuart came in and started the meeting. He spoke for about five minutes, waiting to see if anyone would ask who this young lady was, but nobody did. This was, again, that same crowd mentality coming to the surface that we had seen before. No one wanted to be the first to speak up about how hiding the price increase was wrong, and now no one wanted to be the person who asked why the hell we had a mannequin sitting at the table. So after an uneasy five minutes during which no one would acknowledge the elephant in the room, Stuart explained the concept; everyone then "got it" and embraced the sentiment.

A company's cause should define who it is, and its brand is the general public's perception of the company. So the brand should be a very clear and direct reflection of the cause—if it isn't, then the cause isn't shining through in the company's actions.

Everyone needs to fully understand the cause and what the company stands for, and then every action of the company needs to be true to that persona. Every action should deliver on its cause and help build its brand that reflects the cause. If we'd tried to hide the price increase, we would have been no better than the other guys. Clarissa became a very visible and tangible representation of the people we served and what we stood for. From thereon in, Clarissa was always present and guided us in many a decision.

P.S. I introduced Clarissa's twin sister to Motorola's product room about six years later.

KEY LESSONS

We cannot pick and choose the moments when we want to follow our cause. We should be committed to being a *lighthouse* brand; that is, one who shines brightly, whose position is fixed, so that people can navigate their world trusting in us and our position on things. We cannot achieve that lighthouse status if our actions are based on shifting principles or on anything but a one hundred percent dedication to the cause.

Whether we like it or not, too often we forget the people we go to work for . . . our customers. They are rarely present when we make decisions that affect them. A visual representation of the people we serve helps keep us grounded and focused.

Importantly it also helps build a culture where people are reminded of what our cause is and who we should be focusing on and that encourages people to speak up if ever we deviate.

Do you need a Clarissa?

SO WHAT ARE YOU GOING TO DO ABOUT IT?

Write your thoughts here:

Passionately and Powerfully Articulate Your Cause Every Time

Motorola had signed a contract joining Product (RED) and were in the early stages of planning our launch, which was about four months away. Ron Garriques, Jim Wicks, and I had gone to meet Bobby Shriver and Bono at Bono's penthouse apartment in New York. The purpose of the meeting was twofold. Jim, our head of design, was going to show Bono and Bobby some of our new prototype phones that would, in due course, be available in (RED) versions. We had also scheduled four phone calls with top executives at the big US telecom networks. The pitch we were about to make to them was that there was a crisis unfolding in Africa, and we (Motorola) were going to give a meaningful portion of the profit from the sale of some of our phones to (RED), and we wanted to find a network partner to join us in this endeavor. They would, in turn, give a meaningful portion of the profit they made from each phone call. That would mean the consumer pitch would be stunning and compelling. Buy a (RED) RAZR, and a portion of the profits from that phone go to help eliminate AIDS in Africa, and then every time you use it, a proportion of the cost of that call will also be used to help save someone's life.

Bono delivered the pitch so powerfully: "There is a pandemic happening in Africa, where every day nearly six thousand people are dying from a preventable, treatable disease. We can change that and changing the world is sexy." It was impactful, worthy, and needed. "Our generation will be defined by how we respond to the AIDS pandemic," and this was their opportunity to be a part of that, to have a part in changing the world.

We gave this pitch three times and had a good initial response from all the networks, but like so many other companies they were cautious about giving some of their profits away.

Then we moved on to the fourth and final call; Ron turned to Bono and gave an unusual brief. "Okay, this call is going to be slightly different. There are two words that you cannot use in this call."

Bono looked a little confused and inquisitively asked, "Okay, what are they?"

Ron replied, "AIDS and Africa."

Bono was shocked. "What do you mean? This is all about AIDS in Africa. How can I pitch (RED) without saying AIDS or Africa? Its purpose is to eliminate AIDS in Africa; it's all about those two words that you say I cannot use."

"Yes, that's right," Ron replied.

Bono asked, "Why?"

Ron then said, "Look, there are some people who are rednecks, and they still think AIDS is caused by homosexuals, so they have no understanding or sympathy towards them. They believe charity should start and finish at home, i.e., in the USA. One of those people will be on this call, so please don't say AIDS or Africa."

Bono was stunned that such people still existed. He didn't quite know what to think or do. We started the call, and after a brief introduction Ron handed it over to Bono. Bono explained the concept of (RED), but when he talked about its purpose, he simply stated that we were trying to change the world by creating (RED) and a portion of the profits would go to help people less fortunate than ourselves. I have never seen such restraint. He wanted to blurt out his pitch, but like a good soldier he followed orders.

Needless to say, we made no progress whatsoever from that last call.

Ron was right to warn Bono about the likely reaction from one person we were pitching to, and at the time I thought his guidance about modifying the story was also right. I wouldn't endorse that same advice now. When you have your story—your cause—you know your pitch, and you can emotionally and compellingly deliver it. Don't sanitize it for the shortsightedness of others.

KEY LESSONS

Bono is a master storyteller. He conveyed the stark realities of life and death for thousands of people halfway around the world. He described eliminating AIDS as sexy. He invited people to be part of the group who would define how our generation would be remembered. Punk rock didn't try to please everybody; punks were who they were, and you took them or left them. We should do the same. Bottom line: Don't compromise your message for those who will never follow.

Never tire of articulating your cause; stay true to it, and never tone it down because you worry that it will not be accepted by some as it is. Screw them, they don't count.

SO WHAT ARE YOU GOING TO DO ABOUT IT?

My suggestion: Articulate your organization's story today to someone and gauge their reaction. Do you have a cause? Can you articulate it well? Does it inspire people?

Write your thoughts here:

The Bottom Line

Your cause is vitally important—it should direct everything. What you choose to spend your life doing matters so much more than most people ever realize. So work for an organization whose work excites you—if it doesn't, change it.

Ensure your organization can articulate in an inspiring way what its cause is—if it can't, change it.

Ensure your organization is working on a whole slew of projects that demonstrate how you are delivering on your cause—if it isn't, then create some and cancel the ones that don't.

Ensure that your cause directs every decision your organization makes—if it doesn't today, then change it starting tomorrow.

Finally, use your cause to inspire your people. In 2015 I was trying, for the second time, to hire Ami Silverman into Microsoft; Ami is a talented executive who I first met when she was at T-Mobile. She was very highly thought of at T-Mobile, she had just been promoted to a very senior role, and clearly was in the middle of a great career with them. It seemed that she was going to reject our approach again, so I appealed to her based on our mission and the kind of products we were creating, relative to her existing company. I said, "I guess it comes down to what you want to do with your life: Do you want to change the world or carry on selling a commodity? Do you want to launch holographic computing or a new airtime plan?"

Ami would subsequently tell me that was the moment we had her; that was her you-had-me-at-hello moment. Having a cause inspires effort and fortitude; it guides action, it unites a team, it attracts talent and builds loyalty.

When we look back at the punk movement, we see how it changed the music scene forever—but it also changed society. As the great Vivienne Westwood said . . . "The reason why I am proud of my part in the punk movement is that I think it really did implant a message that was already there . . . punk made it something cool for people to stand up for, . . . we do not believe government, . . . we are against government."[2]

In the same way, I hope that like-minded people will be proud of the impact that their punk rock mentality has in implanting a message that a cause really matters, both to the individual and to the collective organization, and that it's cool for people to stand up for what they are passionate about. Passion is the catalyst that prevents mediocrity, averageness, and things being lukewarm.

Bottom line: Don't waste your precious life doing something that is unimportant to you—find your cause and allow it to direct everything you do.

2 Eric Wilson, "Vivienne Westwood: At 71, Still Not Done Provoking," *New York Times* (March 25, 2013), https://cn.nytimes.com/style/20130325/c25westwood/en-us/.

ELemeNt 2:

BUILD A MOVEMENT

"The revolution is not an apple that falls when it is ripe.
You have to make it fall."

CHE GUEVARA

"All successful revolutions are the kicking in of a rotten door."

JOHN KENNETH GALBRAITH

"Punk is about revolting against a society that
doesn't think we deserve a revolution."

ANONYMOUS

Punk was a movement. The early punks were revolutionaries smashing down the conventional walls of music, society, and fashion. They divided opinion and illuminated the stark divide between young and old, rich and poor, those with prospects and those staring at a dark future.

Punk was a full sensory assault. Before punk the only thing music artists asked you to do was to buy their records. Punk required so much more of its fans! You were expected to sing (or rather shout) politically charged songs, shave off half your hair and brightly color and spike the other half, have your body pierced and put safety pins in those piercings, bounce incessantly, dress radically in ripped clothes, and rebel against almost anything and everything. It wasn't easy to be a punk. Only the committed could do it. In fact, some of the punks who had a haircut that could be spiked at the weekends and then flattened to a more conservative and work-acceptable style come Monday were verbally abused for their lack of commitment and were rightly considered poseurs.

Punk mobilized a section of the youth of the mid-1970s generation. They wanted change, but more importantly they created a change that shook the music industry and the culture of the day. It was able to do that because punk created followership. People associated with the ideology and saw punk as a way to express their anger, frustration, and insistence on fundamental change. Punk, more than the music, was a mindset, and that attracted people.

The power of punk was that it didn't try to appeal to everyone. It didn't tone things down to be broadly appealing, and the last thing it wanted was broad appeal. Its strategy (and there was one, although a large portion of it may be after-the-fact rationalization) was all about the shock factor, and its intention was to offend at every turn. It wasn't trying to be popular; it just wanted a deep passionate followership from a small committed core. The more shocking they were and the more they offended the mainstream, the more committed their followers became.

I've asked myself who were the primary influencers who created the punk rock movement: The Ramones, the Sex Pistols, Malcolm McLaren, or a whole host of other bands? The conclusion I have come to is that they all had a small part to play, but the real creators were the punk fans. The group of committed followers who embraced the fashion, the hairstyles, the piercings, the rebellious attitudes—they were the ones who made punk. Bands like the Sex Pistols had been cut from supporting a headline act after only one show; they'd been dumped by their record label and were regularly booed offstage. That was when people were judging them for their musical qualities. But then people got what they were all about. As I said in the introduction, Steve Jones (the Sex Pistols' guitarist) famously said, "We're not into music, we're into chaos." It was the attitude more than the sound. Once people understood that, they embraced the attitude, and the punk following really exploded . . . certainly in the UK. The hardcore followers created the punk movement. It was about the people. It is always about the people.

Punk Rock Business is all about the people too.

The first punk rock attribute described how vitally important it is to have a cause that you and the people around you can believe in—something that makes you feel you're doing something good or impressive or meaningful. But that cause, however worthy, only creates a movement if leaders can inspire others to rally behind it. In today's fickle world, businesses need to recruit employees who are passionate about their cause, and they need to attract not just customers but advocates or fans. We will look at each of these vital groups.

It is crucial that the people in the movement aren't just passive spectators but people of action. True leaders don't create followers; they create more leaders, both inside the organization and among their customers. Punk Rock Business is about mobilizing people and creating a movement.

Punk Rock Business requires a movement to be truly transformative, and all movements are created by a group of passionate, committed people who are unified, inspired, and who collaborate to drive change. Yes, movements will always have known leaders, but it is critically important that people understand that everyone in a movement who is creating change is a leader.

Building a movement takes huge effort from the early leaders. The problem in the early days of any movement is that, just like all motion, inertia must be overcome, and friction is always there to cause things to come to a grinding stop. That's why this section is vitally important: Punk Rock Business cannot have real impact if it is only delivered by a single person, however senior they may be. Big dramatic changes are almost always impossible to achieve single-handedly. One lone person embracing the punk rock attitude will just be seen as bizarre and out of touch with the organization. There needs to be a group of early adopters. There is always more power in groups, so attracting people within your organization to follow the leader's example is critical and is one of the key activities you must engage in.

We will look at building an internal movement in this section, but let us remember the external group, your customers, who should be your true fans, whose advocacy and support attracts others.

The difference between a customer and a fan is huge and critically important. A customer is defined as someone who buys goods or services, whereas a fan is someone who has a strong interest in and admiration for a person or thing. A customer has a transactional relationship, whereas a fan has a far deeper bond.

We all know how the most potent form of marketing is strong endorsement from relevant word of mouth. Never has that been truer than in today's world of customer ratings and reviews. Consumers don't buy anything these days without checking the level of endorsement from current owners. *Time* magazine called it early by awarding "Person of the Year 2006" to "you"—the consumer. As Lev Grossman of *Time* magazine described, "It's about the many wresting power from the few and helping one another for nothing and how that will not only change the world, but also change the way the world changes."[1]

---

1 Lev Grossman, "You—Yes, You—Are Time's Person of the Year," *Time:* (December 25, 2006), http://content.time.com/time/magazine/article/0,9171,1570810,00. html.

Businesses need like never before to create a movement externally. They need to create something that resonates deeply with their customers, so that the customers aren't just casual purchasers but are, indeed, fans—and a fan base will always do double duty as the company's second sales force. That's the power of people, the power of a movement.

In this section, we will look at stories that are all about gaining people's support for and active participation in creating a movement. You will read about inspiring leaders who mobilized people by creating a unifying purpose, building trust, inspiring others, collaborating with others, nurturing their early followers, demonstrating the behaviors they wanted to see, and turning real-life examples of greatness into legendary stories.

But always remember that the power of the movement comes from the people—it's always all about the people. It always is. And if it is always about the people, then you better get focused on them and give them the attention they deserve.

YOU'RE EITHER A LEADER OR A BYSTANDER

You are either a leader or a bystander just watching from the sidelines. For a great example of this watch the TED Talk by Derek Sivers on "How to Start a Movement." In it he states, "The first follower is what transforms a lone nut into a leader." He talks about the importance of celebrating the first followers and treating them as equals. So, in a movement, having more leaders makes it less risky for others to join. Any movement needs some early activists to get things started; it cannot be a lone voice. Nurture the early adopters.

Your Purpose Should Attract Followers and Be Unifying

When I first joined Motorola, Ron Garriques had recently been promoted to President of the Mobile Devices division. He had secured the job based on an audacious claim and plan. At that time in 2005, Nokia was the clear global market leader, with market share just above forty percent. Sony Ericsson, Samsung, and Motorola were vying for second place, but we were all a long way back with about twelve percent of the market each. Ron believed in the power of a range of radically thin phones that we had in development, and he was convinced that they could enable us to overtake Nokia as market leaders. His pitch to Ed Zander, the Chairman and CEO, was "#1 in 1,000 days." Ron believed that we could gain one point of share or more from Nokia every quarter, and if we could do that we could gain market leadership in three or four years.

I loved Ron's explanation of the 1,000 days. "With the innovation we have coming, we can take more than one point of share from Nokia each quarter. And if we do that every quarter for three years, we will get to be the #1 mobile phone manufacturer. However, we may need a little breathing space in the 1,000 days, so I am not going to tell you if I am counting weekends or not. If we do, then we have three years, if we don't, we will do it in four!" Our goal as a team was clear: We had somewhere between twelve and sixteen quarters to close the thirty-point share gap. We needed to take about one and one-quarter share points each quarter to do it in three years and one point each quarter to do it in four. We had countdown clocks, and every presentation started with the number of days to go. Every quarter, Ron would report a share point gain or more. We recorded thirteen straight quarters of share gains.

While this wasn't a worthy cause that would leave the world a better place, it was a competitive cause that Ron mobilized people behind. We wanted to be the best, the most popular phone brand in the world, and Ron had set the goal that we all bought into. It was energizing and unifying.

The beauty of this goal was that our growth aspirations had been set by default. Each annual budgeting cycle we knew we had to grow by between four and six points of share—and thereby, by definition, each quarter by between one and one and one-quarter points. We could make pretty good forecasts for the market size, so we knew we needed to grow at close to thirty percent every year if we were to achieve our goal. No one questioned our goal—it was #1 in 1,000 days—and we all marched to that tune.

When Ron laid out the audacious growth goals, it was clear that people liked the rhetoric and the ambition, but many didn't believe this bold plan was possible or sustainable. By the time we delivered the third successive quarter of one-point share growth, the doubters and bystanders started to believe. And because people like to be associated with success, they soon joined with the believers. Those early successes that came on the back of the RAZR launch gave credibility to this goal. The numbers spoke for themselves. We had momentum, and we were marching to the #1 in 1,000 days tune.

KEY LESSONS

A well-articulated, unifying purpose or goal reaps huge benefits just by preventing needless discussion. We never debated how many phones we would sell. We had signed up for a three-year goal: The sales and marketing teams knew what our quota would be each quarter—enough to give us at least a one-point share gain, supply chain knew how many phones they were going to be expected to build, and the design and engineering teams knew they needed to innovate more quickly than the competition to give us differentiation. It was simple in many ways.

You will never get everyone on board from day one, but ensuring you get early success demonstrates the reality of the plan and attracts the bystanders.

SO WHAT ARE YOU GOING TO DO ABOUT IT?

My suggestion: Ask ten people tomorrow what your cause or company goal is and what their role is in that. Then see how aligned their answers are. If they don't all articulate the cause well, then how can they be aligned? And if they aren't aligned, you don't have a movement. It will be obvious how much work you need to do to articulate more clearly the company's purpose and everyone's roles within that.

Write your thoughts here:

People Don't Care How Much You Know, Until They Know How Much You Care. Show Them!

Several times during my career I offered to resign if an initiative failed. I did this as my guarantee of success and as a very real demonstration of my conviction that a decision or program was the right one. "If it doesn't work, fire me." "If it isn't a success, I'll resign." The last time I did that was in early 2015 when I wanted to switch over one hundred third-party vendor staff to full-time Microsoft employees to work in the Windows area within Best Buy's stores in the US. We had suffered too high a turnover in the group of outsourced staff. And if you don't keep the people, then you are always in the mode of training new people who move on to a permanent job somewhere else just as they become proficient and acquire the desired level of expertise. We believed we would get more committed, better quality, longer-tenured people if we employed them directly. However, we were making a long-term commitment to this model, and we would incur meaningful redundancy costs if we ever decided we didn't want to continue with this program. So we needed to be certain that this was something that would work for the long term. There were doubters and the inevitable conservative types who wanted the less risky, half-pregnant outsourced solution. I had to argue for this program long and hard, and when I was asked how confident I was that we wouldn't be looking to lay these people off in a year or two, I replied, "Absolutely certain, and if I am wrong, you'll be able to add my name to the list." That conviction and personal commitment went a long way in gaining our CFO's support. If you make that type of commitment, people know that you believe in it, but more importantly they know that you are going to do everything in your power to ensure it succeeds. It will never be one of those initiatives that wither on the vine because of a lack of attention.

A few months later, it was my pleasure to speak to these one hundred new recruits at their initial training session. I was asked to kick off the day by speaking to them about our vision for their role. I was introduced to them by Ami Silverman, who ran our US retail team, and she told them about the personal guarantee I had given to secure the program. She did this, not to praise me, but to show them just how invested in the program we all were personally and how convinced we were that this program was the right thing to do. We needed these new recruits to be tremendous and to be the best they could be every single day in the store where they worked. I appealed to them through my very real commitment to the program, and I dramatized this by flashing up a photo of my family and jokingly saying, "My family are also really interested in this program working, and they send their heartfelt best wishes to all you new recruits."

Later that evening at the welcome reception, I made a conscious effort to walk around the large group and try to talk to as many people as I could. I was staggered by how many people thanked me for believing in them and assured me that my job was safe. Probably eighty percent of the people I spoke to that evening raised the subject of my "fire me if it doesn't work" commitment, and then they assured me I could count on them. Many also told me to reassure my wife and children when I went home that night and to tell my daughters that they would still be able to go to college. The new team could see and feel how important this program was to all of us; they could see how we had staked a great deal on their performance, and they didn't want to let us down.

This is the second benefit of such a personal guarantee. It is my experience that when good people see that you are really betting on them succeeding, that you have confidence in them delivering, and you are committed to their success, then they respond magnificently—they step up and deliver. They repay your personal conviction with their own personal conviction. They repay the trust that you show in them by showing you that it was well placed. Confidence, conviction, and trust all have the tendency to be replicated by good people when they see you showing those characteristics.

I have only ever had one person make the same statement of

commitment to me. That was Deniz Unay when she ran Microsoft's retail business in the Middle East and Africa. I was visiting the region, and I met with her and her leadership team in South Africa. They were talking to me about their far-from-great Microsoft Office sales performance. They explained the work they had done and the challenges they were facing, but quite simply we just weren't getting enough traction. I was direct, but I wasn't threatening or critical; we just needed faster progress. Deniz was passionate and cared deeply about the business and her team. We reviewed their work, reframed the problems, and significantly refined their plans, but I had to reset expectations about what was good and laid out some far more aspirational goals.

Deniz was determined to meet these. She believed passionately in the plans we had just created, and I think she was a little disappointed that her team hadn't come up with such plans themselves. So, Deniz felt a conviction (and maybe a little anger) as she closed the meeting by saying, "Okay Jeremy, I will deliver your numbers by the end of the year, and if I don't, you can fire me." I smiled and responded, "And do you think I didn't already know that?"

Deniz burst out laughing and smiled the smile of a friendly assassin who had just accepted a new mission. Our Microsoft Office sales numbers were now firmly in her sights. There was a determination within Deniz that she mostly hid behind a pleasant smile, but as soon as she made a commitment, there was no doubt that she would deliver—and she did.

KEY LESSONS

People can always tell whether you have conviction or not. They can smell enthusiasm and commitment from a mile away. They want to know if you care. When people know you care (and they always do know), they always give you so much more in return.

People want to know you care about the work they do; they want to know that you care about their contribution and care about them as people. If good people know you are committed to them, then they will respond because they embrace the fact that you have put your trust in them, and they want to show that your trust wasn't misplaced.

Offering your job isn't offering anything that isn't there already. Your boss can fire you whenever he or she pleases (within the laws of the land of course!). But such a commitment makes a huge statement about your conviction; every time I have offered it, people have approved my request and allowed me to go and execute. More importantly, the team behind the initiative saw how I fought for our idea or initiative and staked my job on our plan. That has always resulted in unquestioning support and determination to deliver the targeted performance and protect my employment.

When the time arises, when you truly believe in something and you are faced with naysayers and doubters, demonstrate your conviction by making the ultimate show of confidence. Make it known to your team—you need them to understand that the stakes have just been raised by you. Don't be afraid to make it personal, because it is!

SO WHAT ARE YOU GOING TO DO ABOUT IT?

Write your thoughts here:

Enthusiasm Is Infectious and Attracts Followers

In July 2009, I went to my first Microsoft Global Sales Conference, known as the Microsoft Global eXchange meeting or MGX. With somewhere around fifteen thousand people in attendance each year, the event practically takes over its host city—and that year, the city was Atlanta. The conference lasts three or four days and always culminates in a speech from the company's CEO, who at that time was Steve Ballmer.

I was sitting in my seat, high up in the rafters of the Atlanta basketball stadium, at the end of three days of presentations. Many of us were a little subdued and lacked energy when Steve Ballmer walked out on stage. Well . . . he didn't walk—he bounded, skipped, and roared out on stage. The audience's energy levels switched instantaneously. Steve's enthusiasm was immediately electrifying. What followed was a substantive and inspiring closing speech that clarified exactly what we as a company needed to do, delivered in a way that kept us hanging on every word, and inspired us to go and deliver for Microsoft. Towards the end of the speech, he started to run (skip, bounce, and leap) around the stage shouting at the top of his voice, "I love this company." He was famous for it. There are many videos of it on YouTube, from various events, but I hadn't seen it before. Almost everyone jumped to their feet, cheering, shouting, and screaming along with him.

I sat there a little embarrassed and quite uncomfortable. This wasn't a company; it was more like a religious cult. I was in a state of shock, and it only intensified when Steve closed his speech by running up and down the aisles high fiving and chest bumping people. I left my first MGX seriously concerned about what type of company I had joined. I loved the energy, but Steve was crazy and there was something not quite right. I couldn't put my finger on it, but it wasn't quite right.

The following year I was back at MGX, and when Steve came out to talk to us, I was one of the first ones up, jumping and cheering.

I had been indoctrinated; I'd clearly drunk the Kool-Aid and was a follower and a believer. This time I again left the arena very concerned—not concerned about Microsoft, but concerned about myself and how I now had a very different view of this spectacle.

Steve did an amazing job explaining how we were changing the world, the challenges ahead of us, and what he needed his sales team to go and do . . . but more than that he showed us his passion for what we were achieving, the work we were all doing, and for all of us who worked for Microsoft. But it wasn't just passion—it was love. When he screamed, "I love this company," no one doubted it for a moment. He undoubtedly did. He had been there when he was employee number thirty, and now we were one of the most valuable companies on the planet with over one hundred thousand employees.

What changed between my first and second MGX was that I now understood what Microsoft was all about. At my first MGX, I turned up as an employee—at my second one, I turned up as a family member.

Steve made us all feel more like family members than employees. He showed his passion and energy—he declared his undying love for the company and for all of us by extension. We walked out of that arena feeling ten feet tall and ready to walk over hot coals for him.

I still thought he was crazy, but as I think he once said, "He was our crazy."

I had learned that working for Microsoft wasn't like any other job I'd had—it was more than a job! Steve Ballmer had the ability to make us realize more clearly that the work we were doing was exciting, critically important, and world changing. We knew it was all of these, but Steve's articulation always made it so much more so. Enthusiasm is tremendously powerful for many reasons. It makes everything more attractive; it's more fun; it enables more effective communication; it makes tasks feel easier because people will expend more energy on the things they care about; and, most of all, people of passion are the people who get stuff done.

There was still something a little awkward after that, my second MGX, but once I understood the depth of the enthusiasm that Steve had for Microsoft and how he transmitted it to us like we had been hooked up to an intravenous drip, the small amount of awkwardness was an irrelevance.

As the years progressed, I looked forward to these Steve Ballmer moments more and more. I have never seen anyone energize fifteen thousand people from the four corners of the world the way Steve did. At the end of his presentations, we would leave the arena promising to walk through walls for Steve. Whatever he asked, we would have done; he made us believe in what the company was doing. There was intense love for Steve from Microsoft employees. I suppose if you take a company from a small start-up in the 1980s to this corporate monolith, you cannot help but love the company; it was genuine. Steve always wore his heart on his sleeve. We all knew just how much he truly loved the company, its work, and its people . . . with all his heart and with every sinew of his body.

That phrase, "People won't remember what you said or did, but they will remember how you made them feel," was so true for Steve. He would send us on our way believing we worked for the greatest company in the world and being prepared to do everything humanly possible for it . . . and for him. Steve cared deeply, and as a result he made us care deeply too.

KEY LESSONS

To create a movement, to create intense followership, to gain the greatest level of support from others, you MUST appeal both rationally and emotionally. The rational thought defines the need; the emotional element amplifies the energy and the desire you are willing to invest to get it done. The rational message appeals to the head and convinces someone of the course of action, the path to be taken to achieve the goal. The emotional message is all about the heart and determines how hard someone will try, how much effort they will put in, and the lengths they will go to, to achieve the goal. Enthusiasm is essential. It is the fuel for the cause.

Don't worry about opening up and expressing how you genuinely feel; that's what makes you human, and that is attractive to others.

SO WHAT ARE YOU GOING TO DO ABOUT IT?

Write your thoughts here:

A Successful Movement May Have Many Elements and Architects . . . Embrace Them All

Many successful movements have multiple constituents; if you think of the punk movement you could name the Sex Pistols, The Clash, The Ramones, and many, many more. Pokémon was similarly a movement with many protagonists. There was a television series, a film, trading cards, cuddly toys, the video games, and even Pokémon painted on Nippon airplanes.

Nintendo owned the Pokémon property, so as the Commercial and Marketing Director, I was responsible for the overall brand and all the related properties in the UK. We had some early planning meetings with all the license holders, and it was clear people were looking to compete with each other to make their Pokémon product the preeminent part of the franchise. We ultimately realized (after some petty squabbling) that the different elements were complementary and not competitive. Once we understood that, we stopped being protective of our ideas and plans; instead, we welcomed everyone into the fray and proactively partnered.

By working together, Pokémon attracted one of the most amazing groups of loyal fans I have ever witnessed. It was a cultural phenomenon that burst into our consciousness in 1999. It seems bizarre now that we doubted whether this basic Japanese anime style would work outside Japan, but we did. It first launched in the UK as a cartoon series that aired on a Saturday morning children's TV show called *SM:tv*. The show was presented by Ant and Dec, a young double act, and before every Pokémon episode, they did a humorous sketch about this new phenomenon. They were hilarious, and this helped build the growing cult that was Pokémon. We saw the power and potential of this double act endorsing Pokémon, and we had been trying to work out how we could get them to enhance their endorsement in a very natural non-commercial way without having to pay significant money. We had struggled to solve this dilemma, and we just kept drawing blanks.

I was driving home one evening, and in my six-minute journey, I happened to be in the car when the evening news came on. One of the stories was how Nippon Airways had just won a route to fly direct from London Heathrow airport to Tokyo. I remembered that Nippon Airways had a plane that had been painted with all the Pokémon characters. I quickly put two and two together.

Next morning, I found Shelly, our PR leader, and shared the idea that we go to *SM:tv* and tell them that we would offer a prize to twenty-five of their young viewers to fly to Tokyo, the home of Pokémon, on a Pokémon-branded plane accompanied by one parent with Ant and Dec. *SM:tv* would film the trip and broadcast the experience of Ant and Dec taking this group of Pokémon fans on a pilgrimage. We would pitch to Nippon that we would get them huge publicity for their new Heathrow flights and about £500,000 of PR coverage from the competition and the film. In return, they just needed to give us sixty round-trip flights and arrange for the Pokémon-branded plane to be the aircraft that flew our entourage to Tokyo.

Shelly loved it and so did *SM:tv*. Nippon Airways agreed in an instant.

The competition received huge publicity for the three weeks running up to the start date of the trip. Nippon received beautiful visibility as the group boarded the plane, and then the pièce de résistance was seeing the Nippon Airways Pokémon plane leave the runway at London Heathrow. The trip was an amazing, fun-filled four days. The film of the trip showed how amazing and insane Pokémania was in Japan. This coverage fueled excitement for Pokémon, and it became a key section of that Saturday morning TV show. Those highly influential young TV presenters were now building the movement for us and doing it willingly. Pokémon served us all well.

Everyone was delighted, and it cost us next to nothing. We just traded value. The power of creative matchmaking.

KEY LESSONS

A movement is always a little organic; it is never perfectly defined. Don't try to be too controlling. A real movement may (and normally does) have many followers and protagonists; don't resist those who have a similar goal, even if it isn't perfectly aligned with your version—instead, embrace it. A mass of followers moving in the right general direction is far better than a small number of precise followers.

A key part of business is connecting the dots and seeing how mutually beneficial partnerships can develop. Sometimes other people can be a catalyst for creating the movement you need, so you must stay aware of others in or around your space, understand what they are trying to achieve, and then find the angle for a mutual collaboration.

SO WHAT ARE YOU GOING TO DO ABOUT IT?

Write your thoughts here:

Never Miss an Opportunity to Enlist a New Follower

One of Microsoft's largest Xbox customers was Game, a UK retailer. I had been asked to speak at their Store Managers conference. These conferences are tremendously important because the store managers are hugely influential in driving sales in their stores. When competing head-to-head in a two-horse race, the store manager's preference can make a huge difference on sales and share.

I was introduced at the conference by Martyn Gibbs, their CEO, and he told the store managers how I had flown over five thousand miles from Seattle to be there—that impressed them. While it was technically true that I had just flown in, I was coming anyway for a family event, so it wasn't as impressive as he made it sound. We ended my section by giving away to every store manager a limited-edition Microsoft phone with Master Chief, the hero of the Halo video game, engraved on the back. The place went crazy. They loved the gesture, everyone stood and applauded, and some people were actually crying with joy.

There was a break immediately following our presentation, and all the store managers went into the room next door for a coffee. Our team stayed in the conference room celebrating the fact that we had delivered a very strong hour-long presentation and received a standing ovation—it was such a relief, and we were exhausted from days of preparation.

Then we realized that three hundred of the most influential people in the UK games industry were fifty yards away having a coffee. What were we thinking just standing there congratulating ourselves? So we quickly gathered our team, went next door, split up, and worked the room, thanking them for their support and engaging with them on a much more personal basis. This was the business equivalent of the politicians knocking on people's doors and asking for their vote. I gave out lots of business cards, and several store managers have emailed me regularly every Christmas season to assure me of their continued loyalty to Xbox.

KEY LESSONS

You win followers one at a time. You build a movement one follower at a time. Yes, sometimes we get the chance to speak to a large group of people to expound our message, but one-on-one, or one-to-few, is always so much more powerful. That's because two-way reciprocal engagement is much more impactful than a monologue or broadcast communication. So always solicit followership in two-way dialogue whenever possible.

SO WHAT ARE YOU GOING TO DO ABOUT IT?

Write your thoughts here:

Nothing Says I Care Like Being There

Repeat this after me three times: Nothing says I care like being there. Nothing says I care like being there. Nothing says I care like being there.

There are so many times in life where you must show up to demonstrate how much you care. This applies to your children's activities, your customers' meetings, and your team's social gatherings. Nothing says what is important to you more than how you spend your time, and making the effort to show up in person makes a huge statement.

I had to be in Sydney on a Friday, and then I had to be in Hong Kong for a day on the following Monday, but because I had promised Maddie, my middle daughter who was eleven years old at the time, I would be at her ballet show, I flew back to Chicago for about twenty-four hours. It would have been so easy to have said it was too much, but a promise is a promise, and I wasn't prepared to be seen as a flaky father. So, I flew across the international date line four times in four days. We know being there makes a huge statement to our kids. It's no different for our people.

The beauty of the global teams I've worked with, whether at Microsoft or Motorola, was that whenever we traveled to visit the teams in the various countries around the world we were assured that they would be the most amazing hosts. They would spend so much of their time with us in the evenings and look after us so well. For me that meant that when they visited our events in our country, we had to host them with the same generosity and willingness to engage. After all, these were the people who worked tirelessly for us each and every day in their corner of the world, and we needed them to know how much we valued that. The challenge was that when they came to visit us in HQ, they generally all came at the same time for one of our global summits, so it was much harder to reciprocate the same care and friendship that they showed us.

At Microsoft, we split the world into thirteen Areas, and we often had global meetings where all thirteen teams from around the world would meet. While we would have some big communal evening gatherings, we would normally allocate one evening when each of our thirteen Areas would host their own dinner. The challenge for all the global leaders on those evenings was which Area's dinner to attend. Most would choose to attend the event of the best-performing Area, or the Area that had people they particularly liked to hang out with. But my plan for the evening was to hire a driver to take my HQ team and me around to as many of the dinners as possible, to say hello to as many people as possible, and to be visible to as many of my teams as possible.

As I said, we split the world into thirteen Areas, and so there were thirteen Area dinners or parties that we tried to attend. An impossible task, but that didn't prevent us from trying. They tended to be spread out all over the host city, but many were held in roughly the same parts of the city. Some tended to start early and finish early, like Japan. Others started late and finished late, like the Latin American one. So, it required military-like precision to work out how we were going to get around to attending as many as possible.

The parties tended to start at around seven thirty p.m., and the late ones finished around two a.m. So, we had over six hours to get to all thirteen. The rules of engagement were to target twenty minutes in each party. Grab a bottle of beer on the way in, get around to as many people as possible, have photos taken with the team to show we were there, and then meet at the exit after twenty minutes. As we exited, we had to leave the bottle of beer with at least half of it remaining. We had worked out that by following that rule we would only drink five or six small bottles of beer in six hours, and we could clearly manage that without becoming intoxicated in any way.

Now, sadly, we never achieved our goal of making it to all thirteen parties as they tended to be too spread out, but we did manage eleven on two occasions. We followed up the evening's journey by sharing all the photos with our team as a memento of the week.

The gesture was always tremendously appreciated, and our Area teams recognized the effort we made to come and say hello, even if it was just briefly.

When it was announced that I was leaving Microsoft, I received hundreds of emails from colleagues around the world. It was pleasing to see the consistency of their comments. They thanked me for inspiring them, for being demanding and pushing them hard to be better and achieve excellence, and for doing it while caring deeply for them and the people in the team. That last point was very important to me.

Nothing says you care like being there. I didn't fully appreciate this until I started seeing those leaving emails come in. But it soon became very evident that, because I had always taken the time to visit their team events, say hello to as many people as possible, share a brief drink, and enjoy their company for a few moments, it said to them that I cared about them . . . and I did. Other executives tended not to do that. It was a long, hard evening, but one that was always fun, and it made a huge statement about our relationship that I felt was invaluable.

If your teams don't know you care and feel like there is just an authoritarian relationship between you and them, then your critical feedback is seen as just that, criticism—you being unsatisfied with their performance. However, if they know you care, then using almost the exact same words gets translated into "you pushed me to be better and strive for excellence" and there is never any hint of resentment, all because they know it comes from a place of good intent. A caring relationship allows trust to be built, and trust allows you to push harder without any alienation.

This is something I wished I fully understood twenty years earlier. This is the secret to building a movement. Before people will follow you, they want to know you genuinely care about them. They want to see that your communication with them is caring. Being demanding and caring are not mutually exclusive. Being caring allows you to be more demanding, without resorting to strong-arm tactics. What I have come to realize is that if your team knows you care, then you can push them harder, and they will respond better.

KEY LESSONS

Turn up whenever you can, and when people see you making an effort for them and to be with them, then it goes a long, long way.

Nothing says I care like being there.

Nothing demonstrates what is important to you more than how you spend your time.

SO WHAT ARE YOU GOING TO DO ABOUT IT?

Write your thoughts here:

You Don't Have to Be Able to Measure Your Movement

I was once addressing about seventy-five of my managers, talking about the type of culture I wanted to see in the team, when I was asked a question by someone who tended to have a cynical and pessimistic attitude: "How are we going to measure our culture?"

I replied by saying something like, "I don't really care about measuring it, we will know it exists when you come into work whistling a happy tune while you skip across the office." It wasn't said with any malice or put down, but people understood the sentiment.

It did get me thinking, though, about our fixation with measuring things. I suppose data gives something—preciseness and validity—that many find attractive. When people ask the question, "How will we measure it?" I think they are really asking, "How will we know when we have achieved it?" That's what you really want to know. So, my answer to you is this . . . you'll know when it exists because you'll feel it. Measuring things of the heart and soul are vastly overrated. Can you imagine creating a scorecard every time you had a girlfriend and trying to measure how in love you are? Of course not, so why are we so fixated with measuring everything that moves (or doesn't) at work?

So don't you dare try to measure your movement. Trust your intuition, go for it, and feel the progress. That is far more punk.

YOU CAN'T TRULY MEASURE A MOVEMENT

On my office wall hangs the "Life Manifesto" that I gave to my daughter. It says, "Life is about the people you meet and the things you create with them. So, go out and start creating." At the end of the day (or at the end of your career) what will really matter and will endure are the relationships you created and the amazing experiences you shared with your colleagues and partners—people who, I hope, became your friends. We will all have shared a unique and memorable journey; that is the beauty of work, together with the impact you had on each other's lives. You cannot measure that on a scorecard; in fact, if you tried, you would be soiling something special.

James Cracknell, the British gold medal-winning Olympian, summed up this sense of creating something great with the special people around you when we chatted at a charity lunch many years ago. He won a gold medal as part of the four-man coxless rowing team that included the great Steve Redgrave. I asked him how he feels when he looks at the gold medal and whether the hairs on the back of his neck stand up on end. He said not really, the gold medal is just a piece of metal. What he said meant more to him than the gold medal was the photograph of the four-man crew hugging each other in jubilation in their boat immediately after crossing the finishing line. The gold medal was the ultimate recognition and a very easy way to measure success, but that meant little to him. That photograph for him was far more valuable than the medal, because it summed up the grueling months of training, the raw emotion, the experience, and the achievement that he shared with Steve Redgrave, Matthew Pinsent, and Tim Foster. The photo did something no inanimate piece of metal could ever do, no matter how valuable it is or how hard people all over the world strive for it.

This is the sort of culture I spoke of earlier in this element. A movement where we love striving for greatness alongside those people we choose to spend our working lives with.

I have regularly used the Cracknell photo analogy at work, and I encourage you to do so as well. So whenever you get the opportunity to celebrate a great achievement, do it. But don't do it with some metal plaque or physical representation of the product. Find the photo opportunity that captures the team in that emotional moment of success. Ensure that it has all the team members and is full of emotion, then print it, frame it, put a handwritten personal message on the back, and get it placed in everyone's office. They will display it with pride on their desk. Over time, they will build their collection of great achievements and memorable moments, which will do two things: first, it shows the legacy they are building at the company, and second, it reminds them of their great memories—and each great memory is a reason why they should never leave the company.

As you go through this book, you will realize that being punk and embracing that attitude is passionate, scary, emotional, and intense, and you will need to throw your whole being into it. You cannot achieve that or come through that without caring deeply for your colleagues, for the team that you are part of. That was and is true at every company I have ever worked.

KEY LESSONS

Don't worry about measuring the movement you are trying to create, because it is hard to measure.

If you cannot measure it, it doesn't mean that it is not important. Don't try to measure everything, especially not feelings and emotions. William Bruce Cameron was spot on when he said, "Not everything that can be counted counts, and not everything that counts can be counted."[2]

Find what I call those James Cracknell photo moments and then use them for all they're worth.

SO WHAT ARE YOU GOING TO DO ABOUT IT?

Write your thoughts here:

---

2 William Bruce Cameron, *Informal Sociology: A Casual Introduction to Sociological Thinking* (New York: Random House, 1963), 13.

Tell Legendary Stories

When I joined Orange, I was pleasantly surprised by how everyone at the company believed in what our brand stood for and had a deep sense of understanding and love for it. My predecessors had done a fabulous job of making sure the organization understood the importance of the brand and the competitive advantage it gave us. When I worked for Orange, I used to give a presentation entitled "12,525 People Work in the Brand Team at Orange" for people in our stores and in our call centers. We had exactly 12,525 UK employees at Orange and that was the very point. One line I always used to deliver back then, in 2003, was that "the future of brands will be defined by how companies interact individually with their customers." People weren't going to base their opinions on how a company showed up in their TV ads but rather in how they treated people in their one-on-one interactions. This was just before the explosion of social media and the dramatic upsurge in the power of the voice of the general consumer. It wasn't hard to predict that trend, but looking back, the extent to which that has come true is more than I could have ever imagined. The pitch I was making with this presentation was that we needed every single employee to realize that they had our brand reputation in their hands, and every interaction they had would deliver either a positive or negative impact.

The challenge with those types of presentations is that people on the front line easily understood the point and the importance, but they'd always make the same demand: "So tell me what you really want me to do."

While they say *tell*, they really mean *show*. Showing is so much more powerful than telling. You saw that in the Steve Ballmer story and the Pokémon story already.

One of the most powerful ways to show them is to tell legendary stories that recount examples of greatness by their colleagues. Stories show the type of behavior that we want them to emulate, celebrate their colleagues' actions, and above all else show what is possible in the organization. Stories make concepts real and deliverable.

On the morning of one of these presentations, a customer email landed in my inbox, and with it a gift dropped in my lap. After a little digging, I found a new, hugely powerful legendary story that has since become one of my most favorite and most retold stories.

One of our customers had recently upgraded her phone. However, a few days after upgrading, she rang up and spoke to one of our customer service reps; she was very clearly upset, even distraught. She had started using her new phone, but the photos she had previously taken on her old device were not on her new phone. Our customer service rep explained that the photos were not stored on the sim card that she had swapped but were actually stored on the phone itself. At that time, we would send out a prepaid postage bag for customers to send in their old phones, which we would refurbish and then reuse by selling to a new customer at a lower price. The customer stated that she had indeed mailed her old phone in and asked frantically whether we could get her old phone back for her, before it was refurbished. Our customer service rep explained that was just impossible as they didn't get tracked in, and all were just automatically refurbished where all the data on each phone would be wiped. The customer was now wailing on the phone. After a few minutes of the customer service rep trying to calm her down, the customer managed to explain her distress. She had recently lost a child, just a few hours after she was born, and literally the only photos that existed in the entire world of her baby were on that phone. Without that phone, there was now no physical image of her daughter anywhere on the planet. It was heart wrenching. Our customer service rep sympathized profusely, but there was just nothing that we could do. Clearly, this experience also impacted our customer service rep, and it troubled her for the rest of her shift. When her shift ended, she took it upon herself to go and speak to the refurbishment team and explain the story. She took with her the model details of the phone and the IMEI number (which is a unique phone identification number) and started wading through the thousands of phones that had been sent in. After two or three hours, having checked hundreds and hundreds of phones, she found this woman's precious phone before it had been refurbished. She called her to tell her the good news that the phone had been found and the photos saved, and of course the customer was shocked but ecstatic.

I am convinced that this customer will still be with Orange to this day. The customer service rep showed her humanity by using her own time and her own initiative to find a way to make this happen, and she changed the life of this woman, who had already suffered such tragedy. This soon became a legendary story that swept through the corridors of our call centers. We recognized this customer service rep in a few ways, but for me she became the embodiment of the mentality we wanted.

KEY LESSONS

In creating a movement, you have to not just enlist followers but also show them how you want them to follow and participate. By creating legendary stories, you celebrate the unsung heroes, the ones who create the practical examples that define the followership that you want your people to show, and you inspire others to go the extra mile for your customers. But for us, what this story did even more powerfully was demonstrate that we wanted people to use their initiative to respond to a customer issue, we wanted them to embrace the attitude.

Inspiring stories unsurprisingly inspire others to follow suit. When people are inspired, they try to emulate the behavior in the stories.

SO WHAT ARE YOU GOING TO DO ABOUT IT?

My suggestion: Do you have a large collection of legendary stories that exemplify the type of actions or attitude you want your people to emulate? There is a five-step process to this. The stories must first exist, then they must be found, then be retold, then celebrated, and finally then they can inspire others. If you don't have a large collection that you can spurt out immediately, then start searching now.

Write your thoughts here:

Demonstrate the Behavior You Want to See, to the People Who Will Imitate

François Ruault, a colleague of mine, was taking a few days off from work, and he and his family were crossing from Seattle to San Juan Island's Friday Harbor on the car ferry. While on the ferry, he engaged in conversation with another driver who lived on the island. During the conversation, François asked for a recommendation for lunch on the island; the man recommended the Blue Water Bar and Grill overlooking the harbor and added, "Say you come from David."

The ferry docked, they bid each other farewell, and François searched and found the pub and stopped for lunch. He walked in with his family and saw the islander he had just been with on the ferry at another table. The islander looked across to François, smiled, and said, "See, I told you I thought it was good." The Ruaults had lunch and then asked for the bill, but were shocked to be told that it had already been paid for. François asked who had paid for their meal, and the waitress pointed to the gentleman from the ferry. François went over to remonstrate with the islander and say what a very kind gesture, but that he just couldn't possibly accept it. The gentleman said, "That's how we roll here; you will just have to pay it forward." David didn't think there was enough kindness in the world, and all he asked was that François do the same for a stranger sometime soon.

The kind soul knew how to create a ripple. I am sure he chose François because he could see that he, too, had a kind heart and would be honored to repay the debt to a stranger in the near future.

This islander's cause was to spread kindness and generosity to his fellow man, and he had worked out how one generous act could be multiplied over and over again. He had created his own movement—an act that caused François to follow, and hopefully others to follow in turn, over and over again.

KEY LESSONS

Work out how you can be an epicenter of such a moment so that it causes a ripple effect that spreads and displaces the status quo.

Choose like-minded people who will be inspired to emulate your actions.

SO WHAT ARE YOU GOING TO DO ABOUT IT?

My suggestion: Look at your team and determine whether they are like-minded people who will be inspired by the same things you are, whether they will follow your example, and whether they will also at times set the example for you and others to follow.

Write your thoughts here:

The Bottom Line

If having a cause is the first step in your business's revolution, realize that it will get nowhere without creating a movement. Probably the single most important task of a leader is to create followers, because it is the followers who create the movement.

Creating movements requires far more emotional intelligence than rational logic. It is all about motivating others, showing them that you care, and making them believe that they want to join you on the journey you are going on.

You have to be able to move people and get them to vote for you; each vote is gained one at a time, so realize and appreciate that it is a long, hard road. But as with all matters of motion, once something starts to move, its momentum always makes future progress easier.

Sometimes I didn't pay enough attention to this. My problem was that I was always in a rush to get to the destination. But to get there successfully, it was always important that I brought the team along with me, so my HR partners frequently counselled me to slow down and bring people along. So always be reminded of the old African proverb that says it best . . . "Alone we go faster, together we go farther."

Bottom line: If you are going to achieve something truly substantial, then you are going to need many more committed and passionate people other than yourself. The importance of getting others to join the movement cannot be overstated.

Element 3:

CREATE NEW AND RADICALLY DIFFERENT IDEAS

"Every now and then a man's mind is stretched by a new idea or sensation, and never shrinks back to its former dimensions."

OLIVER WENDELL HOLMES SR.

"Do just once what others say you can't do, and you will never pay attention to their limitations again."

JAMES R. COOK

"... to me punk rock is thinking outside of the box, outside of the program, outside the establishment."[1]

MADONNA

---

1 Madonna, interview by Matt Lauer, "Madonna: An American Life," NBC News, (December 9, 2003), www.nbcnews.com/id/3080045/ns/_dateline_nbc-newsmakers/t/madonna-american-life/#.WyFo2FMv2RY.

It is hard to imagine a music movement that was more innovative than punk rock, or one that was so radically different from what went before. Punk entered the world like a hurricane and blew away the bright and bubbly melodies of disco and replaced them with the full frontal musical assault that was punk rock—while also frenziedly shaking the social culture of the day. Punk didn't emerge quietly over time; it kicked down the front door and screamed, "I am here," and then spread like a virus. Every element of punk (the music, the lyrics, the hairstyle, the fashion, the anger, and the philosophy) was new and entirely different. They were all never seen before and probably never imagined before.

Punk was born out of a fundamental problem the youth of the mid '70s had. They needed music that had more energy and soul. They needed an avenue to not just express their frustration with the dead-end society they saw at that time but to call for a change. They needed to vent their anger. Many wanted to make a statement against consumerism and, in particular, the fashion industry.

Punk met all of those needs to the absolute extreme. Never before had music been played at anything like two hundred fifty beats per minute. Never before had music been played so loudly or aggressively. Never before had the lyrics to the songs been so politically charged or laid siege to taboo subjects like the British monarchy, abortion, fascism, or the Holocaust. Never before had a dance like the pogo allowed people to vent their aggression, and never before had getting a bloody nose while dancing been a common occurrence, let alone a badge of honor. Never before had distressed clothing held together by dental floss and safety pins made a genuine style statement. Everything about punk was so radically different—hated by many—but loved and embraced by the passionate, committed followers.

Punk was rebellious. It was created out of frustration and anger with dull music; but as I said earlier, at its heart, it is about optimism and a passion to change the status quo. People with a punk attitude have never waited for the establishment to change things; they have always gotten up off their ass and created the change. That's the punk attitude: being unaccepting of the unacceptable status quo—stepping forward and demanding change, in fact creating the change.

One of the most iconic demonstrations of a punk attitude in the political arena was the student rebellion in Tiananmen Square, Beijing. The image of the young man stopping the advance of a column of tanks simply by standing defiantly in their way has been seen by billions of people. The context of that moment of rebellion is worth remembering. The previous day, the Chinese army had opened fire on the pro-democracy protestors, who had been camped in Tiananmen Square for several weeks. The army killed hundreds, perhaps more than one thousand, of their own civilians. Yet here was one man who wanted radical change, and he wasn't going to allow the tanks to advance against the people again. He didn't hide in the crowd of spectators. He stepped forward and halted the military power of the Chinese army armed with nothing more than what looked like two shopping bags and a huge sense of defiance and courage. That individual, at that point in time, embodied everything that a punk rock attitude stood for. He was punk.

Punk attitude exists where people want change. It is evident in some of the most iconic statements from people who weren't prepared to put up with the status quo, where they demand something new, different, and fundamentally better. The catalyst for creating something new, different, and better is when optimism, passion, and anger collide to create action and to drive change. Amazing things inevitably happen when these three highly explosive elements come together. In this sense, punk is not just rebellious but entrepreneurial. But punk attitude shouldn't be relegated to those small entrepreneurial start-ups—it should flow through the veins of all commercial enterprises. Punk is about new ideas and innovation, dreaming of the impossible, and then working out how to make it real. It is about creativity and all about the do-it-yourself attitude that punk had. Punk is certainly not incremental improvement, and innovation is almost too small a word. Rebellious, entrepreneurial, disruptive—that's what punk is all about, in music and in business.

Never before in the history of humanity has the world changed as rapidly as it is changing now, and that rate of change is only going to increase at exponential speed. The Internet changed everything. It has evolved significantly since its first incarnation; every evolution changes how we use it, and it will do it again and again and again. The workplace has evolved from an experience-based culture, to a knowledge-based culture, to what is now an ideas-based culture. No longer do you have to put in your years of service to build up your experience to show that you can run a big company. We have never had as many young entrepreneurs as we do today, or so many young companies making such an impact in the world. The 2016 *Forbes* list of "America's Richest Entrepreneurs Under 40" shows that there are twenty people in their twenties and thirties who are worth over $1 billion. Many have been spawned by Facebook, Airbnb, Uber, Pinterest, Dropbox, Stripe, Snapchat, or Instagram. In an incredibly short period of time, these companies have changed the way we all live. Some of the boldest ideas have created some of the most audaciously disruptive companies in the world; I will tell you it has always been that way. We should celebrate them and emulate the innovation that drove their success. Let us celebrate the dreamers, the creators, and the inventors; the people who aren't constrained by current thinking and common sense. Stand up Walt Disney, Bill Gates, Elon Musk, Mark Zuckerberg, and Jeff Bezos. Have your own list of such people, but be inspired by people who ideate, who ask the question *what if*, who are insatiably curious, and who seek to create the new.

WHAT'S IN AN IDEA?

Great ideas are disruptive: Geoffrey Frost (former Chief Marketing Officer at Motorola before his untimely death) used to say, "Whoa! is the new Wow." In the past, wow was the reaction we looked for when we presented our ideas, but wow is so yesterday. We don't just need to surprise people, we need to shock people and cause them to stop in their tracks. Wow is like "that's better than I've ever seen before," whereas Whoa! . . . is more like "Holy mackerel, I've never seen anything like that before!" How many Whoa! projects do you have in the works?

Great ideas are the only differentiator: I will say several times in this book that the only sustainable competitive advantage is to innovate faster than your competition. Innovation is the thread that runs through this element. So, we all better start embracing innovation and the power of ideas, not just incremental ideas, but big disruptive ones.

Great ideas are energizing to your team: There is something magical in experiencing the whole journey: from the conception of an idea, to the reality of it existing in the world, and the impact that it has on people. To be able to be part of that process is a thrilling experience.

This section of the book will look at some of the radically different ideas I have seen, heard, and been part of in my career. I have four goals for this section:

1. To excite you and get you to appreciate the power of ideas and the criticality of innovation in today's world. If a company doesn't innovate, it will surely die.

2. To share some of the lessons I learned from these ideas and hope that they will serve you well as you look to conceive great ideas and deliver them in their purest, most impactful sense.

3. To help you realize that ideas are like newly born babies:

They need nurturing and care if they are to grow and fulfill their potential.

4. To encourage you to dare greatly on behalf of a worthy cause, because that is our calling!

I will recount stories that show how some great ideas came about, and we will use them to identify some key aspects of innovation. We will acknowledge that good ideas don't always succeed, but we will find some lessons on how to protect against that. Finally, we will also look at how good ideas need protecting as they grow from a fledgling idea to their market entry.

Innovation is the lifeblood of business—so let's crack on and see its beauty in some of these stories.

Differentiation Is at the Heart of Radically New Ideas

Orange had enjoyed a love affair with consumers for its first eight years, where it brought fairness, value, and a human style to the UK mobile phone industry. That was when mobile phones were the exciting new technology and more and more people were getting their first mobile phone.

But the sector had become dull and was even resented by consumers. It had become a utility, a commodity that was nearly as dull as your gas or electricity supplier. All mobile phone companies were offering the same phones, almost identical and equally complex rate plans, and the same confusing offers.

As the number of new mobile phone owners started to dwindle because the market was now heavily penetrated, the battle turned from getting new customers who were new to mobile to stealing customers from competitors. In a desperate attempt to compete, it became a short-term promotional battle: Lower rates were offered to new customers while existing customers were kept on higher-rate plans. The inevitable result eroded margins and infuriated existing customers who witnessed, but didn't benefit from, the lower-rate plans; customer loyalty was being destroyed.

Furthermore, the brands were spending millions on advertising trying to create a point of difference in their communications when, in truth, there was little difference. Thus, many firms took the view that "if we cannot be different, then let's be the loudest, the most visible." This meant they were also spending millions on sponsorships: on the sides of racing cars, on the front of football shirts—the irony being that it just compounded the perception that "they are all the same."

That was the environment and the challenge we faced when I joined Orange.

Orange had a longstanding association with the UK film industry: It had sponsored the British Academy of Film and Television Arts (BAFTA) annual Film Awards evening for many years and also owned the prime advertising spot before every movie shown in the

UK. Just as I joined Orange, the Cinema Marketing Agency (CMA) in the UK approached us to see if we could do a promotion with some half-price cinema tickets as they were seeking to drive attendance on Wednesdays, which was the slowest day of the week. Given the telecom's industry fixation with offers and promotions, plus the large-scale nature of Orange, it was no surprise that they came to us.

But this felt like another cheap promotional offer that we weren't overly excited about. It would be just another bribe to tempt customers away from their current provider and get them to move to Orange. However, there was an idea that had been brewing in the company: We wanted to give our customers a sense of being members, as opposed to just customers. The concept was to create a day of the week when Orange members would receive special benefits in several ways and possibly also from some partner brands. Customer churn rates (the number of customers who were canceling their contract with us) were on the increase as people were increasingly shopping around for better rate-plan prices, and we needed to create some unique differentiators that made our services "sticky," and we wanted to appeal specifically to our most fickle group, the youth. Our working title was Orange Mondays, and I think that was inspired by the rock band Happy Mondays, because we wanted to make Mondays happy for our Orange customers. I saw an opportunity for differentiation. This proposed cinema offer wasn't about some cheap tickets—it was a potential ongoing membership benefit. So we went back to the CMA with a far bigger idea than just some half-price promotional tickets.

If I remember correctly, they were pushing us to do this for at least four weeks; there was a look of shock on their faces when we said we wanted to do it for at least four years. We wanted to create Orange Wednesdays, where every week we would thank our customers for their loyalty. If they went to the cinema on a Wednesday, we would pay for them to take a friend, on us. We would pay the cinema industry a multimillion-pound fee for this program over a four-year period. The process would be high tech (for the time), and we would establish the phone at the center of the process. The Orange customer would text the word "film" to the telephone number 241 (an appropriate and easily remembered number), and we would send back a text message which contained a barcode that the cinemagoer would present the following Wednesday. The cinema attendant would scan the barcode, and a free ticket would be given when they purchased another one. That way we could ensure that they were genuine Orange members and also, importantly, track which of our members had gone to the cinema and benefitted from the scheme. We stated how many people we believed we could drive to the cinema on a Wednesday, and the CMA people were blown away by our projection. They were looking to do a small discounted promotion, and we responded with a transformational plan that was beyond their wildest dreams.

They raised several objections to our proposal. The first was the need to have barcode scanners in all theatres—couldn't we just use a paper voucher that we mailed to our customers? Niamh Byrne (my Head of Sponsorship) wasn't prepared to compromise on that important element. So we said no, the technological solution was a key benefit to us as it demonstrated how the phone would soon be used for so much more than just communicating. We needed to ensure that the person who went to the cinema was an Orange member, and since the phone had to go, we reasoned that so did the Orange phone owner. It was also important to us to be able to track who had gone, so we could measure the impact on churn. Finally, it also made a huge statement back in 2003 about how the mobile phone was going to be the key device in your life.

The second objection from the CMA and all the cinema chains was that this could be too successful, and they could end up with too many people going to the cinema through this scheme.

We went through months and months of discussions with the CMA and each cinema chain convincing them of the economics, giving some form of renegotiation clause, developing the technology, and planning the marketing. We systematically went around to each cinema chain and convinced them one by one. It was a long, and at times tortuous, process, and it took about a year and a half from its conception to the first Orange Wednesday to happen in the spring of 2004.

The biggest challenge was getting the whole of the UK cinema industry to agree to the program, and for that accomplishment I must acknowledge the support we received from Barry Jenkins and Diana Berman from the CMA for their tenacity. In Orange, there were many times that we asked ourselves if we would ever pull this off or if we should just cut our losses and move on to something else? It was simply taking up too much time. This program was kept alive internally by Niamh and myself. The thing that sustained us, when we repeatedly bumped into roadblock after roadblock and we were so tempted to move on, was that we were just so excited about what it could mean and how transformational it could be for Orange.

We could have implemented it six months earlier if we had been prepared to compromise on the way in which people received their vouchers, but we felt that the phone as the delivery mechanism was essential—and we were all glad we retained that element as it made a fundamental difference. This deal was never about a promotional offer. That's why we took the audacious step of naming it after a day of the week. Every cinemagoer in town soon knew about "ORANGE WEDNESDAYS."

ENSURE THE PROJECT IS NEWSWORTHY BEFORE PEOPLE START WORKING ON IT

Consumers are extremely savvy these days, and I would argue they have always been savvy. It is vital that we have a clear and compelling consumer benefit defined in all consumer initiatives (clearly articulated in the project brief) long before the work of creating it starts. One technique that is particularly useful in ensuring that we are only working on truly substantive initiatives is one that I picked up from one of my old customers, Amazon. They are a very consumer-focused company, maniacally so, and that is one of the things I admire most about them. Before any project gets started, they have a routine where they write the press release and use that to assess whether the project is worth doing. If the press release does not sound remarkable, then neither does the project. I have adopted this in recent years, and it is a great way to hold every project to the fire to see if it can withstand the heat and intensity of scrutiny.

Orange Wednesdays was undoubtedly a child of a long pregnancy, but its longevity and impact on customer loyalty meant that all the pangs of childbirth were well worth it. The run rate at which customers leave your service is commonly known as *churn*; our churn rate fell by about fifty percent among those who used it, and that helped retain a huge number of customers during the eleven amazing years it ran for. Orange later added to Orange Wednesdays by creating a two-for-one offer with Pizza Express every Wednesday, so you could have dinner and a movie on Orange each week.

The term "Orange Wednesday" remained the most frequently cited term in all mobile network research word clouds for about ten years. That was differentiation!

Sometimes championing a project through to completion is all about getting the naysayers to give the program a chance. However, sometimes the project simply takes a long time to come to fruition. That was true with Orange Wednesdays. It took nearly a year and a half to get to the point where we could launch, but we had the tenacity because we loved the vision and never lost sight of it or the potential benefits for the business, even though there were times when we doubted it would come to fruition.

KEY LESSONS

The first lesson is obvious but vitally important—differentiation is the ultimate goal in most businesses and certainly in a commodity business. Where there is little difference among competitors, do whatever it takes to search out or create points of differentiation.

The second key lesson from Orange Wednesdays is that you often need enormous tenacity to achieve something amazing. Spend time with people who could scupper the project and get them on board. Spend time with the people who can help you make faster progress. Knock off the challenges and the naysayers one at a time and always, always keep the vision of why you are pursuing the project clearly in your mind, because that is what will give you the energy to persevere.

When you question the sense of continuing to pursue a project that is stuck, balance the likelihood that you may not deliver it against the potential impact of your success. If the latter excites you more than the former dampens your enthusiasm . . . keep going!

SO WHAT ARE YOU GOING TO DO ABOUT IT?

Write your thoughts here:

Great Innovation Comes from Solving Customer Problems

When I was at Orange in 2002, we were in the early days of data on the mobile phone. It was post-WAP (for those of you old enough to remember that). WAP was a way of accessing information over a mobile wireless network and was the forerunner to the first real mobile Internet services that were then becoming available. The stock market investors were looking for new growth opportunities from the telecoms and network operators. Investors could see that the huge growth rates driven by the fast adoption of mobile phones were now slowing as the marketplace became saturated. New revenue streams were going to be needed if the rapid growth trajectory of the late 1990s was to be maintained.

Orange had committed to stock market investors, that we would grow data revenue to twenty percent of our total revenue, but data revenue was stagnant and showed no signs of growth. Many previous attempts had been made to grow data revenue, but our UK CEO gave a colleague and me the task of giving it one final shot. He said, "If we cannot shift it from where it stands today (a little over ten percent), then we will just have to admit that."

So, with that brief, we gathered all our creative marketing minds within Orange and within our agencies and started the brainstorming process, mid-morning on a Friday. We asked ourselves the most important question: Why aren't more people using their phone for more than just talking and texting, while we—the in-the-know industry insiders—did so much more with our phones? What you could actually do on your phone was the telecom industry's best-kept secret. I used it for a whole host of things that we now take for granted on our smartphones, but back then my friends were astounded by what you could find out from your phone.

We quickly came to the simple conclusion: People didn't know how to use their phone for more than talking and texting and perhaps taking a few low-resolution photos. So, we started to talk about how we could solve that. Mark Whelan, Creative Director of Cake (an ideas,

PR, and events agency), came up with the idea of turning one of the salespeople in every Orange store into a trainer. The trainer's sole job would be to show people how to use their phones for more than talk and text. A little later in the discussion I piped up, "Well, we have just had some market research back that shows that buying a phone is the second most hated purchasing experience someone goes through—second only to buying a secondhand car. It shouldn't be like that, people love their phones, but they hate buying them."

Everyone was highly intrigued by that research statistic. I continued, "It appears to show that people want to go into stores to look at the new phones that are available, but rather than being able to touch a device and see how it works, we have dummy phones screwed to the back wall, and to get to look at them, they have to get past a few highly commissioned, overly eager salespeople in suits who are trying to sell them an airtime contract rather than show them the phones."

"That's just wrong!" someone interjected.

"Perfect," Mark exclaimed. "We change one sales rep and make him or her into a Phone Trainer, and we advertise the fact that the trainer isn't allowed to sell you a phone. Their only job is to train you on what your phone can do."

We all liked the concept. Showing people how to use their phone was the only way we would ever start to grow people's usage. What we all liked was that it was based in two consumer benefits: empowering people to get more done with their phones and making our stores a less aggressive sales environment.

I hurried straight from our meeting to sell the idea to our Head of Orange Shops, Nick Moore. I had a good relationship with Nick and was confident I could get him to support the new concept: a Phone Trainer in every store. After I'd concluded my pitch, his response was abrupt: "No."

"Why?" I responded, "It's a great idea!"

"I know it is. Why don't we change them all?" he retorted.

"Are you serious?"

"Yes. Let's transform the shops entirely. All sales should start from the question, 'What do you want to do with your phone?' If we show them the phones and what they can do, then I believe they will choose to buy them." This comes back to my long-held belief that people love to buy, but hate to be sold to.

PEOPLE LOVE TO BUY, BUT HATE TO BE SOLD TO

People hate to be *sold to* when that entails facts being distorted and pushy salespeople pressurizing them to commit when they aren't ready to. But people like to buy when they feel in control of the process; when they feel they are getting good, helpful, independent advice; and when the salesperson is helping them come to an informed decision on their own and in their own good time.

We started to talk about what else we could change to really transform the experience. At this point, we got very excited about the concept. It was somewhat crazy, slightly lunatic, but it had the potential to be genius. Now, this is where I believe the powers that be cause certain things to happen when the time is right. It was Friday lunchtime by now, so Nick and I headed to the pub to discuss how we could explode the idea. We stayed there for a good two or three hours, and perhaps the more we drank the more radical the ideas we had. We ended up with twenty changes we were planning for the stores: The facades of the stores were branded Orange Shop; we needed to change them to read just Orange. Shops are where things are bought and sold, and that was not their sole function anymore. We wouldn't display dummy phones—we would have live devices. And we wouldn't have them screwed to the back wall but up front as you entered the store where people could try them out. We wouldn't have salespeople; we would have Phone Trainers, and they wouldn't wear suits, they would have a more casual style. We would scrap the sales training program and instead focus our training on customer service skills. We wouldn't commission them on sales achieved but on demonstrations done. (That was a big one.) I was wobbling now (and not because of the drink). "Are you sure? How do we verify they did the training?" I asked.

"I don't know but we'll work it out," he responded.

I love that attitude. Let's embrace an idea, do what's right, resist the temptation to pour cold water on it, and trust that we can work out the details in time.

Mark's fabulous idea had been boosted and enriched.

That was one of the most beautiful afternoons of my career. Free-flowing ideation without a hint of negativity. We left the pub with an even greater sense of optimism and excitement. Nick was to go to his team and get them to work on how to make these twenty things happen. Meanwhile I'd pitch it to our CEO, John Allwood, the following Monday.

I wasn't thirty seconds into my sales pitch when I saw the color draining from John's face. By the time I had mentioned that we were going to pull all our salespeople out of the store, he was quite pale indeed.

"John, I know this is a brave idea, but it's not stupid. Remember I trained as an accountant.

"What we want to do is to try it out in five stores in London for five weeks. We believe that by the end of that trial we can get sales to remain flat, and if we do that then we want to roll it out nationally."

I ultimately gained his agreement to the trial, but he was clearly skeptical, as were most people we shared the idea with. They held the view that it was interesting but insane and probably doomed to failure, but it would be fun to give it a try.

I gave Nick the good news, and we hastily concocted the five-week trial. We set up after-hours briefings for the stores where we served beer and pizza. I went to every one of them to explain the idea. At all of them, I stated how we were going to make the store

employees the heroes of our advertising campaign, so everything
was resting on them. I did everything I could to stress to them the
importance of making this work. Nick and I and our teams were
regular visitors at the stores over the next few weeks as we sought to
learn how it was working and, more importantly, what we needed to
refine to make it truly work.

THE MISSION, THE MOVEMENT, AND RADICALLY NEW IDEAS ARE INTERLINKED AND BUILD OFF EACH OTHER

This story could have appeared in any of the first three chapters, but I have
placed it here in chapter three, as a radically new idea, because that was
really where it started. What we saw was that this transformational idea
helped us reconnect to our original mission of being a consumer champion, but we also knew that it would never get traction if we didn't inspire
the people who worked in our stores—we had to build a movement with
them. That's why we toured the country asking for our people to buy into
our idea and deliver on our cause. We weren't launching a marketing campaign—we were creating a movement.

In the first week of the trial we saw sales fall seven percent in our
five test stores compared to the control stores, but by week four we
were just two percent below the other stores' run rates.

I went to John again and said, "John, I need to extend the trial by
two weeks. We are back within two percent, and it's getting better
every week, I just need two more weeks."

"No," he said emphatically.

"What?"

"No, I am not giving you two more weeks," was his very stern
response.

"Why not? It's working, and we will have it sorted in two weeks."

"I know," he said far more warmly. "That's why I am not giving you two more weeks. I have been in the stores, and I can see how the atmosphere has changed. I can see the trends. Roll it out now; we're going for it." That was a high-quality piece of leadership.

So, everyone jumped into action—we had eleven weeks to plan and implement all these major changes. We created an advertising campaign that communicated that we were there to show people how to use their phones and that described the changes inside the stores.

These new Orange locations—we didn't refer to them as shops anymore—had a very different vibe to them, and consumer reaction was fabulous. We even had some people lining up outside our stores on the morning after the first evening airing of the adverts asking for their training session. The momentum continued to build as more and more people heard of the program and embraced the concept. Nine months after we had launched Orange Phone Trainers we saw that the average customer who had been trained was now spending an extra £5 (about $7) with us every month—that was way above expectations. Usage on data services had skyrocketed, we had grown foot traffic in our locations (previously known as stores) by a staggering fifty-two percent, and sales were up thirty percent. The idea had worked beyond our wildest dreams.

THE KEY REASONS WHY ORANGE PHONE TRAINERS SUCCEEDED

1. There was a core consumer benefit at the heart of the proposition, it addressed a genuine need that existed back then, and we translated that into a fundamentally different experience for the consumer.

2. We had a bunch of retail salespeople who were already a competitive advantage for us (they were the best on the high street), and they excelled when we made them the heroes of our campaign, not least because we made their jobs far more

enjoyable. We saw staff turnover rates fall by a third, because the trainers loved their jobs more.

3. We had a team across the organization who championed the initiative, and everyone was excited to be part of it.

4. We lit the spark of human passion across the company. This was one of those Bright Orange initiatives that we so desperately needed to rekindle our mojo, and it was so true to our brand essence. Everyone could sense it, and you could literally reach out and touch it in our stores . . . I mean locations!

KEY LESSONS

The process for creating a truly innovative initiative is fairly simple. Identify a consumer problem, find the real thing that is stopping progress, ideate on a solution, and then let the team go and explode the idea before executing flawlessly.

You need to allow the core idea to expand and stretch in every direction—don't place constraints on it in the early days.

When you have a potentially huge idea, but also a potentially risky one, test it in a microcosm. Put it out there fast and watch the reaction, watch it evolve. Learn, adjust, learn, adjust, and then decide.

SO WHAT ARE YOU GOING TO DO ABOUT IT?

Write your thoughts here:

Ideas Don't Happen on Their Own

I had just joined Microsoft and was driving to work one day in 2009, listening to a radio program, and I really don't remember who he was or why he was on the radio, but this is the essence of what the speaker said . . . "People in the media are talking about: What will Tony Blair's legacy be?" This was during the final few months of his prime ministership that lasted over ten years. The speaker continued, "When I think about the legacy I create, I look at it in a far shorter timescale. I am not even contemplating my legacy over a decade. I am asking myself what is going to be my legacy of today? What am I going to do today that will have a lasting impact?"

I thought about this for the rest of the car journey in. I loved the attitude. I reasoned that so many people go to work each day with no significant goal for that day. If we get through the meetings, clear our inbox, and check that our sales are on track, then we can go home feeling progress has been made. But I knew I wasn't like that—I mean I hate emails, that's the last thing I could be accused of focusing on. So, I rushed up the stairs to get to my desk and turn my PC on, so I could look through my agenda for the day to see what opportunities I had to create something that would have lasting impact. I was disappointed to see that there was just a bunch of dull meetings that I had allowed to clog up my schedule. I looked at tomorrow, sure that this was simply a random occurrence—it wasn't. Looking at the day after and the day after that, I became appalled by what I saw. I didn't have dedicated time planned to address any of the biggest challenges we were facing.

The guy on the radio had sparked a thought in my head about the need to create something valuable and enduring each day. The excitement I gained from that mentality and the thought of what radically new idea our team could create that day was quickly quashed when I saw my schedule. How had I allowed that to happen?

I asked Liz, my PA, to clear two hours that morning and apologize to the people affected. I was going to create a legacy for that day.

Now I just had to work out what it was! I tackled one of the issues that was troubling us: how to simplify the way in which we assessed our retail partners' execution of our Office Attach motion. (Office Attach is the sales process Microsoft uses to try to get every new PC buyer to also buy a copy of Microsoft Office for their new machine. It was our version of "would you like fries with that?")

There wasn't a framework or a systematic approach to drive greater quality of execution, and it was very hard to see what each retailer was doing and coach our sales teams on where their focus should be. In the next two hours, I created something that we would call the "5-star attach framework." I shared it with my team, and they liked it, so we trained the broader team on how to use it to provide focus and grow our business. In the following few months, it helped us grow sales meaningfully. Then several months later we exported it from my Europe, Middle East, and Africa (EMEA) region to be used on a worldwide basis, until I killed it four years later, when it had become outdated.

The legacy of the day was evident, but it wouldn't have existed if it were not for the reminder I received from the car radio that morning.

So many of us spend so much of our time on the day-to-day issues and not enough time on the transformative ideas that would ultimately make the biggest difference.

TRANSFORM WHILE YOU PERFORM

There are two jobs for leaders in a company at every level of the organization. Clearly, we must deliver the business performance that is demanded for the time period—we all have budgets to deliver and targets to hit. But we also need to innovate and plan for tomorrow, because tomorrow is going to be very different from today in many businesses around the world. We all must invent the future while taking care of today. At Microsoft, we referred to it as *transform while you perform*.

There are times when transformation is vitally important and needs lots of focus. One of my bosses once shared with us how he was taught to focus on the "tomorrow." In his last year or so working for the previous CEO, he had been told that his personal performance and bonus were no longer going to be assessed on the business performance of his division—that was being taken for granted. His performance was only going to be assessed based on what innovations he brought. That is a great way of getting people to focus on tomorrow.

KEY LESSONS

We all must create time, space, and an environment where we and our teams can ideate and innovate. Ideas are the source of innovation, and innovation is the lifeblood of our companies, so we need to dedicate time to the formulation of ideas and innovation.

My experience that morning during my drive into the office taught me that I needed to dedicate time to innovation. Since then, on my way into work I always ask myself: "What is going to be my legacy of today?"

We all must look after both the business performance of today and the business creation of tomorrow, and in today's rapidly changing world, that balance has never been as skewed to tomorrow as it is now. That's why we must perform and transform.

Holding people accountable for the innovation they bring is a fabulous way of bringing focus to tomorrow.

SO WHAT ARE YOU GOING TO DO ABOUT IT?

My suggestion: Look at your schedule for the last two working days and ask yourself what the legacy of those days was. What did you create that will stand the test of time? Look at the next two working days; do you have the opportunity to create a legacy for those days? If you don't, then ask yourself whether you are having enough impact in creating your company's future. If you have lost control of your time, reclaim it now. If you have an assistant who manages your schedule, share this concept with them. Then start every day with a clear goal of what you are going to create that will have a lasting impact.

Write your thoughts here:

Show, Don't Tell—Especially When Something Is Radically Different

In the late 1990s, Pokémon was a cultural phenomenon in Japan, but it was very much a Japanese property. It was a low-resolution anime-style game in a world where graphic quality was the rage. In addition to the game, Pokémon was a television series, playing cards, soft toys, and a whole host of licensed products. After a couple of years of doubting whether Pokémon could work outside Japan, Nintendo made the decision to give it a try. In the spring of 1999, we were told that Pokémon was coming to the UK that fall. We had heard about Pokémon, but none of us had really understood it, and we were skeptical. The graphics were so basic: How could it be a good game?

To try to understand it, I sat with our product manager on an hour-long train journey from London, and I made him take me through the game. After about thirty minutes, I understood what Pokémon was all about. Here's the long-winded explanation: Pokémon are strange-looking creatures of all shapes and sizes who live in the wild or alongside humans. For the most part, Pokémon (with the exception of the villainous Pokémon, Meowth) can only speak their name. The players in the game, called Pokémon Trainers, journey from place to place in the Pokémon world, catching and training their Pokémon and ultimately battling against other Trainers' Pokémon. When Pokémon battle with other Pokémon, they grow, become more experienced, and evolve into stronger Pokémon. There were originally fifteen types of Pokémon: water, fire, electricity, ground, etc. The art of the game is selecting the right Pokémon and the right abilities to use when competing in a battle against another Pokémon. As you can imagine, a water-based Pokémon does well against a fire-based Pokémon but struggles to beat an electricity-based Pokémon. The goal is to capture all the Pokémon and become the Pokémon League Champion. It is like a very sophisticated game of rock-paper-scissors with a key collecting element included too. In the first series, there were one hundred fifty Pokémon to collect, and the tag line was, "Gotta catch 'em all."

It took me thirty minutes to understand (and probably took you a couple of minutes to read that last paragraph). We'd have just thirty seconds to explain that same message in a TV commercial—and that was our issue.

After a few weeks struggling badly to make progress on working out how we would do that, I was on the phone with one of our Japanese colleagues in Nintendo's supply chain. "How are you Takeshi-san?"

"Oh, today has been a bad day for us in Nintendo."

"Why?" I inquired.

"We unveiled that there was a secret one-hundred-fifty-first Pokémon, called Mew. We promised to give it away to the first one thousand consumers who lined up at this trade show, and we had seventy-two thousand people show up for it."

"That's brilliant. What's the disaster?" It didn't sound like a problem to me.

"It caused chaos. It closed many roads and caused traffic congestion in Tokyo, and the police had to come."

"I still think it's brilliant. Do you have TV footage?"

"Yes, it was all across the news," he said in a very despondent way.

"Brilliant, can you send it to me please?"

He reluctantly agreed.

I then rang our PR team and told them the story. We quickly hatched our plan. We weren't going to explain Pokémon to anyone—it's simply too complex. Instead, we'd show them the phenomenon that Pokémon was causing in Japan and tell them that it was on its way here for Christmas.

We started to leak this footage of the Tokyo roads being blocked to the UK press, and we told them that we would be launching in September. The day after we sent out our release, the phones rang off their hooks at Cake's office (they were our PR agency). I was there, and I remember one journalist rang up and his first line was, "I hear there is a tidal wave about to hit Britain and it's called Pokémon, tell me all about it."

SHOW DON'T TELL

Showing is always more powerful than telling.

Imagine trying to tell someone about what a punk rock gig was like. "Well punk rock is where a group of people who have minimal musical ability and who cannot really call themselves musicians play basic songs (which only have three chords) very loud and very fast. The lead singer shouts particularly offensive lyrics about a whole load of previously taboo subjects. The fans have weird hair that they dye a variety of bright colors and spike up. They wear ripped clothes, they have pierced various parts of their bodies, and they have inserted safety pins into these piercings rather than real jewelry. The fans dance by jumping up and down at a very high tempo, and it is not unusual for fights to break out at these concerts. Oh, and the band shouts obscenities and abuses their fans. It's so much fun!"

Telling recounts the facts and articulates the information, but showing communicates so much more. It's more visual, emotional, impactful, and memorable. Access these critical elements and stimulate the senses.

With Pokémon, we realized that it wasn't about telling the story of the product itself, but rather it was showing the story of the pandemonium that was kicking off in Japan. We didn't have to explain it; we just needed to create the intrigue so that the press, the kids, and their parents would do all the research themselves. It worked fabulously; before we even launched Pokémon in the UK, there were Pokémon clubs established in schools across the country. They had done the digging themselves and were hooked before the first Pokémon landed in the UK.

So, our launch campaign was all centered on showing the Pokémon phenomenon and thereby creating intrigue for Pokémon. If we did that well, and with Pokémon there was certainly enough to warrant the intrigue, people would do the hard work for us.

One way we did that was to show a few five-second TV adverts (that we called *blipverts*) in each advertisement break inserted between various other commercials. In each blipvert we showed one of the Pokémon, with no branding or explanation. So everyone started to ask: Who or what are these weird-looking creatures? Why were people seeing them? This was a genius idea by our media agency and was born out of our core concept. The Pokémon had never been seen before, and they grabbed people's attention and created intrigue.

The day before we launched, we again showed the nation a glimpse of Pokémon. We staged the arrival of the first Pokémon products. Two black lorries carrying the Pokémon logo—and allegedly the first Pokémon games—rolled off a ferry at Dover. The lorries were protected by Japanese ninja-style security guards travelling in blacked-out SUVs, with eight motorcycle outriders and a helicopter overhead. The convoy proceeded up to London where we held an impromptu press conference on Westminster Bridge with the Houses of Parliament and Big Ben as a backdrop to two of the Pokémon characters in full-size costumes. That was broadcast on all the major news stations that day, culminating in about £10 million of media coverage.

Everything we did was about creating fame for Pokémon by showing a glimpse of the Pokémon phenomenon and thereby stimulating intrigue.

KEY LESSONS

Radically new ideas need to be brought to life.

Show, don't tell, wherever humanly possible and especially when something is as visually different as Pokémon was (and punk for that matter). Showing is so much more impactful. Remember the old adage that a picture is worth a thousand words—that is so true.

A product story must be a simple one that can easily be explained. If it is too complicated, you will not retain people's attention. The truth to marketing a product is always in the product somewhere.

You just must keep looking for it. If it doesn't sound simple and straightforward, then you haven't cracked it yet—so keep exploring.

For so long we had worked on how to tell people about Pokémon and how to explain it to them, but that wasn't the story we needed to tell. The story to be told was the impact it was having in Japan and alerting people of its impending arrival. You must always ask yourself what story you are really trying to tell and be open to the fact that it isn't always the obvious one.

You never know where the solution will come from. The inspiration for shifting the focus area came by complete coincidence from a side conversation with our friends in Japan. You have to constantly be searching (even subconsciously) for the solution.

SO WHAT ARE YOU GOING TO DO ABOUT IT?

Write your thoughts here:

Champion Big Ideas through the Organization

As part of the rebranding of ONdigital to ITV Digital, we came up with the "Al and Monkey" advertising campaign idea. I will tell more of how that campaign came about in a different story shortly. But for now, let me ask that you understand that the campaign involved two characters: One was a man called Al and the other was a knitted monkey, appropriately called Monkey. Our advertising agency had written the scripts and created the Al character with Johnny Vegas in mind. Johnny was a stand-up comedian who had started to appear in a few television series. We shared the scripts with Stuart Prebble and Rob Fyfe, my CEO and COO respectively, and they both loved the campaign.

They proved to be huge advocates and supporters of the campaign, although Stuart did suggest we swap Johnny out for Hugh Laurie, who was contracted ITV talent. I didn't have to fight too hard with Stuart to keep Johnny; he was prepared to allow us to decide that. But if I thought that was where that battle would end, I soon realized I was sadly mistaken. ONdigital was owned by two of the ITV franchises: Carlton and Granada. They weren't the best of friends, and in those days engaging with them was like being a child of divorcing parents.

It soon became evident that there was going to be a battle with the shareholders to get this advertising campaign through. Johnny Vegas was, at the time, earning critical applause for his portrayal of a fat drunk in the show called *Happiness*, written by Paul Whitehouse. His character, Charlie, which had been written specifically for him, was a heavy-drinking, heavy-smoking, overweight, jobless waster. There was one article where Johnny's friends reportedly commented, "That's not acting; that's your life." The shareholders were likewise concerned that Johnny was very much like Charlie in real life. I assured everyone that Johnny wasn't like that, and I remember saying he had to put on a few pounds for the role and clearly didn't drink to the same extent as Charlie. I think I managed to say that with a straight face.

Then I got a message that the shareholders didn't like the campaign; they objected to us portraying our viewers as a stupid fat man and a knitted monkey. I had to prove that Johnny was not an unshaven, fat drunk if he was to keep the role. I remember the call to the agency. I said, "I need a photo of Johnny looking slim, smart, clean-shaven, and sober—and I need it quickly." They knew the challenges I was having internally, so they sprang into action.

A little later I received the news that there was a hastily arranged photo shoot with Johnny for that afternoon. He was wearing a black suit (black is very slimming), he was clean-shaven, and the photographer was taking a photo from the top of an eight-foot ladder with Johnny looking up at him—apparently, that is the most slimming angle you can have. Oh, and of course Johnny was sober.

The next morning, I had the most amazing photograph of Johnny Vegas. Smart, sober, and clean-shaven . . . and if you squinted hard enough, slim. Unrecognizable from the Charlie character. This helped convince the shareholders that Johnny would be okay. Many other concerns were raised, and we rebuffed each of them. Eventually we received the go ahead, but not before I had said, "You can fire me if this goes wrong." I also think my COO had made a similar commitment to the shareholders. We knew we were onto something huge, and we weren't going to let some uniformed authority screw it up.

Now, it would have been easy to have given in at any point along the way. I could have allowed the switch of Hugh Laurie for Johnny, accepted that we were never going to get a smart photo of Johnny, or just agreed to go back to the drawing board—and I wouldn't have had to put my job on the line. There are a few reasons why I just couldn't do that:

- I believed in the campaign like no other in my career. I always believe in doing what's right for the business, and this was so right.

- A lot of people in my team and in the agency were enormously invested in this campaign. They needed, and were looking for, a leader to champion this campaign through the organization. How could I "bottle it" and let it die? If I had done that, how could I look my team in the eye again? If I did that, we would be destined to forever play it safe in all our future work. Leaders are defined by where they stand in times of difficulty and adversity.

- I have never worried about putting my job on the line, because the truth is, it is always on the line, as it is for all of us. If we hadn't made "Al and Monkey," we would have done some average work that would have led to the same ultimate fate. Maybe playing it safe enables you to drag things out, so you may get a more drawn-out death spiral, but I am not one who believes in long painful deaths.

KEY LESSONS

Big ideas need protecting. Big ideas by their very nature are often new, unusual, challenging, certainly different, and often scary. As a result, you can always find someone who doesn't like it, or wants to adapt it, or is more concerned by the downside risks than the upside opportunities. That isn't always bad. It is good to test the ideas and work out what could go wrong, and what you would do if the worst happened. However, when you have an idea with great potential, you must stay true to the idea, and you must ensure that you aren't too accommodating of people who want to water down your idea in order to minimize risk in their eyes. If you are too accommodating, you can quickly create a camel with seven humps and lose the magic of the idea.

Big ideas that are transformational risk being killed before they are even born. These ideas need caring for like an unborn baby;

protecting them when they are vulnerable is essential, and it's your duty. If you believe in them, then you cannot let them die.

Believe in the power of ideas and champion them throughout the organization. As Oscar Wilde said . . . "An idea that is not dangerous is unworthy of being called an idea at all."

SO WHAT ARE YOU GOING TO DO ABOUT IT?

Write your thoughts here:

Don't Let the Proposition Get Diluted

Around 2003, Ralph Peedy headed up engineering at Motorola. During that era, several people in the design and engineering team were frustrated by the trend of mobile phones that were narrow, but fat. The group was inspired by the concept that things shouldn't be narrow and fat, but wide and flat. Apart from the obvious aesthetic beauty, it would also provide more real estate for the phone's screen and keyboard, which would create a richer experience for the user. Motorola was an amazing hardware engineering company, and the development teams rallied around the concept of becoming the *Kings of Thin—with no compromise.* The no-compromise part was really important, as you will see later.

The iconic RAZR was the first of the thin phones conceived under this Kings of Thin mantra. It was designed to be the thinnest phone ever; its z-dimension was set to be a maximum of 13.5 mm. The design required some revolutionary innovations: The antenna was moved from the traditional place at the top of the handset to the butt of it, which represented a far greater challenge than you might imagine.

During the engineering process, there were the customary reviews, and as the story goes, the product engineers came to one meeting asking for the z-dimension to be fractionally increased. This was denied as the RAZR's one nonnegotiable was that it was going to be 13.5 mm thick. Later in the development cycle the engineers again came back and said they wanted to increase the z-dimension to 14.5 mm so that they could include a 1-megapixel camera in it, rather than the 0.5-megapixel camera that they could accommodate in the current structure. That request was again rejected—this had to be the thinnest phone ever, not the thinnest 1-megapixel phone ever. No one wanted to be the Kings of Thin-ish. The engineers went away despondent, but as was so often the case, they returned to the next meeting having found a way to squeeze a 1-megapixel camera into the nonnegotiable 13.5 mm limit.

This is where the no-compromise part of the mantra came in

useful. If it hadn't existed, we would have accepted only putting in a 0.5-megapixel camera, but because of the no-compromise barrier, the engineers went away with a mentality of: We have to find a way if we are going to live up to a principle. And of course, they did just that.

It soon became clear that the 13.5 mm could only be achieved if it had a low-profile keyboard—no keys that needed to be depressed. Some amazing innovations from the team of engineers led to the development of an entirely flat keyboard, backlit, and made from spun metal. It was an engineering masterpiece that redefined mobile phones.

Geoffrey Frost was Chief Marketing Officer in 2005 when we launched RAZR. He, as well as others, championed the device and became one of its leading evangelists. While he christened RAZR with its funky four-letter name, he didn't create the phone. RAZR's project code name was the *Razor*. It had been called razor from its conception, and as time went on, it became evident that its code name summed up the phone perfectly; to some extent, the name helped keep the teams true to the essence of the original idea.

If the RAZR's original proposition had been "let's build a phone as thin as it could be," RAZR would probably have ended up about 15.5 mm thick, still pretty slim for those days, but not sleek and beautiful like it was. The 13.5 mm nonnegotiable helped make RAZR the icon it became, and it was proof that we had become the unequivocal Kings of Thin. Not one of the leaders who oversaw the RAZR ever questioned the proposition; all the work went into solving the challenge, and no time was wasted debating resetting the parameters to make the challenge easier. The real beauty of the RAZR is the story of how it truly delivered on the concept of wide and thin, and how no one wavered from the 13.5 mm nonnego-tiable. From its genesis to the end, RAZR was true to the brief, and the team's single-minded focus and good stewardship ensured that the RAZR became the icon that it did.

HOW TO DELIVER ON A BEAUTIFULLY CONCEIVED IDEA

A beautiful concept only becomes a beautiful reality if the original proposition is protected and its purity is retained. With all the naysayers who circle around innovation like vultures, these ideas need protecting. I have generally seen four key things that keep a proposition pure:

A great brief and alignment to it—A well-defined goal, clearly articulated, plus a single-minded focus from the entire team on achieving it are so powerful. If the brief isn't good, it will rarely provide the clarity of purpose that is needed. If the team doesn't fully embrace the brief, then they will never achieve it.

The no-compromise mentality across the team—The no-compromise part of the Kings of Thin mantra can so easily be overlooked, but it was so important. It stopped people from being accepting. The engineers could have accepted they were only able to fit a 0.5-megapixel camera into the chassis, but because they believed in no compromise, they went back and found a way.

Obsessing over the critical decisions—It's an art knowing which decisions are really important and which aren't. I don't think it can be taught as it isn't a precise matter. I believe it is an art—part intuition, part experience.

Good stewards—People who sometimes sit outside the immediate fray and can impartially identify if a bad compromise is ever being considered can be so valuable. With the RAZR, there were enough good stewards (like Geoffrey Frost and others across the team) who wouldn't allow the original proposition to be compromised.

I once asked Geoffrey how we had got it so right with RAZR, yet hadn't for some time before. He told me that he had once asked a leading Hollywood director a similar question: Why are there so few really great movies made each year? The answer he received was very enlightening. The Hollywood director said that in making a movie there are literally thousands of decisions that need to get made, and the director cannot possibly make all of them. He has to delegate and rely on his team to make most of those decisions so, clearly, you have to make sure you have a great team. But the great film directors have an intuition about which decisions in the making of a movie will be the defining ones, and then they obsess over getting those right. Geoffrey likened that story to the role our product designers and engineers went through during the phone's developmental journey.

It's all about getting the crucial decisions correct, and a key part of that is knowing which decisions are the really crucial ones.

KEY LESSONS

Every project should have a vision and some nonnegotiables. The nonnegotiables are so important, because not only do they prevent the willingness to compromise, they also act as the catalyst for intelligent people to seek creative solutions when the inevitable challenges arise.

Don't reset goals when faced with what, on the surface, appears to be an insurmountable obstacle. When the goal is nonnegotiable, creativity is the only alternative.

Don't dilute the proposition, and especially on matters of great importance within the proposition, don't budge at all.

SO WHAT ARE YOU GOING TO DO ABOUT IT?

Write your thoughts here:

Watch Out for Those Who Could Scupper a Great Idea

We were in the midst of Pokémon mania. We had launched the first two Game Boy games, *Pokémon Red* and *Blue*, and they had blown away all UK sales records for video games at that time. We followed that up with *Pokémon Yellow*, and the whole thing was going insane —in a good way. We came up with a great idea that was an absolute certain success. The concept was that we would hold a tournament in the stores of the UK's leading video game specialist, Game. The winning players would represent Great Britain in a Pokémon world cup and compete against teams across Europe and against Japan, the home of Pokémon. I had run the idea by a few of my daughter's friends from school (they were six or seven years old), and they nearly started hyperventilating with excitement. I knew we were onto something huge.

We made a big announcement advert to launch the competition and explain how players could sign up. We had a full PR campaign, and we had thousands of people on hand in call centers around the country to handle the inevitable mass of calls we were going to get.

We created huge hype through our pre-announcement PR campaign, and people knew that there was going to be a big Pokémon piece of news. We ran the TV ad unveiling the opportunity to represent your country as the ultimate British Pokémon Masters. We then sat back and waited for the landslide of calls we would undoubtedly receive. In the first twenty-four hours we received just over one hundred entrants, whereas we were expecting ten thousand. We had a sophisticated system where player would play against player over the course of several weeks, but at this rate we could select our team in just a few hours. It was a complete and utter disaster. The worst day of my career by far. Even now as I type this story seventeen years later, I cringe at the pain I feel once again. An old scar has been opened and it hurts.

We conducted a hastily arranged postmortem that included interviewing children and their parents who were shopping for Pokémon products in some of our friendly retailers' stores. The postmortem was enlightening. Kids were desperate to enter, but their parents wouldn't let them. Their thinking was that their child had so little chance of winning that they didn't want to subject their kids to the pain of losing and the inevitable heartbreak. Why allow them to go through the trauma that would come after their inevitable elimination? We'd never even contemplated that possibility, yet with hindsight I totally understand it. Why had we got it so wrong? Why hadn't we even considered that risk?

I think we had failed to even consider this possibility because we had been carried away with the euphoria of Pokémania, and perhaps we had thought we were invincible. Specifically, what we failed to do was to check out our idea with all those involved in the decision-making process. While kids were desperate to participate, parents just put their foot down and vetoed any prospect of that happening.

Even now I cannot believe my stupidity in not thinking about how the parents would react. Clearly, I overestimated the strength of pester-power. Parents just refused, and we needed them because they would be the taxi drivers to get their children to the shops every Saturday morning for as long as they progressed in the tournament.

This was the biggest failure in my career. We wasted a lot of money creating a concept that was great in many ways but flawed in a critical one. We all learned a valuable lesson.

KEY LESSONS

Always consider all the people involved in the decision to buy or participate. Don't overlook the tertiary participants when they have a huge impact on the decision. Assess their attributes and the impact they can have.

Don't allow success to give you a sense of invincibility—always challenge your plans and continually ask, "What could go wrong? What could scupper this idea?"

I have seen this time and time again in my career. A great idea may be great for many constituents, but often one group loses out, and not enough consideration has been given to how they would react and respond. Role play the likely reaction of those who may lose out, and ask yourself how you would scupper the program if you were them.

SO WHAT ARE YOU GOING TO DO ABOUT IT?

Write your thoughts here:

Radically New Ideas Are Always Born from a Team, Not Individuals

For ideas to move from an initial thought in someone's mind to a physical incarnation, many people with unique skills are needed. I would come up with some ideas, but I was rarely the one who generated the big transformational idea. I loved people who could do that, and I eagerly gathered them from all our agency partners and ensured they loved working on our business. At times, I felt a little bit of a fraud in this group of creative heavyweights. Then, when I moved to Orange as Vice President of Brand and Strategy, one of the marketing journals ran an article on me. They interviewed some people I had previously worked with to get some insight on me. Robert Saville (founder of the advertising agency Mother) was quoted as saying, "When Jeremy sees the wonder in great ideas, his eyes light up like an excitable kid."[2]

Robert helped me understand my value to the group. My role was to ensure that the great ideas hit the business need and then also see how we could expand them beyond their original concepts to make the ideas even larger. For example, many of the ideas may have been generated with an advertising medium in mind, but I tried to see how we could push the concept into our stores, our call centers, and even our internal communications.

So, to create big daring initiatives, you must engage with those people who can deliver that spark of genius from within their imagination. Ask yourself who the creative geniuses are that are working in or on your business. If you cannot readily name a list of people who excite you and fully meet the description of creative genius, then you have a problem. You also need those people who can expand the idea and ensure it delivers the business advantage or goal you are looking for. You also need people who can deliver on that idea and turn it into

2 Ravi Chandiramani, "Profile: Stunt Man—Jeremy Dale, UK Brand and Marketing Director, Orange," *Campaign* (July 18, 2002), http://www.campaignlive.co.uk/article/profile-stunt-man-jeremy-dale-uk-brand-marketing-director-orange/151169.

reality. You also may need people who have the tenacity to champion the idea throughout the organization since brave, daring ideas magnetically attract naysayers and snippers, but more of that in a moment.

KEY LESSONS

They say, "Success has a thousand fathers," and that was certainly true with all the great products, initiatives, and marketing programs I was fortunate to be part of. So, let me say here and now: Thank you to all the creative geniuses, the deliverers, and idea champions who made the ideas come to life. It couldn't have happened without all of you; it couldn't have happened without you all believing in the idea and being inspired to deliver it. It can take a village to pull off something huge.

Ensure you have these types of people in abundance working in or with your team. You need people who create value through their imagination, and you need the people who can turn an idea into a beautiful reality.

SO WHAT ARE YOU GOING TO DO ABOUT IT?

My suggestion: Ask yourself, "Do I have the people I need?"

Name your creative geniuses—now.

Name your deliverers, those people that you know you can count on to execute an idea—now.

Write your thoughts here:

The Bottom Line

Radically new ideas are the way businesses truly differentiate themselves from their competitors. In a world where there is intense competition in almost every business sector, the ability to provide customers with meaningful new innovation has never been so necessary. The twenty-first century is an ideas culture, where the speed of change has never been faster, and it will only increase. The victors will be those people and organizations who innovate most dramatically, most quickly, and in the most meaningful way for their customers.

So we all should take a moment and consider our team and our organization and ask: Is our environment one that inspires transformative ideas, that allows them to grow, and has the capability to bring them to fruition? And from a market perspective, is it more innovative than our competitors in terms of the changes we are bringing and the speed we are delivering them at?

So take a moment and ask yourself these critical and specific questions:

- Do you have a rich pipeline of ideas in the works today—ideas that genuinely excite you?

- Do you have the talented people you need to ideate, to expand, and to execute?

- Would someone describe your team as an ideas factory?

- Are you too busy managing the issues of today to invest sufficient time to create the whoa projects of tomorrow?

- Do you have the strong organizational capability needed to consistently deliver innovative projects to market at great speed?

- Do you have an advantage over your competitors in systematically bringing radically new ideas to market?

. . . If not, get on with making it so.

I just asked you to take a moment to answer these questions, which was fine for here, but it's not sufficient. If you cannot answer a categorical "Hell yeah!" to these questions, then you absolutely need to take a few days with your team and really drill into these critical questions and build your Innovation Plan.

Bottom line: Innovate; stand out from the crowd; be different; and embrace radically new, never-seen-before ideas. Then make them a reality by protecting their essence and championing them throughout the organization at high speed.

ELEMENT 4:

DRIVE SPEED AND ACTION

"Speed has never killed anyone. Suddenly becoming stationary, that's what gets you."

JEREMY CLARKSON

"Do it or don't! It's amazing how many things in life are that simple."

HENRY ROLLINS

S peed and action are two halves of this vital element of punk rock, and they were very evident in the punk rock movement. Let's look at each half of this element in turn. First, speed. Punk rock music upped the tempo. It was fast and loud, and there were no long introductions. The chorus would often occur within the first thirty seconds of the song. There was a brevity to punk; many songs lasted only two minutes in an era when all other songs lasted between three and four minutes. Punk's speed was much faster than anything that preceded it. The music of the disco era, which immediately preceded punk, played at around one hundred thirty beats per minute, which is similar to a person's walking heart rate: perfect for dancing. Punk rock, on the other hand, would hit something approaching two hundred fifty beats per minute—enough to lift the heartbeat of its live audience so much so that a person's body would naturally release adrenaline, producing over-charged energy levels. No wonder there was so much fighting on the dance floor. A person jumping around in the pit was the most abbreviated move possible, and brevity of movement was essential to keep pace to the music.

Some punk songs lasted less than a minute—"You Suffer" by Napalm Death consumed all of 1.316 seconds. Punk didn't mess around for the sake of it—no art for art's sake. In one interview included in the punk documentary *Decline of Western Civilization,* the interviewer asks Black Flag band members about the brevity of their songs. One reply was that when you looked at all the notes in their songs, they weren't any shorter than a regular song—but the fast-paced tempo meant "we just got done quicker." I love that. It's not less—it's just quicker. And if you can get through it quicker, why not?

The second half of this element is action. In the early days of their band, Black Flag lived in a communal space, and a bunch of hippies lived there too. When asked how they got along with the hippies, one band member replied, "They're ok, 'cos they just get loaded and they're pretty mellow dudes." Another band member added, "They smoke so much pot that they're neutralized. Even if they get pissed off, they have a joint (and) talk about it—instead of doing some-thing about it." That was the difference with punk. They sang about what was wrong and wanted to do something to put it right. Punks acted on their thoughts. **Talk Is Cheap—Take Action.**

Speed and action are core components of punk—and they should be core components of your business, too. Both parts are critical, and both are required. Speed without action is just motion with no progress. Action without speed is normally pointless in today's high-paced world. Speed and action are inextricably linked, and both are absolutely essential.

In a world where speed of innovation is often the only thing that keeps you ahead of your competition, we need to strip away all the paraphernalia that surrounds, constrains, and suffocates the real business activity. In a world where speed is so often compromised because people are too scared to act and be decisive, we need to learn how to drive for action and make substantive progress every minute of every day.

The future belongs to the swift and nimble companies, whose pace of innovation should scare the living daylights out of the big, fat, and happy establishment.

SPEED OF ACTION IS A HUGE COMPETITIVE ADVANTAGE

Probably the ONLY sustainable competitive advantage is the ability to innovate faster than your competition. So you better get good at being fast, fast! It must become a core competency of yours: What are you doing to build that capability? Do you move faster than your competition? If not, then you need to. If you cannot even answer that question with a good depth of understanding, then you need to find out. FAST!

If speed of action is such an advantage, why do so few of us act on this principle? General George S. Patton said, "A good plan violently executed now is better than a perfect plan executed next week." Well said, General Patton. Put that quote on the wall of your office. Etch it into the meeting room tables. Apply it every day of your life. I am deadly serious about this . . . get that phrase out there, and train your team on its importance and how you expect them to execute in that way. Many people think the most important element when making decisions and driving action is for them to be of the highest possible quality. However, I would almost always compromise some quality for speed. Fast and good trumps prolonged and perfect. This applies to decisions, and it applies to execution. People cop out of making a decision because they claim they don't have all the information, facts, or insights. Of course you don't, and you never will. The question isn't: Do you have ALL the information? It is: Do you have ENOUGH information to make a good call? Far too often we have way more information than we really need, but unconfident, timid, and fearful managers like the security of more data, more facts, more opinions, more analysis. Analysis paralysis! Aaaarrrgghhh!

Another popular excuse for not making a decision is that too many people believe that they need more time to ponder and think things through if they are to make good decisions. That is also rubbish in my view. It's not that they aren't equipped to make decisions; it's that they are too scared they'll make the wrong call. And because they are scared, they are impeding themselves badly.

Like the punk rockers knew well, there's an adrenaline kick to making quick decisions that can be both addictive and highly beneficial. People of speed make decisions fast, they sometimes make them alone, they are fine with some decisions being wrong, and they aren't afraid of tripping up, because they know if they're moving at speed and they trip, then they still fall forward and make progress. They just get up, brush themselves off, and start running again. These leaders also expect their people to do likewise, to *seize* the initiative and create momentum. They ensure that their people don't fear getting the occasional decision wrong—the only fear is of moving too slowly.

SPECIAL PEOPLE BRING SPEED AND ACTION

There are two critical factors in determining the speed in your organization: your processes and even more important, your people. More than anything else, find those special people who bring speed to your organization. Those people who devour work and drive speed have a number of key characteristics. They can easily be identified by the following qualities:

- They have a bias for action.

- They aren't scared to roll up their sleeves and get their hands dirty.

- They are tuned in to their environment and teams at all levels, so they can quickly identify blockages and work unrelentingly to remove them.

- They know how to maneuver projects and programs through the organization.

- They are uncompromisingly intolerant of people who slow things down and put in extra hurdles.

- They have a great ability to know how good something needs to be, so they don't waste time overengineering parts of the solution.

- They have an inherent knack for simplifying issues and breaking down complex problems into manageable chunks for their teams to work on.

- They are committed to their cause, they are prepared to do whatever it takes, and they have the grit to battle through when needed.

The business world needs more people who are in a rush, who are impatient as hell, who make things happen at breathtaking speed, and who create an environment where their teams are also empowered to make things happen. When people of passion have a cause they believe in, they don't hesitate in driving change; in fact, they cannot help themselves from driving action and pushing to see their goals get fulfilled. The pages in this section spotlight a few of the people I admire greatly for their speed of decision-making, their bias for action, and their reasoning—in other words, they are comfortable making fast decisions. These are the beautiful people who just *get stuff done*. They have a unique ability to churn out good work at speed and devour task after task after task. These people aren't just busy—they make fast, high-quality progress.

As Ernest Hemingway said, "Never confuse movement with action." In the following stories you will read about aggressive decision-makers and their attitudes towards decision-making; leaders who created action in their team; people who worked out how to make things happen at speed; punk rock people who thrive off the adrenaline rush of being the doers; the people who bring speed and momentum to their companies. They're the people the bosses turn to when they just have to get something done fast. You should be one of those people.

ONLY HIRE PEOPLE WHO MAKE THINGS HAPPEN

As the old proverb goes, "Some people make things happen, some watch things happen, while others wonder what has happened." Whenever I interview someone, I always look for people who get turned on by execution, who talk passionately about the execution detail, and who can recite examples from their career where they clearly explain how they removed blockages, freed up "stalled" projects, and made stuff happen. Review your people, every single one of them. Anyone who isn't clearly in the "some people make things happen" group should be told they need to go find a job outside your company. Seriously, why would you allow anyone to remain on your payroll who doesn't make things happen? The watchers and the wonderers exist, in all companies. They are commonplace, and if you look at your team, trust me they are there—but they shouldn't be.

My hope is that this section helps you get comfortable moving at speed, and you can only do that if you can get over the fear of getting some things wrong. Stop using more data and more thinking time as excuses. Reset expectations with your team about speed trumping perfect by building trust and creating the right environment, so that they will not fear getting a single decision wrong. Everyone on your team should be describable by you as a person who makes things happen, rather than as someone who watches or wonders what goes on. Check every name on your team, and be ruthless when assessing them to ensure that they all meet those criteria convincingly.

Above all, remember: Speed and action are the currency of the digital age.

When Time Is Tight, Great Things Happen

It was five weeks before our rebranding of ONdigital would go live. We would introduce ourselves to the world as ITV Digital, and we were excited about the TV advertising campaign that we would run. I was in a final concept review meeting with our advertising agency when I was presented with a quote and a request for approval of the costs of shooting the films. I was stunned to see that it was twice as high as the £1 million budget we had given in the initial brief.

The agency argued that this was the absolute minimum cost they could execute the agreed-upon scripts for. We had a long and heated argument. We had told them the budget up front, so they should not have presented an idea that they couldn't deliver for that amount. We pushed them to reduce the cost, but it became evident that they were not budging. And while they didn't say, "You don't have a choice other than to approve this, because we are only five weeks from launch, and we cannot start on another idea," that certainly was the undertone emanating from their side of the table. After a few more phone calls during the following twenty-four hours, it became apparent they weren't going to budge.

About noon the following day I was sitting with my recently appointed Advertising Director, Alison Victory, and discussing our options. I hated that we had been backed into a corner, and my natural reaction was to rebel and resist, but I couldn't see an alternative other than to give in. I said I was resigned to having to roll over and accept that we were about to be shafted for an additional £1 million.

Alison offered up, "I know the guys at Mother, a hot new creative agency. They would die for a shot at this brief. They would work round the clock to give it a go. If anyone can do something great in five weeks, it's them. Shall I call them?"

I was open for anything, so I readily agreed. Five hours later at the end of the day, three of their founders (Robert Saville, Stef Calcraft, Mark Waites) and two other creatives (Jim Thornton and Ben Mooge) were in our offices. We had the very best people from Mother, this recently formed young and vibrant creative agency, and they were excited to be meeting with us. They would all become firm friends of ours, but I didn't know that back then. We spent about two hours briefing them. The most exciting element about the meeting was how ruthless they were in their questioning. They didn't have time to do extensive research; they had to suck as much information out of me as they could in a very limited time frame. It was like a grueling interrogation with hundreds of questions, and if my answer to any one of them wasn't good enough, they kept hammering on it. It was evident that while they knew of the company and broadly what we did, because we had generated great awareness, they had no understanding of our value proposition. The question they kept coming back to was: Why would people choose to buy ONdigital (soon to be ITV Digital) over the market leader Sky?

Everything I had learned from our customers, from other research studies, and from my own experiences was sucked out of me in two intense hours of questioning. Eventually they appeared to have a good understanding—and a much better one than they'd had two hours before.

"How long do we have to come back with a concept and scripts?" they asked.

I replied, "Five days, including the weekend. Let's meet next Tuesday. Come in at the end of the day after most people have gone home. This needs to stay confidential."

My feelings oscillated during those five days more than I had ever experienced before. One moment I was convinced they were going to come back with something fabulous, and then realism set in and I reminded myself that all they knew about us was what we had told them in two hours. How could we expect something even reasonably decent so quickly?

Day five arrived. Reception called me to tell me I had some visitors, and I remember saying to Alison, "The cavalry has arrived."

That was more in hope than expectation. We entered the meeting room, and as I looked around I realized that I had never seen so many tired-looking people. One of the creatives, Jim Thornton, looked particularly shattered and was visibly lacking any color in his face. He looked like he had aged five years in the past five days. I was genuinely worried for him. What had we done to these people?

The presentation started. "People have heard of ONdigital, but they don't know what it is or why they should care. There are compelling reasons why people should choose ONdigital over Sky, but they simply do not know what they are, and that is not surprising as you have never told them in your communications."

He was right, we hadn't.

"We will do this through a creative construct of a comedy double act. We will use a smart guy and a stooge, where the stooge will ask all the questions that the confused British public wants to know, but don't; and the smart guy will answer them. The dialogue will be funny and informative. We don't want the smart guy to come across as a smartass, and for reasons of memorability, the smart guy will be . . . (dramatic pause) . . . a knitted monkey!"

I looked at Alison. Telepathically, she knew what I was thinking, "Did he really say knitted monkey?" But we were desperate, so we kept believing.

At this point Mark Waites started presenting the scripts. After the first one, we were startled by a noise from the couch in the room. Jim was now asleep, and he was snoring loudly. Someone apologized and stated that Jim hadn't slept for forty-eight hours. No one was offended, and I loved the informality in the room. I actually was glad he was snoring as at least I knew he was still breathing.

The scripts were presented, and Alison and I were laughing out loud at the dialogue. We were seeing a piece of work that was pure genius. Perfectly crafted to deliver the specific value propositions as to why someone should choose ITV Digital over Sky. Funny and memorable, so our message would cut through, and they were so endearing that I knew we would gain brand love. The campaign was straightforward and relatively easy to create, so we had time to deliver them, and we could do it within the £1 million budget.

This was the shortest time I had ever given an agency, and yet it was the best work I had ever received by far. I believe strongly that great things happen in short time frames. I think there are two underlying causes of this. First, "necessity is the mother of invention." When there is a desperate need, it is amazing how focused people can be, and focus always brings good results. Second, simplicity is highly underestimated and short time frames force simplicity, so I am convinced that there is an indirect correlation between time and quality.

The agency came back the next afternoon, and together we presented the scripts to Stuart Prebble (CEO) and Rob Fyfe (COO). Stuart sat straight faced through the entire presentation while I had been biting my hand to stop myself from laughing out loud. Surely, he must love these scripts? How could he not find these funny and perfect for the communication task we had? When the last script had been presented, Mark Waites, the lead creative, was a little confused at his lack of any sort of a reaction, so he turned to him and said, "So what do you think?" We all held our breath in hopeful anticipation.

He looked at Mark and simply said . . . "genius," before breaking into a huge smile.

That was all Stuart said.

We were on! I think we all floated out of that office on a huge high, excited about what was now going to happen. The relationship with the guys at Mother had been forged in the intense fire of the past six days.

My sales and marketing team thought I was stark raving mad when I told them the new plan. Unsurprisingly, there was much nervousness in the next few weeks, from both the team and myself, as well as a dose of uncertainty about what was to come. We literally received the finished adverts a few hours before they went live on the evening we rebranded. However, as soon as the first airing ran, we knew we had something truly special on our hands. The Monkey campaign went from strength to strength. Our market share shot up to the point where we were outselling Sky two-to-one, whereas they had been outselling us four-to-one when I had joined nine months earlier. Some stores reported that kids were coming into the store and stealing Monkey signage and sales posters. We received hundreds of merchandising license requests, from stuffed toys to ladies' lingerie. Our brand metrics went through the roof, and our research agency said, "We have never seen any lines (on our brand charts) move like this ever." It won advertising campaign of the year in the leading marketing journal. There were theses written on the campaign at universities. It wasn't just a great campaign, it was one of the greatest marketing campaigns ever.

Let's take a step back. This decision was insane, or certainly bordering on it. It was crazy to believe that we could do all this in the short time frame we had, but I would argue the short time frame made this possible, and without that time crunch, we would never have created something as magical as Monkey proved to be.

KEY LESSONS

When you see people who think something is impossible, tell them to get out of the way of those of us who are proving that it is not. When time is tight:

- People speak in a much more direct way; they get right to the point, because there is no time for skirting the issues.

- People push for the decisions that need to be made and the decision-makers are held accountable to make them.

- People simplify, and simplification tends to bring other advantages in terms of clarity.

- There is no time for bullshit, bureaucracy, or politics.
- People realize they need to lean on each other, collaborate, and work more productively together.
- People get very focused, and focus is so often the key to success.
- Great things happen.

Never doubt what can be achieved in short time frames by motivated, talented, and focused people, but remember: For those of us in a rush, time is always tight.

SO WHAT ARE YOU GOING TO DO ABOUT IT?

Write your thoughts here:

Decision-Making Is a Portfolio: Not Every Decision Needs to Be Correct

The fastest, most aggressive decision-maker I have ever worked with is Ron Garriques, who presided over Motorola's mobile phone business during the RAZR heyday. I loved Ron's no-nonsense, fast-moving leadership, and his decision-making was lightning fast. I had always thought I made quick decisions, but Ron's speed blew my mind.

He didn't always make the right decision, and if he made an incorrect one, it didn't seem to concern him greatly. At first, I thought his speed of decision-making was impulsive and almost reckless, but he rarely made poor important decisions. One day I asked him how he could make so many big decisions so quickly. He said, "First of all, I process data very quickly. Then I also know that if I make quick decisions, I have a strike rate of about eight out of ten. If I take more time, my batting average goes up to about nine out of ten, but I only make half as many decisions. So I can either make ten decisions and get eight right and two wrong, or I can make five and get four and a half right." He went on to say that he believed we made more money from the extra three and a half right decisions even though there were an extra one and a half wrong decisions. Ron continued, "And when I make a wrong decision, I generally find out before it costs me a lot of money, as I can generally fix it without huge cost."

Ron's confidence came from the fact that he had a good sense of his strike rates, and he knew he could course correct if a bad decision was made. However, the thing I admired most was that he didn't obsess over always being right—he obsessed over making money and moving at speed.

What was evident from Ron's explanation—and what I have endeavored to religiously follow ever since—were these five things:

1. Intimately know your business and your business model. You can only process data if you know the "formula" in your business—how the money flows in your organization's

business model. Having a good grasp of how a change in one thing ripples through your company's P&L and cash flow is vital for fast decision-making.

2. Understand that not all decisions are created equal, and allocate thoughtfulness and time accordingly. We all have finite time each week, and in a normal world we would follow the correct process for each decision. But that's not possible anymore given what we want to fit into our work time now. We need to be able to shoot from the hip on decisions that have less of an impact on the business. I want to have my highest strike rate on the biggest decisions.

3. Be confident and capable in your ability to process data quickly. It's not just about being capable; it's about having confidence in your ability to do this at speed and also about knowing when you are confident. Mental agility and mental arithmetic are skills that can be trained and honed. But more than anything else, for me it has been about learning to understand when I am confident in my processing and when I am not.

4. Realize that there is always a Plan B. If something goes wrong, you often find out before it is really too late; even if it is too late, ingenuity will find a way to recover the situation or at least stop it from being disastrous. Ron believed in Plan B—he didn't need to know what it was at the time, but he had confidence that we would always be able to work one out.

5. Accept that not every decision will be perfect. Ron wasn't perfect in his decision-making. His own self-declared stats showed that, but he didn't worry about getting some wrong. Too many people think that if they get something wrong it will mean that they will lose face and respect with the team. He didn't need constant reassurance, and I don't ever think he worried about what we thought of him.

Ron wasn't fearful of making a decision; there was never any dillydallying; we always knew which direction he had committed us to.

John Lydon hit the nail on the head. "Making wrong judgments is not a problem. Making mistakes is not a problem. These are things we can deal with and move on from, but lack of commitment is a serious error."[1]

KEY LESSONS

Invest the time to intimately understand your business model and get fast at processing data. Or if that isn't your strong point, get a trustworthy, commercially astute partner who can.

Understand your strike rates and how they change as you speed up your decision-making.

Know that there is almost always a Plan B that you will find if things go wrong.

Stop dawdling on small, relatively inconsequential decisions.

Believe in yourself, back yourself, and understand that you are being paid to make decisions, so stop copping out or "bottling it" as us Brits would say. And more than anything, go for it!!!

SO WHAT ARE YOU GOING TO DO ABOUT IT?

Write your thoughts here:

---

1 John Lydon, *Anger Is an Energy: My Life Uncensored* (New York: HarperCollins, 2014), 236.

When You Have Momentum, Make Big Bets

The business plan for the RAZR had a lifetime volume of 600,000 units. It wasn't a huge volume for a phone, but it was large for a $600 device back then. It was slim and stunningly beautiful, and its price point made it exclusive.

The RAZR was a success from the very first moment we unveiled it, and it was soon very clear we would beat our 600,000-unit goal. One day soon after launch, Ron Garriques announced to us in a meeting that we were lifting our target volume. That didn't surprise anyone, and we were all well up for pushing our expectations for this device. I certainly felt we could reach 1 million units within the first year. What shocked us was the number Ron announced: 10 million units. That was unheard of for a high-end phone like this. There were initial exclamations of horror and surprise from around the room and more intense questioning once we were outside the meeting. For about forty-five minutes, we debated the number Ron had demanded of us, but that conversation was very short lived. We knew Ron had committed to 10 million units with the parts manufacturers, and in so doing he had reduced the pricing to about $400. We quickly realized that there was no point arguing the 10 million number—that was locked in. He had bought the parts, and we were going to build them, and if we built them, then we sure as hell were going to have to sell them, one way or another. We weren't entirely sure at that point whether he was insane or a genius.

From feeling like we would beat our target by nearly double, things had been reset; we now had to work out how to increase our run rates tenfold. There was a naïveté to what was playing out, and after the initial shock, everyone just started working out what it would take to sell that many.

No one I spoke to at that time said that Ron had discussed his 10-million-unit commitment with them in advance. I do believe he just went and laid the bet. He was betting on the RAZR, and I suppose he was betting on us as a team as well.

Ron was great at making us work out how we were going to do something rather than wasting everyone's time debating whether we were even going to try. We didn't have a say on some of these things; he just made some big bets, pointed the team in a direction, stated what the expectation was, and then let us go. He was demanding, but he was always with us, fighting alongside us.

The postscript to the story is that we sold over 160 million RAZRs, so we need not have been too worried about the first 10 million.

When it is evident you are onto something, when you start to see things moving in your favor, that is when you need to seize the momentum. People talk a lot about momentum in sports but less so in business; yet it is just as valid here. When you start to see good things happening, look to double down on the bet you made. Set big bold goals, make the bets, and focus the team's energy on working out how to deliver. We waste too much time deciding whether we are going to make the bet. The balance is so far out of whack it is crazy.

> "In a startup, it doesn't matter if you're 100 percent right 100 percent of the time. What matters is having forward momentum and a tight fact-based data/metrics feedback loop to help you quickly recognize and reverse any incorrect decisions. That's why startups are agile. By the time a big company gets the committee to organize the subcommittee to pick a meeting date, your startup could have made 20 decisions, reversed five of them and implemented the fifteen that worked."[2]
>
> —STEVEN GARY BLANK

---

2 Steven Gary Blank, *The Four Steps to the Epiphany: Successful Strategies for Products That Win* (K&S Ranch, 2nd edition, 2013).

KEY LESSONS

When you have momentum, seize upon it immediately and exploit it for all its worth.

SO WHAT ARE YOU GOING TO DO ABOUT IT?

My suggestion: If you had three big bets to make in your business tomorrow, what would they be and what is stopping you from making them? Assess the best upside, the worst downside, and the likelihood of each, and then just decide whether it is worth betting on your team to deliver them.

Write your thoughts here:

Have Plenty of Canaries: They Protect Against Bad Decisions

As we have discussed, most of the time you can change a bad decision before it costs you a lot of money. One bad decision that cost one of my companies a lot of money was when we made a particularly aggressive pricing decision to crush the momentum of a small competitor. The decision was made quickly with plenty of senior people in the room. To many of us it felt like using a sledgehammer to crack a nut. Some months later, my colleague who was responsible for that particular area of the business got badly criticized by his boss for that decision when it became obvious how much money it would cost us. He argued to his boss that his boss and many other more senior executives had been in the room when the decision was made, which was true. The response he received was that his crime was that he "didn't have enough canaries in the coal mine," and that was a fair criticism. The low price was maintained for far too long, and too much of our business shifted from a highly profitable product to this very aggressively priced product. The forecasts that had been made were wildly inaccurate, and it was allowed to continue for far too long before someone noticed things were out of control. Clearly there were insufficient checks in place to ensure that the gutsy call didn't play out badly. I would argue that, while the decision wasn't the correct one, the real crime wasn't the decision he made. The crime was the lack of monitoring, which meant we didn't pick up on the magnitude of the pending disaster soon enough; it should have been seen earlier. If the decision had been carefully monitored, there would still have been plenty of time for someone to throw themselves on the tracks to stop the pending disaster.

I am always slightly slower in making a decision when it is a pricing decision, enhancing a partner's margins, or matters of brand reputation. It is always good to be slightly more circumspect about decisions like those that are hard to reverse, and which have potentially long-lasting consequences. Don't avoid them, but do think twice and watch them play out.

When making big calls and moving at speed ensure you have the listening mechanisms (the canaries) to detect if something starts to go wrong. The damage from most big decisions that turn out to be bad can be limited if the right monitoring processes are put in place. But you also need to have people who are watching the numbers like hawks and who know they absolutely must shout quickly and loudly and, if need be, throw themselves on the tracks as soon as it looks like it is all going horribly wrong.

KEY LESSONS

Be more careful about irreversible decisions or pricing decisions as these have huge consequences very quickly.

Ensure bold calls have good listening mechanisms and are being watched by people who fully understand their role and obligations as watchmen.

SO WHAT ARE YOU GOING TO DO ABOUT IT?

Write your thoughts here:

Anxiety and Fear Are the Enemies of Decisiveness

One of the most amazing experiences of my career, and almost certainly the greatest story I have ever heard, came when I met Nando Parrado.

In 1972, Nando was a twenty-two-year-old university student and a member of a rugby team that was flying from his native Uruguay to Chile. The plane carrying the team crashed at 18,000 feet. The search and rescue operation for them was abandoned after eight days. But seventy-two days after the crash, Nando and his friend Roberto descended the treacherous terrain and walked off the mountain to raise the alarm and get help. Nando, Roberto, and fourteen others survived, while twenty-nine people perished on that mountain.

This is a story that you must hear. Read the book *Miracle in the Andes* or watch the film *Alive*. (The book tells the story so much more fully.) There are so many lessons from that experience that you will be able to glean by reading that book.

I have been lucky enough to hear Nando personally tell his story twice. The first time had such an impact on me that when I had the opportunity to get him to come speak to my Microsoft team, I did not hesitate. He gets over three hundred requests each year to tell his story, and he accepts about ten. To hear Nando tell his story personally was one of the greatest gifts I have ever been able to give to my team. About six hundred people were in the room, and for ninety minutes you could hear a pin drop . . . literally. I have never known anyone who could hold the complete attention of so many people for so long.

I had the distinct pleasure of spending time with Nando at dinner the night before his talk and at lunch on the day of. I asked Nando how the experience had shaped his life since then. He talked about how he makes very fast decisions: "When you get used to making twenty life or death decisions every day for nearly three months, decisions back in real life don't seem quite as important and not worth agonizing over." He gave several examples, including meeting his wife of many years, Veronique, for the first time on a Thursday and marrying her the following Thursday. He said he just knew she was the one, so why wait?

In an extract from his website, Nando explains his experience in the mountains and how, because of one incident, he became far more confident and able to make decisions quickly and easily. That incident came from a conversation he had with Roberto Canessa, while they were sitting at 18,000 feet on the top of a mountain peak, surrounded by a wilderness of snow and rock as far as the eye could see, knowing no one was looking for them and there was no way out.

> . . . we knew we were going to die. There is absolutely no way out.
>
> We then decided how we would die: we would walk towards the sun and the west. It was better than freezing at the top. This decision took us less than thirty seconds. . . . Other decisions made later in life seemed no more difficult than deciding about my own death.
>
> I have gained confidence in myself, a quiet tranquillity that has given me a better perception of the world around me. Making decisions became easier because I knew that the worst thing that could happen would be that I was simply wrong. Compared to what I had gone through, that was nothing.[3]

There was a freshness and vibrancy in Nando's whole being that was infectious. He shouldn't have been sitting opposite me having dinner, because by all odds he should have died on that mountain. But here he was, larger than life, loving life. He shouldn't have had a

3 Nando Parrado, "Letter," *About Nando* (accessed October 16, 2017), http://www.parrado.com/about.html.

beautiful family, he shouldn't have gone on to be a racing car driver, a television broadcaster, or own a production company. He had a lot to be grateful for, as we all do, but we just don't see it as clearly as he does. I honestly believe that because of the perspective he gained on the mountain he doesn't stress over making decisions; he isn't riddled by anxiety. His mantra is "What's the worst that can happen?"

I learned many valuable lessons from Nando during our interaction, but one of those that affected me most was this mindset of trying to rid yourself of the anxiety of each decision. "What's the worst that can happen?" has helped me greatly.

This thing about freeing yourself from your anxieties is vitally important, and I would suggest it may be the biggest secret to making decisions far more freely. All the best and fastest decision-makers I have known have never appeared worried about getting decisions wrong. Nando had accepted he was going to die and that he had no way out; nothing worse than that could happen to him.

Now, I recognize that it is easy to say, "don't be anxious," but a whole lot harder to change your mindset. As I sat there and listened to him, two things he said really struck a chord with me and helped me embrace more of his "freedom of decisions." One was asking yourself this question: "What's the worst that can happen?" The second was a quote that was born out of his realization that he was going to die on the mountain. He told us . . . "As we used to say in the mountains, 'Breathe. Breathe again. With every breath, you are alive.' After all these years, this is still the best advice I can give you: Savor your existence. Live every moment. Do not waste a breath."

How marvelous that mentality is. I have found that embracing it does, indeed, make it so much easier to make critical decisions freely. When faced with difficult decisions, I embrace the mentality of "I'm going to savor my existence, I'm going to live every moment, and I am not going to waste a breath." Then I find that I am far more willing to make a decision so that I can return to my breathing, savoring, and living.

And once we have made that decision, we then need to be comfortable with our decision and stop agonizing over it—it has been made and it has gone. Move on, next!

KEY LESSONS

Understand what is important in life and don't become paralyzed by unimportant decisions.

Have more confidence in yourself and your decision-making capability. Look at your success rates; look at how few bad decisions you make.

Decide what you are going to do and do it. Don't revisit it—it's done. That is what you are paid to do—to lead, to decide, and move on.

Embrace a tranquility that helps you understand your world and make decisions easily because the worst that can happen is that you are wrong . . . that is all.

Remember, "Breathe. Breathe again. With every breath, you are alive. . . . Savor your existence. Live every moment. Do not waste a breath." Remember Nando's advice.

SO WHAT ARE YOU GOING TO DO ABOUT IT?

My suggestion: Order the book online now. *Miracle in the Andes* by Nando Parrado.

Write your thoughts here:

Some Things Require a Zero-Tolerance Attitude

Sometimes you just cannot allow something unacceptable to continue for another day. The urgency to see dramatic change and an immediate difference is often the greatest catalyst for transformation.

I hate the word improve. Obviously, it is better than deteriorate in that it says you are going in the right direction, but it has a tone of incrementalism that I am allergic to. Instead, I like transformation or dramatic change. Now, dramatic change doesn't only come from new ideas, it can also come from the quality of implementation, when there is focus and a zero-tolerance mentality.

The most dramatic transformation I ever heard of was when a CEO of a large UK life assurance company spoke at a conference I was attending many years ago. He had joined about three years before and had been horrified to find out that, in the year before he joined, there had been something like 18,362 complaints, and most were related to how the customer was treated or the fact that they didn't get a satisfactory answer to their questions. He said that he found it horrifying that there were so many complaints, especially when the person who generally rang in to contact them was the loved one of someone who had just died. He said that when someone was in such a devastating period of their life and going through such trauma, it was unacceptable that they didn't receive first-class service with care and consideration one hundred percent of the time.

So he set out to remove every single complaint. Nothing incremental about that. In the first year, the complaints fell to just 281. Down by over ninety-eight percent. In the second year, complaints were down to 73. Staggering! Amazing! I was on tenterhooks to find out what sophisticated solutions they had implemented to drive such an astonishing change.

He said he implemented just two simple rules.

Rule One: If the phone rang, whoever was by it had to answer it, and then they were personally responsible for making sure that all the customer's questions were fully answered. They could pass the phone call to someone else if that person was better equipped to answer, but they had to check that THEIR customer's question had been fully answered.

Rule Two: If there was a customer complaint in this new era, then the manager of the person who had handled that call had to go meet that customer face-to-face the very next day. The manager had to knock on the customer's door, apologize, and resolve the issue there and then. The CEO said, "It didn't take many trips to Middlesbrough (a place about five hours' drive away from their head office) on a rainy Saturday morning for the managers to take responsibility for how their teams handled their customers."

The CEO had concluded that the root of the problem was that people were not taking responsibility on the calls for resolving their customer's questions, and the managers were not managing their teams to the standard that he expected. Ultimately, those were the only things he needed to address.

Dramatic, transformative shifts drive change quickly. Rule #2 was a simple yet transformative rule that had a dramatic effect on the number of complaints because it had a substantial consequence for the manager. For the employees, it spoke oceans about how important customer satisfaction was now regarded in the company. For the offended customers, it showed the depth of what their satisfaction meant to the company, and I am sure the rule resulted in these complainers speaking glowingly about the company rather than negatively.

I love the zero-tolerance approach to something important.

Now, this example reflects so many of the punk attributes. The CEO had high ambitions and didn't settle for incremental improvement. He didn't try to reduce complaints by twenty-five percent per year, which to most leaders would have been a huge success. He dared greatly, he was unaccepting of treating people badly at such a traumatic time in their lives, and he radically changed the status quo.

I first heard this story over twenty years ago. It has stayed with me for all that time, and I have recited it probably over one hundred times.

KEY LESSONS

The speed of change is set as much by the extent of your expectations and the timescale you dictate. If you don't set goals that need lightning-fast speed, then I will bet you will never see that speed.

A zero-tolerance approach to something fundamentally important speaks volumes about what matters to you and the standards you demand.

SO WHAT ARE YOU GOING TO DO ABOUT IT?

My suggestion: Ask yourself what you want your teams to really focus on. What is the cause of the problem, and what zero-tolerance steps can you take to address it?

Write your thoughts here:

Everyone Needs a Paddy

In April 2001, after months of procrastination, parent companies Carlton and Granada finally backed the rebranding of ONdigital to ITV Digital. We had spent considerable time planning it, but no decision had been made and as a result the process had stalled for several months. I was informed of this late change of heart at the eleventh hour—and we now had just eleven weeks to do a full rebranding of the company. Normally, something of this magnitude—which was not just a simple logo change, but a fundamentally different positioning and appeal—would take twelve months to do. In fact, they'd offered that as a time frame, but because of other scheduling issues, it simply didn't make sense; we had to do it in eleven weeks. I was furious—how could we now be expected to rebrand an entire company in such a short time frame and do it well? We all knew the eleven-week deadline was ridiculously ambitious, but we were a team that did what was right rather than taking the easy option. So there was never really a debate about whether we would go for it.

Chris Moss (who was the main marketing man behind the launch of Orange, Virgin Atlantic, and 118118) was working with me as a consultant at the time, and he was there when I came back to my office agitated and frustrated at the bureaucracy that was now causing us to try to pull off the impossible, when it would have been so much easier if the pettiness had been sorted months ago. I told him the news that we now had permission to rebrand.

His reaction was, "That's great."

I told him the implied timeline. His response . . . "You need Paddy."

"Who is Paddy?" I asked.

Paddy was the person who had planned everything for the launch of Orange. Before that, he had been in an elite military group and had been a key member of the team that had planned the logistics for the Falklands War in 1982.

He repeated himself, "Everyone needs a Paddy. You need Paddy. I'll get Paddy for you."

Next day, Paddy walked into my office. I liked him immediately: He was one of those people who have a presence about them. He was very slim, probably in his sixties, and he looked just like the retired army lieutenant colonel he was, decked out in a blazer, open neck shirt, and cravat. We spoke about the scope of the rebranding program, the vision of what we wanted to achieve, and the amount of work required in such a short space of time. I didn't try to hide the magnitude of the task, and I was delighted that he immediately agreed to do it, starting the next day, but he demanded four things.

"I need a project management team seconded to me from across the company—ideally each person needs to be able to make decisions for their group, but probably more likely get decisions approved quickly. I need to take them on an offsite for two days at the very beginning. I need access to you every evening at the end of the day, and you need to make the decisions of the day. I need to know what date we are launching."

"Okay," I said, "Let's go through those. A dedicated project management team—I will get that for you. Easy. A two-day offsite—do we really need that, we don't have many days as it is?"

"Yes, absolutely essential. We need to be absolutely aligned on the mission."

"Okay—done." You tended not to argue with Paddy.

"End of the day you and I meet, perfect."

"Launch date—we want to launch on 11 July if at all possible."

He stood bolt upright as if he were going to salute. "We will launch on 11 July, the only thing that can stop that is the weather." And he walked out of my office. I swear it was nearly a march, but I will give Paddy the benefit of the doubt.

Chris popped his head in and asked if everything had gone all right with the meeting with Paddy. I said, "Yes, he'll be here in the morning. But I don't understand what the weather has to do with our launch date?"

"That's just Paddy's military training. The only permissible reason to ever not deliver on a date when people's lives were at risk was if the weather made it too hazardous."

So, Paddy was in next morning to meet his newly created project management team. They went off on their essential team-building two-day offsite, and then the following week everything kicked off with real purpose.

Paddy instigated two daily standing meetings, one at the start of the day, which he called Morning Prayers. This was for the seconded team where everyone would close all the agreed-upon actions from the previous day and assign new actions. This was a mandatory daily meeting for thirty minutes; there were no chairs in the room because he didn't want to extend the meeting at all. As Paddy told me, a no chair meeting always ends earlier than if chairs are present. Damn chairs.

Everyone held Paddy in such high regard that it was inconceivable that anyone would come to Morning Prayers without having achieved their daily goals. This was partly because of how he conducted himself with unfailing precision and as a perfect gentleman, partly because of his past accomplishments at Orange and in the Falklands War, and partly because we were scared of him—even though he was in his sixties, I am sure he could have taken any one of us out in a blink of an eye. He also could make himself heard across a loud and large room without ever shouting. He had a penetrating voice that would cut through the din.

The second meeting was at the end of day with me. This was the meeting where he needed decisions, and he didn't allow any procrastination. He used to say to me that I had clear authority for the rebranding, and so I needed to make the decisions. On some decisions, I was not as confident as I wanted to be, but with Paddy, no delay was ever allowed, and he forced me to decide. I know my decisiveness increased significantly as a result of this process, and I have always appreciated Paddy's influence on that aspect of my leadership.

During this intense eleven-week period, I learned that there were two types of project managers: genuine project managers worth their weight in gold and process managers who call themselves project managers.

Process managers are great with critical path planning. They walk you through the right processes to get you to the end destination, and they even tell you if you are on schedule with beautiful green, yellow, and red color-coded status charts. Project managers do all of that, but also when the project starts to stall or hits a speed bump (which is an oxymoron as it does the opposite), they trace the issue blocking progress back to its source and then they clear up the problem themselves or escalate the issue quickly to the leader who has the authority to remove the problem and force that person to take action.

Paddy had five great qualities that made him the most masterful project leader I have ever met:

1. He had great experience with tracing issues back to their sources and finding the blockages.

2. He quickly understood people and the dynamics involved, so he learned very quickly how to navigate our organization and find the real decision-makers and the people who would drive progress.

3. He had a beautiful blend of charm, professionalism, and determination that meant no one could resist his request to drop everything for a moment and seek a resolution.

4. He was fabulous at simplifying the decision at hand and explaining the pros and cons for the alternative courses of action. When Paddy articulated it, I often wondered why there had been so much debate before, because the answer always seemed strikingly obvious to everyone in the room.

5. With Paddy, there was rarely an option to not make a decision. On a couple of occasions when I tried to categorically

tell him I couldn't make a decision, he told me I was putting the completion of the mission at risk. He'd sit me down, take me through it step-by-step, explain the consequences of each decision or non-decision, and we would then make the call together. He was a master at forcing closure.

As the launch day approached, everything fell into place and we comfortably achieved all our goals. What many of us thought was impossible was delivered thanks to Herculean efforts from the team and the rigor that Paddy brought. Without Paddy, I really don't believe we would have achieved the deadline. Launch day passed, and Paddy's work was complete. Never have I known someone to come into a company and have such an immediate impact on such a wide group of people. But then, just like that, he was gone. We had rebranded on time, and the weather hadn't caused any delay; in fact, it was a beautiful sunny summer's day. Just like Mary Poppins, he had blown into our lives, had a huge impact, and then before we knew it, he had gone. But also like Mary Poppins he left a lot of himself and his spirit behind, and we were by far the better for it.

Looking back soon after the rebranding, we all recognized that the limited time frame had forced us to move with such speed and agility that it had helped us in many ways. If we had been given nine months, we would have taken nine months, and I honestly believe it may have resulted in poorer execution. We built a fluidity to our business that kept us focused on what really mattered, and in many cases, we decided with our hearts, and we decided as a small empowered group—and this was so much more effective than if we had been given nine months and everyone could have had an opinion on everything.

KEY LESSONS

Focus is a critical element for driving speed. The simplicity of daily action plans and daily check-ins drove a fluidity I hadn't seen before.

Project managers need to have accountability for hitting key deadlines; too many times they consider themselves support functions to the business leaders. No, they have to hit deadlines—that's their job. Anyone can be minute takers and meeting organizers, but those people aren't real project managers.

Time crunch often means that clear accountability is established, and this forces managers to decide and stops them from hiding behind the need to get consensus.

SO WHAT ARE YOU GOING TO DO ABOUT IT?

Write your thoughts here:

Sometimes Everything Else Just Has to Stop

It was late on Friday afternoon, about four p.m. in Chicago. We were at the point of closing the deal where Motorola would join Product (RED) as their mobile phone partner, and everything was set for a signing the following Monday. I was winding down for a relaxing weekend after a long and hectic week. I then received a phone call that disrupted all my plans.

Bobby Shriver rang me to tell me that Nokia had just offered a huge minimum guarantee if they were given the (RED) contract, and (RED) had no alternative but to give the deal to Nokia rather than to Motorola as that minimum commitment was transformational for the Global Fund and would secure the lives of millions of Africans.

The altruistic part of me was pleased—but in honesty that lasted about two seconds. The commercial businessman in me was pissed. Everything we had worked tirelessly for was now in doubt. We already had some (RED) phones in production. Had we jumped the gun? How could they ditch us at the altar like this? CRAP!

Ron Garriques (our president) was on vacation that day. I texted him, and he called me straight back. I explained the news I had just received. In about five minutes on the phone, we quickly hatched a plan:

- I was to call Charles Dunstone (the founder of Carphone Warehouse and a high-profile UK entrepreneur). Charles was a "friend of (RED)" and had been helping Bobby and Bono as a special advisor to (RED) for the mobile phone category, and I was to try to ensure he would support us over Nokia. He was also a long-standing friend of Motorola as we had given him the exclusive rights to the Pink RAZR in the UK the previous year, and that had been a huge success for us both.

- I was to invite Bobby to be the guest of Ed Zander (our Chairman and CEO) at his house in Carmel for the weekend where we could discuss what Motorola could offer. I had to get him to agree to that. The plan was that the three of us would try to keep him there until he had signed with us.

- I then had to put together a compelling PowerPoint presentation of why (RED) should choose us over Nokia. I was to call Allan Burns, who was responsible for our Africa region, and get all our African credentials, as we knew that was important to (RED). We would make the pitch that we wanted to be helping people in Africa to help themselves, and by taking some of our commerce to Africa, we would be doing that. We were not just about donations; we would add some commerce to their region and double the impact that our (RED) phones would have in Africa.

- Finally, after securing Bobby's commitment to join us for the weekend, I was to arrange for the company jet to fly me to pick Ron up on Saturday morning. He was somewhere in the US on vacation, I don't remember where. We were then to fly to Santa Monica late on Saturday, and we would collect Bobby on Sunday morning and fly him up the coast to Carmel to stay with Ed for a day or so.

Having gained Bobby's agreement to the trip to Ed's house, I then called Charles Dunstone. Ron had suggested that I ask just one question. So, I called Charles. It was now just after ten p.m. on a Friday evening, and I was calling his mobile phone.

He answered, "Hello, Jeremy. What's up? Is it urgent? It's just that I have ten friends over for a dinner party."

"I think it is, but you can decide. We just heard about the Nokia counteroffer, and Ron wants to know one thing." I paused for dramatic effect. "Ron wants to know: Are you for us or against us?" Ron had phrased this in a deliberately provocative way but had cleverly distanced himself from it by making me deliver the line.

"Okay, let me excuse myself for five minutes, and I will call you back," Charles replied.

A couple of minutes later he called, and I simply reiterated my question . . . "We just want to know, are you for us or against us?"

"Well, it's not as easy as that," Charles said. "They have put a very large commitment down and, well, that's not easy to walk away from and . . ." This was the only time in all the dealings I have had with Charles where he was a little stuck for words.

"Charles, Ron is just looking for a one-word answer. For or against. That's all I need."

Charles was again struggling to get his words out before I heard him inhale deeply and say, "FOR. I am FOR Motorola. I will call Bobby."

"Thank you, Charles, have a good evening."

Charles knew better than anyone how we, like no one else, could and would get behind an idea and make it big. We had done that together with the Pink RAZR just a few months before.

I rallied my team and told them the predicament. Many volunteered to cancel their Friday evening plans, and they stayed with me into the early hours of the morning as we tried to piece our pitch together and create a compelling deck. I rang Allan Burns at some unearthly hour on Saturday morning to get a whole load of facts about our activities in Africa. We decided there and then that we would commit to making our packaging for the (RED) phones in the region; we didn't know how, but we would work it out. We also stated that our intent was to build assembly capabilities in Africa for the (RED) phones in due course, but that would take more assessment. We knew it was important to (RED) that we helped people in Africa to help themselves.

I fell asleep at my desk sometime after two a.m. I woke at three thirty a.m. with a terrible cricked neck. I literally couldn't turn to the side. I drove home in agony and got into bed just after four a.m. I set my alarm for six a.m. as the jet was wheels up at seven a.m. I drove to the private hanger in a neck brace that I had at home; I was in terrible pain.

We landed a few hours later, and Ron boarded the plane. I felt like crap, and I know I looked like it too; Ron didn't hesitate in telling me so. A few hours later we landed in Santa Monica. We went to the hotel, and I collapsed into bed.

I managed to ring my wife at this point. The last time I had spoken to her was about five p.m. on Friday evening from my office. I had rung to say I would be home a little later than planned as a problem had cropped up with the (RED) deal.

"Where are you?" she asked.

I told her I was now two thousand miles away in California.

She was trying to hide her disappointment, but I could tell she wasn't overly happy. She has always been so supportive, but the prospect of now having a weekend of looking after our three kids on her own was a little frustrating. She said something like, "I know you came home at some point last night as your side of the bed had been slept in, but I don't know how long you were there for."

"Not long," I replied.

"And when are you coming home?"

"I don't really know. We have a problem."

It wasn't a very long conversation.

Next morning, we wandered down to the beach and pier area; we planned to meet Bobby later.

I managed to call Charles again, and he said he had talked to Bobby and reiterated his support for us, but it would be Bobby's decision.

We flew to Carmel, and Ed and his wife Monica were perfect hosts. They welcomed us and allowed us to settle in. Before dinner I took Ed and Ron through the PowerPoint presentation. I had entitled it and structured it as "Ten reasons why only Motorola can meet the Product (RED) objectives."

Ed and Ron liked the deck, but they both wanted one change each. One was bold and one I was unsure about, but I made the changes overnight.

Our plan was to do everything we could to keep Bobby at Ed's house (short of holding him hostage) until we had gotten him to sign the contract. I had the previously agreed-upon contract papers with me.

We had an enjoyable dinner on Sunday, and then on Monday we had some initial discussions before I made our pitch.

"Ten reasons why only Motorola can meet the Product (RED) objectives."

Number one, I reassured Bobby that we would make the same monetary commitment as our competitors had. That clearly reset the balance, and I do think he was a little surprised by how that significant decision had been made so quickly; he saw we weren't messing around. If he was a little off-balance by that, we knocked him over with our next shot.

Number two. This was Ron's change from the night before. While Ron acknowledged that I had added in that we will match the Nokia financial commitment, guaranteeing the same money for the Global Fund, Ron wasn't a "match them" kind of guy. He wanted to "raise them." He wasn't going to allow someone to have to decide between us.

So, number two (I paused for dramatic effect), we will write a check for $10 million up front as an advance, so that we get the ball rolling and put this show on the road. Bobby was now reeling.

I later found out why this had such an impact on Bobby. Up until that moment, (RED) had been an idea, a concept, a bunch of plans. But here was one of the preeminent companies of the day prepared to give ten million dollars to the Global Fund there and then. That gesture made (RED) tangible and real. We could start to save lives immediately. Bobby would subsequently tell me that was the moment he really knew for certain that (RED) was going to become a reality and Motorola were the ones who had the courage to put up before anyone else. The advance was bold and very punk.

I then went on to talk about points like RAZR being the sexiest phone on the planet; the fact that the Motorola brand was one of the coolest in the world at that time; we made a commitment to making the packaging for our (RED) RAZRs in Lesotho, because (RED) felt it was important that it wasn't just aid we were giving, but commerce; and another bunch of reasons.

Then number ten. This was Ed's change. The previous evening he said, "Make reason #10, the last reason and our last slide . . . because we are Americans." I wasn't sure Ed was being serious. I questioned it, but he was adamant. I told them that one of them was going to have to say it. I couldn't say that with my English accent.

I got to the final slide and looked for support from Ed or Ron to jump in and deliver the message in a genuine American accent, but no one came to my rescue, so I said (with a straight face and in my best British accent) to Bobby, "This is an American idea, based on America ideologies, and we are American. So by choosing Motorola, you're choosing America."

Appealing to the American in him was another master stroke; the money commitment had won us the deal, but this was an American idea, and stating our American credentials helped seal the deal. I really think someone else needed to deliver the message, but Ed was spot on in appealing to his American patriotism.

After all of that, surely there was no way he could say anything but yes to us.

We departed early Tuesday morning for the airport. No contract signed, but a firm belief that Bobby could not say no to us, his fellow Americans who overnight had turned his dream into a reality.

We arrived in Chicago late on Tuesday. Gerry was always so supportive of my career, but she did make the point that the last time she had seen me was Friday morning when I was supposed to be coming home early to go out for dinner with friends. And apart from seeing that I had lain in our bed at some point on Friday night and a rushed two-minute call on Saturday, she had no idea where I had been or what had gone on, other than that it was about (RED).

A day or so later we each signed the Motorola and Product (RED) contract. We had saved a deal that was very close to falling through our fingers. We did it because we responded with a "whatever it takes" mentality and the team jumped into action. I loved working for Ron.

There was a period of time when we felt like we were unstoppable, and for that I will always admire, respect, and thank him. He left for Dell around 2008, and Motorola was never the same again.

The following Saturday Ron and his wife, Karina, invited Gerry and me to a charity dinner at the Chicago Bears stadium, along with some other colleagues including my great friend Jim Wicks (mentioned elsewhere in this book) and his wife Sue. Ed and Monica were at another table. While they were serving coffee, the Live Auction started; Ron was always very generous in such events and always keen to contribute. He had bid on a few items, winning a couple, and then a week's vacation in a beautiful villa in the US Virgin Islands came up. He was very persistent with that item and secured it for about $8,000. The hostess came over, took his credit card details, and gave him an envelope that I presumed contained the voucher. He borrowed her pen, scribbled something on the envelope, and then threw it across the table to me. He had written, "Jeremy and Gerry, Thanks for closing the (RED) deal, Ron and Karina." It was a gesture that meant everything to Gerry and me. For Gerry, it showed that Ron, despite his demanding work ethic, was human and kind, and it was a very public demonstration of his appreciation. In all my working years, it was the most special recognition I had ever seen. It was spontaneous and very public. On the way home that evening, Gerry was so excited and said, "When can you disappear again for five days and do another one of those deals?"

KEY LESSONS

Great teams need grit. There are always moments when things look like they are going to be snatched from your grasp. You can allow them to slip through your fingers, or you can spring into action. If things matter and you care deeply, you jump into action and so do your teams.

Know your audience. Ron and Ed both made substantive changes. Too many of us when preparing our pitch, fail to adopt our audience's mindset and fail to think how they would think. Too often we are too fixated in telling our story, rather than reframing it to show how we can help them tell theirs.

Ron knew not to just match the competition. He raised the stakes but did it in a way that was most appealing to (RED). He had worked out that the naysayers and skeptics would be circling if (RED) didn't make a meaningful donation soon after launch, and this gesture removed any risk of that.

Ed's change to appeal to the American in Bobby (a Kennedy) was important and, in honesty, obvious to an American. That aspect of who the audience was and its role as a compelling argument for Bobby hadn't occurred to me. That's why I should have thought about the presentation as if I were in his shoes and making that decision.

The $10 million advance helped (RED)'s story become a reality, and the American angle would help (RED) to rally the American people who were their primary focus.

There are times when you need to call on your relationships. Our close relationship with Charles meant that he answered my call at ten p.m. on a Friday evening when he had a house full of guests. Ask yourself how many of your best customers, suppliers, or partners you have that type of relationship with. If the answer is too few, then you need to fundamentally change things.

SO WHAT ARE YOU GOING TO DO ABOUT IT?

Write your thoughts here:

Time Is Our Most Precious Asset and Focus Is Our Most Powerful Tool

While working at Microsoft, we brought in a coach who normally operated in the world of sports. His name was Mike Gervais, and he, among other things, was the sports psychology coach for the Seattle Seahawks. He helped us greatly. We brought him in to work with our team when he was first starting to take the science and practices of training elite athletes and apply them to businesses. One of the things he called us out on was our behavior in some of our meetings. He was shocked that there were so many other meetings going on within the meeting in addition to the actual meeting. People were IMing each other, there were side conversations, and other people weren't mentally present because they were writing emails or texting on the phone. He asked, "How the hell do you get anything done? So many bad practices have crept into our culture, and I see it in every company I visit. People seem to have lost the ability to focus."

He explained that science says that the brain cannot do two things at once in situations where we are required to think. We can walk down a street and talk, because we have learned to walk without thinking, but you cannot listen to something someone is saying to you and talk to another person in a different conversation. You can switch between the two very quickly, the brain allows you to do that, but you cannot be engaged in both at exactly the same time. The brain just isn't good at multitasking, yet we all try to do it, we all think we are good at it, and we all put up with it happening around us. It is a huge source of inefficiency. To do great things you have to focus.

You may have heard the story of the day when Bill Gates first met Warren Buffett. They were having dinner, hosted by Bill's parents. I am not sure whether this was some kind of after-dinner discussion starter, but the dinner guests were asked to write down the one word that was the single most important factor in their success. Both Bill and Warren wrote the word *focus*.

HOLDING MULTITASKERS ACCOUNTABLE

Mike's line of thinking was echoed in the advice Patrick Lencioni (the highly regarded author of, among other works, *The Five Dysfunctions of a Team*) told us at one of our conferences. Someone in the audience asked him who he thought was the best CEO he had come across and why. Patrick responded, "Alan Mulally at Ford." I had met Alan briefly a year or two before when he had been on Microsoft's board of directors and he came to talk to the company's corporate vice presidents.

"And why? . . . because he holds people accountable in the most joyful way." I wondered what that meant.

Patrick gave an example. "When Alan first went to Ford, he was in a leadership team meeting, and one of the team members kept being distracted by emails on his computer or other things. Alan asked him afterwards if he would concentrate on the meeting more and do whatever he was doing later. This leader said, 'Well, I am very busy, I am highly productive, and multitasking is how I get so much done.' Alan replied, 'Oh, that's ok then.'

To which this guy replied, 'Oh, so it's okay then?'

Alan then cheerily stated, 'Yes, it's ok, we can still be friends, you just can't work here anymore.' Accountability in the most joyful way.

This obsession on focus was also one of Mike's key principles. He told us one of the principles of the Seahawks is that there is only one play you must focus on and that is the next play. You cannot change the last play, you cannot get ahead of yourselves and think about a future play, the only play you can impact is the present one. That really hit home with me. No wonder so many meetings are far from effective; it is because no one is focusing. What a complete and utter waste of time!

A few months later Mike invited me to a Seahawks practice session. It blew my mind to watch how disciplined they were with their time. I entered the indoor field, and there were about three or four different groups, each doing a separate exercise. Play after play was being rehearsed like clockwork. The team appeared in constant motion. Then, after the designated time, a horn sounded, and everyone ran to their new pre-assigned station and immediately commenced their next practice routine. Fifteen minutes later and the same thing—everyone runs to their next station and immediately they are up and at it again.

The team's clockwork-like efficiency was clear for all to see. Two days later I ran into Nicole Davis, a two-time Olympic silver medalist who works with Mike. I told her about my revelation. She acknowledged it as common practice. "You know why we are all like that? It's because the difference between winning and losing is small, and we are constantly driven on by the fact that we worry that our competition might be practicing harder or more efficiently than we are. If we are sitting around, they could be working."

I went into work on Monday with this thought about how efficiently we could be using our time. Every meeting that day I decided to ask myself: If our competitors could see this meeting, would they be concerned, or would they be sitting back feeling extremely confident about how they were far more prepared and ready? I was horrified at the way I had to answer, meeting after meeting. I had been invited to irrelevant meetings that were focused on unimportant internal stuff that meant nothing! Apart from being irrelevant, these meetings failed to even achieve the unimportant goals that had been set. It was three p.m. in the afternoon before I had been in any kind of useful meeting. I went home traumatized. The blanket of fog had swept in over my world and had consumed my agenda without me even realizing it.

I took control back.

I stopped attending pointless meetings as they were a waste of my time. I banned other meetings from happening entirely as they were a waste of everyone's time.

I stopped having my PC open in meetings as it was just a distraction, and an email popping up would inevitably take my attention away from what should be my focus.

I pushed for thirty minutes as the standard meeting length, not the obligatory hour.

I was unaccepting of presentations taking up ninety percent of the allotted time, because I didn't want only ten percent of the time to be focused on the discussions and decisions that were far more valuable.

I started telling the meeting owner at the end of each meeting how effectively I felt that they had used the time. Each meeting was a huge investment decision, and I wanted them to know how well they had spent that money.

KEY LESSONS

Look at every activity of your working day through the lens of: If your competitors could see you now, how would they feel? Try it for a week and see how you feel. If you are disappointed, you have to force change.

You have to constantly assess how effective each part of your day is. You cannot allow pointless, ineffective activities to take place. You are obligated to use your time on the things that are important and deserve your focus.

Having seen the Seahawks practice I cannot un-see that level of efficiency now. My eyes were opened. Again, it was like taking the red pill in the Matrix. I saw a reality that is hard to live up to, but I cannot stay in the comfortable, closeted blue-pill world. We all need to take the red pill and try to dramatically increase our productivity.

SO WHAT ARE YOU GOING TO DO ABOUT IT?

Write your thoughts here:

Meeting Productivity Comes from Ruthless Cutting

"People who enjoy meetings should not be in charge of anything."

THOMAS SEWELL

Endless research studies get published every year with sensational headlines like "Managers say twenty-five to fifty percent of their time in meetings is wasted" or "American businesses lose $37 million in ineffective meetings." I say one hundred percent of research studies that try to quantify this unquantifiable phenomenon are a waste of money. We all know the inefficiency, but rather than calculate the cost, let's focus on the solution. I am appalled at the number of bad practices that turn meetings into wastes of time. It is horrendous that we even have to discuss this here, but sadly we do. Punk attitude is highly beneficial in creating more effective meetings. The secret for more effective meetings is to cut and to cut deeply. These are the ten cuts to start making today:

1. **Cut people from meetings.** Keep the list of meeting attendees lean. Invite players, ban spectators. More people equals more opportunity for distracting questions, deviation, and pointless discussion—and less accountability by the real participants.

2. **Cut the length of meetings.** Meeting activities expand to fill the time available. An hour, in my experience, is the standard scheduled length of eighty percent of meetings. In my opinion, that is too long ninety percent of the time. Instigate thirty minutes as the default meeting length, and make the hour-long meeting the rare exception.

3. **Cut meetings into specific time chunks.** Too often the way the time in a meeting is used is totally disproportionate to how it should be used. Time slips away as people try to establish the facts and wallow in the backward-looking analysis. Then, before you know it, just five minutes are left to discuss

the recommendations and actions. Cut the (hopefully rare) one-hour meeting down into specific time sections and keep to them: fifteen minutes to understand data and facts, fifteen minutes for the recommendation to be heard, fifteen minutes to decide the actions, and fifteen minutes for any follow-up emails necessary to start implementing the decisions.

4. **Cut the owners of an action to one individual.** Multiple people may need to be involved in completing an action, but there needs to be only one person ultimately responsible. Apple obsesses about this. They have DRIs (Directly Responsible Individuals), which is a beautiful name with meaning in each word, none more so than the third one. I will always bet on one person who is on the hook rather than two people who are doing something together. A single responsible person always feels more empowered and accountable than when an action is shared between two or more people.

5. **Cut the chairs from the room (sometimes).** Hold meetings in chairless rooms—a lesson I learned from Paddy and told in a previous story. Nothing makes meetings go on and on like people sitting down and feeling comfortable. Making them stand always ensures people get on with the business at hand.

6. **Cut the meaningless questions that go nowhere and add no value.** My biggest frustration is people who ask pointless, irrelevant, or at best tangential questions. Don't allow people to suck up valuable time by asking irrelevant questions that are often stimulated by their desire to appear clever. Cut them off.

7. **Cut the distractions that take focus away.** As you read in the previous story, people cannot focus on more than one thing at once. Focus is a skill that needs to be trained, but

it is also something that can be helped by simple meeting rules. During the meeting, ban having Outlook open on anyone's PC, ban Instant Messages, get everyone to put their phone in the middle of the table, and eject anyone who breaks these rules. If a meeting doesn't justify a participant's one-hundred-percent attention, then they shouldn't be there at all.

8. **Cut the number of dial-in conference call meetings in favor of face-to-face or video meetings.** If a call has more than three participants, face-to-face communication is always more productive. Clearly, geographical restrictions do not always allow you to be there in person, but video calls allow face-to-face communications, and you can check people's attentiveness and gauge so much more of their reactions from seeing their facial expressions and body language.

9. **Cut bland meeting names that don't inform.** People end up frustrated and disappointed if a decision cannot get made because someone doesn't turn up to a meeting—and often they don't turn up because they don't realize the meeting's importance. To combat this, name the meeting with the decision that is being made. Don't call it a "pricing meeting," don't even call it a "pricing review meeting," call it the "Next year's pricing decision meeting." Even add the word FINAL in for impact. Then ensure that if those people who must be present for the decision to be made decline the meeting, don't hold it. Reschedule instead.

10. **Cut the passive-aggressive post-meeting sniping.** If you have a different opinion than what is being decided in a meeting, you have an honor-bound obligation to speak up there and then—not out in the hallways afterwards. In my

office, I have a sign on the door that people have to pass as they walk out of meetings with me. It references the three roles of leadership that Satya Nadella advocates. It says this: "Create Clarity—are you clear about the actions we have agreed and your role in delivering those? Generate Energy— are you excited and energized to go and do the work that we have agreed? Deliver Success—do you believe that we are taking all the necessary actions to be successful? If you cannot answer yes to all three questions, sit back down—you can only leave this office when you can answer yes."

The root cause of ineffective meetings is that people are not prepared to cut. They don't want to have to throw uninvited guests out of meetings, hurt people's feelings by not inviting them, offend them by cutting them off from their distracting and pointless comments, call people out for their rudeness in not concentrating, or throw them out if their attention is elsewhere. None of these should be a problem if you have a punk attitude; you just have to say it as it is. You may hurt someone's feelings, but they'll get over it, and the rest of the room will applaud internally. It doesn't take many instances where you are unaccepting of this bad behavior to set the rules of engagement for your meeting and your organization.

Whoever runs a meeting, determines the attendees, sets the length of the meeting, or prepares the content for the meeting is making a huge investment decision, and most have no appreciation for the cost. If you are calling a meeting, do the rough math and estimate the cost—then ask yourself, is it worth it? An hour-long meeting with eighteen people can cost six times more than a thirty-minute meeting with six people. I am appalled at the waste that occurs in this way. These ten cuts, ruthlessly but skillfully executed, have huge potential for reducing costs, increasing satisfaction, improving results, increasing speed, and most importantly, maintaining people's sanity.

KEY LESSONS

Train your team on the ten cuts or whichever you feel will help your organization.

Start every meeting with an appreciation of the total cost to the company of holding this meeting. I do the rough math in my head; it takes me about ten seconds, and it makes me far more ruthless about getting value out of the meeting.

Close every meeting by asking everyone: Has the meeting created clarity, generated energy, and put you on track for delivering success? And get a definitive answer to these questions.

SO WHAT ARE YOU GOING TO DO ABOUT IT?

Write your thoughts here:

The Bottom Line

I trust that you have seen that there are three things that primarily drive speed and action: people, focus, and decisions.

We saw how decisiveness obviously increases speed of action, but the most important lesson in my eyes was the realization that decision-making should be looked on as a portfolio, and we should embrace the fact that we don't need to be right every single time and we need to rid ourselves of the anxiety that inhibits our freedom to decide.

Focus is another key contributor to speed. Tight deadlines, by their very nature, provide a focus that is useful. I remember hearing one story of a well-known leader who would cut thirty percent of the headcount from any team whose project fell behind schedule. He reasoned that fewer people helped provide focus and remove unnecessary deliberations. Time constraints, apart from bringing focus, also help because they remove the paralysis of choice, which can be so debilitating.

But at the end of the day it all comes down to people, and the fact is that there are some people who are highly productive and get things done, and then there are those who don't. There are many ways in which certain people get through huge amounts of work and consume tasks with an insatiable appetite. They may do that because of their decisiveness, their work ethic, how they remove blockages, cut through the crap, drive for closure, or focus on the stuff that really matters. Whatever the skills they use in getting stuff done, find those people and hold on to them like the precious stones that they are.

Bottom Line: Take action and move things forward at speed or get out of the way of those of us who are.

Element 5:

SAY IT AS IT IS

"Be a voice, not an echo."

attrib ALBERT EINSTEIN

"Our message is simple: Where our music is welcome, we will play it loud. Where our music is challenged, we will play it louder."

EAST BELFAST PROTESTANT BOYS

The irony of punk music was that you didn't need to be a musician—you just had to have something to say. The Sex Pistols certainly had something to say. Their lyrics were aggressive, straight-talking, and they didn't pull any punches. They became the unofficial voice of the alienated British working-class teenager of the mid '70s. The Pistols were four guys who used to work (or hang out) in a London clothes shop called Sex. All had limited musical ability, and the lead singer was hired for his anarchic look alone, rather than his voice. Throw in the fact that they were managed by that clothes shop owner, and it was that clichéd accident waiting to happen. Yet from that accident, a band rose like no other, that spoke to the disaffected youths of that generation with a voice that resonated with their sense of hopelessness and with an attitude that reflected their anger.

The Sex Pistols said it as they saw it. They got straight to the point; they said it plainly, and they didn't just say it—they screamed it with all the volume that their lungs could produce. In their song "God Save the Queen," it took all of seven words to reveal the whole message of the song: "God Save the Queen, the fascist regime." Juxtaposed against the generic love songs of the disco era, punk rock's plainspoken message was nearly unfathomable in the musical realm: Nobody before had sung of the fascist monarchy, abortion, anarchy, apathy, Nazis, and the Holocaust. Clearly, their lyrics offended many people and still do today. So while I am not endorsing what they said or many of those sentiments, I am commending them hugely for how clearly they got their message across. Their lyrics were direct and forthright. They didn't leave anything unsaid.

This lesson is not about replicating the shock value of the punk rock movement, and offense clearly isn't our goal. However, I believe corporate culture would be far better off if people integrated some of the punk movement's most authentic, say-it-as-it-is traits more often. For instance, the most notable punk rockers exhibited the following:

- They had an original point of view, and nobody was ever unclear about their stance on a subject.

- They were willing to jump forward and express that point of view irrespective of how contrary it was to popular opinion. Popular opinion never concerned them.

- They wasted no words and didn't dillydally in getting to the point. They said it simply and clearly.

- Their words drove change. They felt compelled to speak their mind because they weren't prepared to put up with the status quo.

In this section, you'll read of some occasions where lack of sincerity and biting your tongue may avoid short-term confrontation, but it usually just means a larger bust-up later on. You'll see how straight-talking saves so much time, so much emotional energy, and brings so much clarity to people. You'll also see how strong relationships are the bedrock of being able to express yourself honestly and bluntly. The skill (and it *is* a skill) of "saying it as it is" is one of the things I improved at in recent years, and I so wish I had learned to be better at it earlier in life.

Having something to say and saying it are two entirely different things. The first is useless if you don't do the second. Punk rockers weren't afraid to say it like it is—and you shouldn't be either.

In Lester Bangs' essay about The Clash, and Joe Strummer in particular, he writes, "Their simple, straightforward honesty, their undogmatic insistence on the truth and why worry about stepping on people's toes because if we're not straight with each other we're never going to get anything accomplished any way . . . It seems like such a simple thing."[1]

That is so true and is the essence of this section. Too often in the corporate world, we're afraid to express ourselves, afraid to offend, afraid to say something wrong. We need to find our voice, and we need to say it as we see it, whatever the consequences may be, because if we don't, "we're never going to get anything accomplished any way"!

GOOD COMMUNICATORS CAN EXPRESS THEMSELVES WITHOUT OFFENDING

Encouragingly, what I see from the good communicators I know is that you can almost always express your honest point of view without offending—no matter how different your perspective may be, or even if that perspective is critical in nature. Good communicators can critique without being disparaging; disagree without being dismissive of others' point of view; and argue without attacking. And they do that without toning things down.

Are you someone who confidently says what you feel loud and clear—or are you diluting it or toning it down for fear of offending? Don't be afraid.

---

1 Lester Bangs, "The Clash," in *Let Fury Have the Hour: Joe Strummer, Punk, and the Movement that Shook the World*, ed. Antonino D'Ambrosio (New York: Nation Books, 2012), 88.

"What Is the Real Purpose of Your Trip?"

In 2009, shortly after I joined Microsoft, I flew to Moscow on one of my first country visits. Our Russian business had been particularly affected by the economic turmoil of 2008, just when we had invested in growing our Russian team by hiring several new people.

The trip's itinerary had me spending the first day visiting stores with the leader of our Russia retail business, Alexey Badaev. At the end of the day we went to dinner with the Russian leadership team. As is typical in Moscow, traffic was horrendous, and we arrived late. I walked into the room to see about six people from the Russian team seated around a dinner table in a private room. At the head of the table sat a very striking woman—six foot tall, attractive, and with bleached-blonde hair. I was to subsequently learn that she was Inna Zaytseva, a senior member of our Russian team, and I was not surprised to hear that she had previously been a model. I was directed to sit in the seat next to her at the corner of the table. As I was sitting down, and in all reality probably just before my cheek touched the seat of the chair, Inna leaned across the table and said in a very imposing way, "So Jeremy, tell me what is the *real* purpose of your trip?" I loved her directness and no-nonsense approach. At that moment, I wouldn't have been surprised to learn that apart from being an ex-model, she had also been in the KGB. It felt like the interrogation had begun.

"I am here to understand why the planned growth in Russia is not materializing. Is it just down to the recent economic crash or are there other factors we can overcome? Also, we need to assess whether we are right to continue to invest in the additional headcount in Russia in this difficult economy." I was relieved that I had replied with a substantive answer to her direct probing, rather than trying to deflect it or avoid it.

I also commented on her style of questioning. I joked that while I might have first liked to have been given a drink, or at least been allowed to fully sit down, I loved her directness and the fact that

I instantly knew where we stood. Acknowledging the style, showing I was comfortable with the approach, and being able to laugh about it gave anyone seated around that table permission to take that approach any time they wanted.

The conversation over dinner continued in this forthright tone, balanced with a friendliness that had quickly developed and a sense of humor, which I always appreciate. I quickly gained respect for the team and loved their honesty and directness.

The following morning we met at the office for a series of business reviews and meetings. First on the agenda was Inna, who was due to present on the state of our Microsoft Office business in Russia. Before she could put the obligatory PowerPoint deck into slideshow mode, I saw that she had fifty-four slides in her presentation. Before she could speak, I jumped in . . . "So Inna, tell me what is the real purpose of your presentation?"

She smiled a smile that said, "Smartass," but she diplomatically verbalized, "I am going to review our Office business."

"That's what you're going to do, but I am asking what is the real purpose of your presentation?"

"Well if you allow me to start I will show you," she replied.

"I just want to know what your purpose is before we start."

"Well Jeremy, at the moment, the investment restrictions being placed on us are preventing us from growing, and if you were to invest a relatively small sum of money, we could demonstrate how we could drive growth."

"That's interesting, how much investment do you need and how much return will you generate?"

"Let me show you," she said as she reached for the clicker.

"We were doing so well just talking," I said.

"Okay, then." She put the clicker down and proceeded to articulate her business situation, the opportunity she saw, the incremental investment she was asking for, the return she would commit to, and how she was going to deliver it. After a ten-minute conversation where she demonstrated a good understanding of her business, articulated what she wanted to do, and gave good answers to my basic questions, I turned to the rest of the Russian team and asked, "Do you all support this?"

They all did.

"Okay, let's do it then," I said.

There was a sense of confusion, and some people asked for clarity of what had just happened. I explained that Inna had asked for a $20,000 investment and promised to deliver $100,000 upside from that. Everyone said it was a good plan, so I said we are doing it.

They realized that this was happening. Inna picked up the clicker, and for the first time, she seemed a little unsure about what had happened. "Do you want me to do the presentation now?"

"Why would we need to? I thought we just fully met the real purpose of your presentation?" I responded.

I recounted the story of that dinner and the incremental Office investment many times to my teams all around Europe. I wanted them to realize a few things:

- I wanted everyone to know they had permission to be direct with me and say it as it was—actually, they didn't just have permission, I wanted it and even demanded it.

- I wanted to send a message about speed of decision-making. I didn't need to go through a fifty-four-page deck to make a $20,000 decision, and I certainly didn't want my team spending hours and hours creating such a deck for such a relatively small investment request.

- I expected my team to be able to talk coherently about their business without reading from a script.

- I wanted my team to know that I would back their collective judgment; I just required them to have a well-thought-through plan that was commercially logical and be unified in their conviction that it would be successful.

Among the broad and widely dispersed EMEA regional team, "What is the real purpose of your _____" became shorthand for "Let's get straight to the point and say what you are thinking." The humor that accompanied the retelling of the story showed everyone that "what is the real purpose" was a safe and friendly request that could be made top down or bottom up in the organization.

QUESTION #1: WHO ARE YOU?

So . . . who are you? Are you someone who will step forward and speak your mind or are you someone with a lacerated tongue because you've spent your life biting it, as you shy away from expressing what you believe?

Be direct, straight to the point, and say it as it is. Don't waste time skirting around an issue. Don't waste time softening your words to mollycoddle your team or colleagues.

So, again, who are you? Who have you been? Who are you going to be?

Some people have so much to say, so much to offer, yet fear is stopping them from fully contributing and being everything they could be. So the big question is . . . are you going to be a voice or just the echo of what others have already said because you're more interested in fitting in rather than going against the flow and speaking your mind?

Don't compromise your opinions for acceptance. Clear your mind, by speaking it.

KEY LESSONS

Say what is on your mind because it brings clarity to the conversation.

Create a culture where people are comfortable speaking openly.

Get straight to the point and strip away all the superfluous dialogue.

Applaud others who speak their mind.

SO WHAT ARE YOU GOING TO DO ABOUT IT?

Write your thoughts here:

Get Comfortable Calling People Out

At one point in my career, my boss took a new job, and I was asked to cover the role on an interim basis. To do the role full time would require relocating my family to a new country; at that time, it just wasn't possible to do that, given the stages of my eldest two daughters' education. So I had to pass on the role, but I commuted a long distance to lead the team for about five or six months while an external hire was sought.

Eventually the new hire (who would be my new boss) was announced (we'll call him Simon), but before he even started working for us, I was contacted by mutual acquaintances expressing their surprise at his hire. From the very moment Simon arrived, it became evident that he wasn't up to the job and just wasn't suited to the company. Within several weeks, it was clear he was an absolute, unmitigated disaster. Members of our team inundated me with stories about what this new leader had just done, and people were saying he was a complete joke. In his fourth month, we were at a big industry trade show, and my phone was being lit up almost every hour by people imploring me to come into a meeting to save it and recover the situation or to pop into a dinner and apologize.

We flew back on Thursday evening, and on Friday I asked my boss's boss if I could get thirty minutes with him that day. We had a good relationship forged during the period when I had been covering the role. He asked if a beer after work would be better, and I quickly agreed. He drove me to the bar, and I started to tell him about the disaster that was unfolding. I stated that I knew I had nothing to gain; in fact, I had everything to lose. If he didn't believe me, then I was going behind my boss's back with a call for him to be fired, and that would leave me in an untenable position because he would inevitably find out. If my boss was fired, then I would have to once again cover the role on an interim basis and return to the pleasures of the very long commute while a replacement was found. So I told him it was a lose-lose situation for me, but I was doing it because the company and the team needed Simon to go. The most confrontational line I delivered to my boss's boss was that I was doing it because the team members were now questioning his credibility for not seeing the disaster that was unfolding because it was as clear as day to everyone else. So out of loyalty to him and out of responsibility to the company, I had no option other than to say it as it was, whatever the consequences.

It was a strange evening as I recounted horrific moment after horrific moment. I retold all the painful stories, and we cringed at just how embarrassing they were. They were ridiculous, and we found ourselves laughing, not because there was anything funny, but because if we didn't laugh, we would cry. Now, fair play to Simon's boss, he appreciated the honesty, and the following week he conducted six skip-level meetings and heard all the same stories retold painful detail by painful detail. By the Friday of that week, Simon was gone, never to be seen again.

Now this may sound mean-spirited to you, but I didn't feel bad about what I did in the slightest. My motive was honorable; many of the team members and I had suffered greatly from Simon's randomness, it had hurt the company, our customers were appalled, the end result was inevitable, it was just a matter of time, and quite honestly, I cannot help but believe (although I have no evidence) that he had exaggerated his credentials greatly during the interview process. So when you consider all the elements, I didn't see any other choice. The only thing that was stopping others from doing likewise was the fear of recrimination. I was the most senior member of the team; I was the one with the best relationship with his boss, and it was my responsibility.

KEY LESSONS

There are moments when you need to stand up and be counted and say it as it is. What are you going to do? Be true to the person you want to be or shy away from your responsibilities because you are scared of consequences? Step up and show some backbone!

When you make a bad hire, and it is evident we had, move quickly. A senior bad hire often costs you three years. You give them a year to settle in. You give them the second year to show what they can do, and when you realize that they will never deliver what you really need, it takes you another year to manage them out and find a replacement. At least in this story he was gone in four months.

SO WHAT ARE YOU GOING TO DO ABOUT IT?

Write your thoughts here:

Get Comfortable Calling Yourself Out . . .
A.K.A. Know When Your Baby Is Ugly

Motorola's biggest marketing campaign of 2007 was always going to be for the RAZR2 launch. We had allocated $75 million of media to be put behind the advertising campaign that we were developing. We had commissioned an Academy Award-winning director to shoot the TV commercial. During the pre-production meetings, we started to have some concerns, but we were using this top director, and our advertising team was adamant it was going to be brilliant. I kept assuring myself it would all come out all right. However, it didn't. It was a disaster! It was an artistic film that may have won a prize in some arty film festival, but as a piece of marketing communication, it was, as one of my team said, "far too far up its own backside." There was no way we could run it.

I had to go to my boss at the time, Ray Roman, and tell him that the film we'd made was going to be confined to the cutting-room floor. I was dreading the meeting, I'd wasted $2 million, and the work was so bad. It wasn't going to be a good meeting. The only good news I had to offer was that in a hectic week we had scrambled a different agency on our roster and created an alternative campaign that we felt much more confident about; the bad news was that we would overspend our budget by $2 million because we would have to fund a second film shoot, but that paled into insignificance against the $75 million we'd waste by running this piece of artistic garbage.

I told the whole grim story, and I even refused to show the film as it was so inept and I was so embarrassed.

I was shocked by Ray's response: "Thank you." He then added, "Many people would have kept going with the first idea and tried to convince everyone that it was the right thing to do. I am glad that you weren't so wedded to the first campaign and that you were able to keep a good sense of perspective as to what was right for the consumer." He was spot on.

I think I have only had a couple of occasions when I tried to argue that something I or my team had done was good, when I really knew it was weak. I stopped doing it when I realized that I never fooled anyone and I was only making myself look foolish by trying to defend the indefensible. You gain far more respect by being your own biggest critic, and self-criticism reassures people about your judgment, which builds your credibility.

This also comes back to your credibility as a judge. People will not respect your critiquing of their work if you don't critique your own work with the same high bar and honesty. In the previous story, I called out my boss; in this example I called out myself. Both required an honesty that is uncomfortable for entirely different reasons, but both were vitally essential.

KEY LESSONS

There are times when our work is substandard; be the first to identify it. Calling yourself out shows class and shows the high performance bar that you set for yourself.

SO WHAT ARE YOU GOING TO DO ABOUT IT?

Write your thoughts here:

Teams Who Banter Have Tested the Edges and Know How Far They Can Push Each Other

I love banter, and I believe the Brits are the world champions at it. For instance, Lady Astor once criticized Churchill by saying . . . "You are drunk." Churchill quickly responded, "And Madam you are ugly. But I shall be sober tomorrow." Lady Astor at another time attacked Churchill, "Sir, if you were my husband, I would poison your drink." Churchill again replied, "Madam, if you were my wife, I would drink it." That is good banter. Churchill always had a witty riposte.

The traditional definition of banter is "the playful and friendly exchange of teasing remarks," but the Urban Dictionary articulates it perfectly: ". . . a term used to describe activities or chat that is playful, intelligent, and original. Banter is something you either possess or lack, there is no middle ground. It is also something inherently English, stemming as it does from traditional hi-jinks and tomfoolery of British yesteryear."

So why do I mention this? Well, during my tenure at Microsoft, a group of us Brits were close-knit, worked well together, and understood each other. Banter was at the heart of our relationship and our camaraderie. Relatively soon after I had joined, while I was based in the UK, we had a senior leader from Seattle visit us, and he wanted to travel around and see some of the European markets. We were to accompany him on the tour of our largest markets. We spent many hours during that week on a minibus travelling from city to city and visiting many of our retail partners' top stores. During that week on the road, we had soon resorted to banter to relieve the tedium of the bus journeys. After a few days of relentless and sometimes quite brutal banter, we were on a long stretch of our journey, and we had all started to doze off when the visiting exec blurted out, "I am concerned by the fact that you don't like each other. It must impact the power of our team, and we need to do something about it."

We were all staggered. "Why do you think we don't like each other? This is the best group of people I have worked with," one of us responded.

"Because of what you say, it's cruel," he challenged.

"No, it's not, it's funny. It's banter!"

"What's banter?"

So we tried to explain banter, without a great deal of success. He couldn't understand it was something you engaged in with your friends.

What I have since realized is that the banter between this group had helped us to test the edges and understand just how far we could push each other. Because we felt comfortable being direct and (to some extent) being brutal with each other in banter, we were also much more comfortable being direct and challenging with each other in our work conversations. Banter had allowed us to test the soft edges of our relationships and refine them in the fire. This meant we weren't ever trying to discover how much we could push each other in a really difficult and challenging business situation. We already knew. This was a huge advantage for us as a team.

Teams need to be able to say things as they are to each other and be direct, and because you don't want to be working out how blunt you can be with someone for the first time in a real pressurized business situation, testing the edges first in a friendly environment in advance is very beneficial.

KEY LESSONS

Good-humored banter helps you test the edges with your colleagues, so you know how far you can push them when there are challenging business decisions that need to be fully discussed.

Use good-humored banter and self-deprecation to show that you don't take yourself too seriously, and that will help give your teams permission to speak freely.

SO WHAT ARE YOU GOING TO DO ABOUT IT?

Write your thoughts here:

Learn How to Be Truly Honest, Constructively

Early on in my career, I wasn't always as direct and honest in my conversations with people, most often with people in my own team. I pulled my punches to some extent. In hindsight, I did this because I wanted to be liked, and I worried that being too honest wouldn't win me any friends. That changed for me when I joined Microsoft, and it changed because of one key realization. At Microsoft, it was the first time in my career that my boss was not in the same building as me—he wasn't even anywhere close to being in the same time zone. He was in Seattle, and I was in the UK. So he was asleep when I was awake and vice versa. My boss was Mitch Koch: He was smart, brilliant in many ways, and he was very hands off. He was a teacher who taught us how he thought, and then he expected us to implement his philosophy. He always used to say, "You can do whatever you want, as long as it's what I want." It was up to us to learn what he wanted. So I soon realized that the buck stopped with me. There was no one who could step in; it all ended with me. It was a stark realization, and for me it meant that I suddenly became far more comfortable saying it as it was. If I didn't, no one else would.

I also learned the power of the phrase "I am concerned that_____ and I am worried about_____." Those are nine beautiful words that give you a framework to say exactly what is on your mind, but in a caring and supportive way. "I am concerned that some people in the team are beginning to think you are a jerk, and I worry that despite your natural talent that could derail your career here." "I am concerned that you aren't hitting your quota, and you know how that is just a *nonnegotiable* in our company. I am therefore worried about the impact that getting fired could have on you and your family."

I realized how far I had come in speaking my mind three years later. We were doing a personal development session, and I had been asked what skill I wished I had learned earlier in my career, and I recited this story. My team just laughed and thought I was winding them up. They couldn't imagine me not saying what I was thinking. Now my old team from my Motorola days will be reading this and thinking, *I wish he had got there sooner.*

KEY LESSONS

You have to say it as it is; otherwise, everyone else thinks you are chicken because you are copping out of addressing the issue. If you invest a little time in refining how you use those beautiful words, "I am concerned that . . . " and "I am worried that . . . ," then there is no reason to hesitate to have the conversation.

If I had my time to do over again, this is the one thing I would put at the top of my "I wish I had learned this earlier" list. For goodness' sake, embrace it now. It is a career accelerator and, more importantly, it is what your team needs.

SO WHAT ARE YOU GOING TO DO ABOUT IT?

Write your thoughts here:

False or Exaggerated Praise Is Cancerous

In all the companies I have been in, there are countless emails where people share their work. In all honesty, much of the work is mediocre or, at best, what I describe as good-ish. I am not a fan of these emails, but what I do hate seeing with a passion are loads of emails responding back with messages of "great work," "awesome job," and "really fabulous execution." We see the same with presentations: Average or even flat-out bad work receives praise, because people fear saying anything less will make others feel disappointed that their work is not being recognized.

I detest people who give false praise. I think it sends all the wrong messages. First, people think they have done a good job when they haven't, and by definition, it starts to lower the performance bar, which is a very slippery slope. If people haven't met my performance bar, I want them to know. Second, if others see you congratulating someone on something that is average, then that's the standard they will look to and try to replicate.

Doing anything that threatens to lower the performance bar is dangerous, but the most fundamental problem with it is that if you react to average thinking as if it were breakthrough thinking, then you are far less likely to get truly breakthrough thinking. You get what you celebrate. If you celebrate mediocre performance, you get more mediocrity.

If your performance bar for giving praise is high, then when you do give praise, it means so much more to the recipient. I was in a workshop in Mexico with our Latin American team, and Nuno, one of our category managers, presented some truly high-quality work. At the end of the meeting, I went up to him and said, "Nuno, that was really brilliant." Within ten minutes, I had someone come up to me and say, "Nuno is walking around in a kind of stunned state. He said to me, 'Jeremy just said that my work was brilliant. Jeremy doesn't give praise easily. Wow!'" In the next thirty minutes, three other people came up to me and said Nuno had had almost exactly the same conversation with them. My praise, because I don't hand it out like confetti, is more valued than if I said awesome job to every email that shared work of varying standards.

Now, I have questioned my attitude towards praise. Why do I dole it out far more sparingly than others? I think the answer is because I don't like lying. I think I am cheating myself and cheating the person by exaggerating my perception of their work. Instead, I try to give specific feedback. "I thought this part was very good, but this part needed more options considered, and I would have liked to have seen more of this or that." That shows that you have really looked at the work and really understood.

KEY LESSONS

Only give deserved praise. It says a lot about your performance bar, and when you do give out praise, it is so much more appreciated.

If you celebrate mediocrity, then get used to it, for you are far more likely to get more of it served up from your team.

SO WHAT ARE YOU GOING TO DO ABOUT IT?

Write your thoughts here:

Be Unaccepting of Mediocrity

I am a firm believer in meritocracy. As I've told my teams in the past, "Good enough isn't good enough—not in the twenty-first century, not in a recession, not in my team." A meritocracy is a much better culture and is defined as:

- A system in which the talented are chosen and moved ahead on the basis of their achievement

- A system in which able and talented persons are rewarded and advanced

- A social system in which people's success in life depends primarily on their talents, abilities, and efforts

The idea is that people are recognized and rewarded based on their achievements. If you believe in that, then you have a responsibility to be consistent and transparent—to say it as it is, in other words. With this in mind, in advance of one of Microsoft's internal conferences in the EMEA region, I started to construct a league table showing where each individual country stood based on a simple ranking system using six core metrics. I said I was going to share this with all participants attending the conference, including the country leaders, so they could know where they stood relative to their peers. This was met with great concern and a load of alternative suggestions. "Why don't we just show the top six performing subsidiaries?" There was a real allergic reaction to showing who was in the lower positions, and it was especially concerning to some that we were going to reveal who was at the bottom.

I didn't have a problem with this. "Why wouldn't anyone want to know where they stood?" I asked. "I would like to know if it were me." From my perspective, I wanted everyone to try to move up that table. Getting to the top six may be impractical this year for some countries, but moving up the ranking was always achievable. So I was adamant that I was going to show it.

Now, maybe my willingness to see the whole table may stem from the fact that my favorite football (soccer) team is Birmingham City, who for much of my life has resided in the lower half of the division they were playing in. To scan for my team, I naturally started at the bottom and would work my way up; that is what I became used to.

So against all advice I went for it and shared the whole table. Before I revealed the table, I took the time to explain why I was doing it and how I wanted everyone to try to improve their ranking and that all progress was good. I then shared the table. There was a mixture of obvious delight and alarm, a combination of whoops of joy and gasps of horror. It took about five minutes for everyone to fully absorb the table.

After my presentation ended, Jon Grimes, who had put the slide together for me, was approached by Alexey Badaev. Now, Alexey was a great guy whom I have huge respect for, and like even more. But he is an intimidating figure—a large, strong man who spoke in a gruff voice. He approached Jon and said, "The league table. I want a copy now."

"Alexey, I have checked all the scores, and I am sure it is correct," Jon hastily said, expecting a dispute over the rankings.

"I am not doubting the ranking. I am going to pin it to my desk, and I will only take it down when we get into the top six countries," Alexey said in a calmer voice.

That was exactly the reaction we sought. We wanted people to know where they ranked. We also wanted leaders who were intolerant of anything but exceptional performance. Alexey received the information just as we had intended. It was a motivator for himself and his team.

KEY LESSONS

If you want to celebrate the top performers, then publish the top performers' league table. If you want everyone to understand where their performance ranks, and you want to inspire everyone to be better than they are today, then show the entire league table. As a manager, one of your top jobs is to improve the performance of your lower performers (people and teams) . . . so why wouldn't you want them to see the table?

By publishing the full league table, you are likely to get two types of reaction from those at the bottom. They will either be determined to change their position (as Alexey was), or they will be upset or offended by being called out in public. The reactions are very telling. I will bet that the people who fall in the first group will change their position and the people in the second group never will. I use it as a very effective tool to help determine who I should believe in to turn things around and who I would do better cutting quickly.

SO WHAT ARE YOU GOING TO DO ABOUT IT?

Write your thoughts here:

Don't Let Your Team Waste a Moment Wondering What You Think

When one of your team leaves your group, and particularly if they leave the company, this is the moment they are most honest with you. They have nothing to lose by saying it as it is.

When François Ruault decided to move to our corporate offices in Seattle, he came and thanked me for what I said to him on our very first meeting three years before. Not surprisingly, I couldn't remember what that was, and I had to ask. He told me that I had said, "I don't want you to waste a single moment worrying about what I think of you or how you stand in my thoughts. I will always tell you what I think and be honest. So if I don't tell you I am disappointed with you, then I am not." He said that statement had relieved a lot of anxiety throughout the time he worked for me, and he realized how much he had worried about what his previous bosses had thought and how much time he had wasted wondering and worrying about how he was perceived.

Being honest and promising to be transparent is a great liberator. It frees your team from second-guessing you and allows them to focus their attention on what matters. Your team may be wasting a lot of time worrying about what you think. But if they see you always saying it as it is, if they know you will never keep your negative perceptions to yourself, then you are saving them from a huge chunk of anxiety.

KEY LESSONS

I remember the old man on his deathbed who said he had had a great many troubles in his life, but most of them never happened. My philosophy is that people don't perform at their best if they spend too much time worrying over pointless things. Put them out of their misery tomorrow. Seriously—go in to work tomorrow and commit to your team that you will always, always, always, say it as it is, and demand that they never waste a minute worrying about what you think of them. But you will need to follow it up by being honest and transparent. You have to back up your promise, and if they see you do that, then you have given your team a truly great gift.

SO WHAT ARE YOU GOING TO DO ABOUT IT?

Write your thoughts here:

External Advice Should Be Strong and Honest

Let me tell you the most horrendous story I have ever heard. I promise you it is a true story. When I joined Orange, I met with one of our marketing agencies as part of my induction, and they complained that my team was using them for everything and never did anything themselves. He told me about one time when a relatively junior member within my team had rung up one of their team and asked if they could nip out to buy a sandwich and drop it round as they were going to be in meetings over lunchtime.

I was absolutely appalled. I asked, "What did your person say?"

"What type of sandwich would you like?" was the reply.

I didn't know who I was madder with, my team member for asking or the agency for complying.

Whenever I have taken up a new post and been introduced to an incumbent external agency, I'm amazed and disappointed at how they try to make me feel important. They nod and hang on my every word; they wave me off from reception and tell me what a pleasure it was. These types of agencies assume a subservient position from the very first meeting. I assume that is because they think it's what a new boss will want. But I'm always suspicious of agencies who adopt a subservient attitude towards me—because if their first priority is to make me feel happy and important, will they really have the backbone to argue with me when I am wrong?

There is a second cause of this master/servant relationship, and again it is the agencies' fault. When the agency presents substandard creative work to the client, the client quite rightly rejects the work. But does it work the other way around? When the client presents the agency with a substandard brief, where there isn't really a compelling product or differentiated proposition, how often does the agency critique that? Rarely, but they should.

In my mind, the agency/client relationship must be a strong, trusting, collaborative, and equal partnership where frank opinions are traded and where all parties are involved in the collaborative development of the strategy, the propositions, and the work.

KEY LESSONS

If you are going to employ external agencies for their expertise, you have to ensure that they never contemplate diluting their opinion because it may be unpalatable to you or your team.

If your agency partners are more worried about keeping your business than providing strong and honest advice, then their value has been lost. Fire your agency at the first sign that they are diluting their views to please you. They are of no use to you anymore.

SO WHAT ARE YOU GOING TO DO ABOUT IT?

Write your thoughts here:

You Don't Need to Hold Back with Your Friends

Megan, a dear friend of our family, was visiting us in Seattle from Chicago with her daughter Gwen, who was a freshman in college. Gwen shadowed me at work for half a day—she wanted to see what a business environment was like because she was unclear as to the profession she wanted to enter.

We had a few good early meetings then we headed back to my office. After a couple of minutes, Kevin McCarthy (the CFO of our consumer group) popped into my office for an impromptu conversation that soon deteriorated into a heated stand-up argument. I was very unhappy with something his team had failed to do, and he had a different point of view. The conversation was loud and aggressive, but ultimately constructive, as we managed to agree on the appropriate course of action, but not before some expletives were thrown around.

At home that evening, Gwen was recounting her day, and she was a little traumatized about the row I had been involved in. "Clearly you guys don't like each other, why is that?"

I responded, "No that's not true, Kevin is one of my best friends in Seattle. We regularly play golf and have a beer. We go on golf trips together. Kevin is great."

Gwen couldn't understand that. How could good friends argue so vociferously?

But that is the magic of close relationships with colleagues. You can say it as you see it and argue intently while knowing that both of you place a high value on the relationship and have a great deal of respect for the other. Our close relationship meant we were able to resolve a major dispute in about fifteen minutes, because we both said everything we had to say, no one pulled any punches, we were prepared to listen to the other's point of view, and—because of our friendship—we trusted that neither of us had any malice. It could have taken days to really understand all the issues and ultimately resolve them if we hadn't had the relationship that allowed us to say it all as we saw it.

To help you understand a little more about what that argument was like, let me explain a little about Kevin's family. He is from Ireland and his wife Analese is from Italy. Both nationalities are stereotypically renowned for talking and fully expressing their feelings. As Kevin has regularly said, nothing is ever left unsaid in his house. One day a colleague was telling us how she had a small row with her husband, and he had given her the silent treatment, to which Kevin immediately replied, "I'd love the 'silent treatment,' that would be so good. Rather than being shouted at, I could just go and play Xbox on my own in peace for a couple of hours."

Kevin always tells the story of when he first met his wife's family. It was the typical large Italian family dinner; all the sisters, brothers, and partners were seated around a long table, with multiple loud conversations going on across the table in Italian. It all meant very little to Kevin as he didn't understand a word of Italian at the time.

Suddenly a very heated argument broke out with people standing up, shouting, and gesticulating; someone even held their head in their hands in despair. Kevin was perplexed at what could cause such an uproar. Analese eventually sat down, still very agitated. Kevin asked, "What's going on, has someone slept with someone's sister?" That was the only reason he could think of that would cause such an outbreak of hostilities.

Analese responded in a very angry voice, "No, it's my sister. She is stupid. Stupid, stupid, stupid. She thinks last year's tomatoes are better than this year's. Unbelievable!"

That's why nothing ever gets left unsaid in Kevin's house, and why I always knew we would never leave anything unsaid to each other.

KEY LESSONS

Strong personal relationships with your key colleagues, where you share deep trust and respect, mean that everything will always be said, and nothing will ever get hidden away.

SO WHAT ARE YOU GOING TO DO ABOUT IT?

My suggestion: Do you have similar relationships with your closest colleagues? If not, what are you going to do?

Write your thoughts here:

The Bottom Line

I believe you get three things of huge value when people "say it as it is."

The first benefit is speed. Plain speaking saves time. "What is the real purpose of your trip?" will always be my shorthand for this and is the perfect demonstration of that mindset. In essence, it is just saying, "I don't need the preamble, let's just get straight down to business." Honest dialogue where everyone quickly volunteers their point of view and immediately argues their position is a key accelerator and drives speed. You cannot truly move forward at speed until everyone has said what they need to say.

The second huge value is that it brings clarity. No one is left in any doubt about where they stand or where you stand on a particular issue. Also, stating your point of view clearly and concisely on a particular issue allows you to verify your understanding. Others have the opportunity to correct you if you have misunderstood something or challenge you where they disagree. People need constant reminders that you want challenges and corrections.

The third significant benefit is that you set the performance bar where you want it set. False praise or gratuitous recognition only lowers the bar and misleads people as to the standards you demand. Saying it as it is, normally results in high quality performance; compromising that ensures mediocrity.

Saying it as it is won't always be easy as some people may be put out by what you say, and others may be disgruntled by your lack of praise. However, in my experience, not saying it as it is may make the short-term conversation easier, but it will make the future conversation far more painful. The need to say something rarely disappears by turning a blind eye.

Bottom line: Trust me. Saying it as it is makes life one hundred times easier.

ELemeNt 6:

BE AUTHENTIC

"Authenticity is the alignment of head, mouth, heart, and feet—thinking, saying, feeling, and doing the same thing—consistently. This builds trust, and followers love leaders they can trust."

LANCE SECRETAN

"I'd rather be hated for who I am, than be loved for who I'm not."

KURT COBAIN

Authenticity is at the heart of punk rock. This was something I didn't immediately appreciate, but upon closer inspection nearly every punk band fits the criteria. Let me turn to the Sex Pistols and The Clash for the proof points.

As the story goes, John Lydon was walking down a street in London when Malcolm McLaren (the Sex Pistols manager) saw him. Lydon was a striking figure with his spikey green hair and doctored Pink Floyd t-shirt—he'd written the words "I HATE" above the band's name. The t-shirt had seen better days . . . it was ripped and held together by a safety pin. McLaren convinced him to audition as the

Sex Pistols' lead singer. Lydon's audition was so bad it was met with cries of laughter from the existing band members. McLaren hired him immediately. Lydon didn't try to hide his cockney accent as so many singers did (and still do). He spoke like a cockney and sang like a cockney and was true to his London roots. Like Lydon, the Pistols never tried to be anything they weren't. It was simply: "Look at us, this is who we are, take it or leave it—your choice."

The Clash were equally committed to being who they were; they were authentic. One manager's alleged song writing advice was for them to "write about what's affecting you, what's important," and they did. The band members fought their management whenever management tried to manipulate the band. They fought to keep ticket prices down at their gigs so that they could be more accessible to their fans. In a post by Ray Philpott he summed it up by saying, "They were so punk, that the punk purists complained when they moved on from the iconoclastic three-chord style of songwriting. And that's what made them authentic."[1] The Clash knew who they were, what they believed in, and what they stood for—and they weren't going to allow that to be compromised.

> "Punk is all about being yourself, liking what you like, doing what you do and not having to live up to someone else's expectations, only your own. There is no dress code, hair colour or rules to be punk, since punk is about being true to yourself."
>
> **URBAN DICTIONARY**

Punk is about being true to who you are and being happy with that. As Kurt Cobain wisely put it, "Wanting to be someone else is a waste of the person you are." This is one of the most beautiful things about applying a punk attitude in your professional life. Life is about

---

1 Ray Philpott, "The Clash Taught Me Everything I Know about B2B Copywriting," *The Marketing Practice* (January 18, 2017), https://themarketingpractice.com/insights/the-clash-taught-me-authenticity-in-b2b-copywriting/.

self-discovery, learning who you are, and then being comfortable with that. People flourish when they can be who they really are. They are always happier, more content, and more motivated, and as a result they are far more productive. More organizations need to encourage people to be themselves. People waste so much of their lives trying to be what they think they should be, putting on a mask as they second-guess what they are expected to be like. It is pointless, futile, and self-defeating. If you are nothing else, be authentic—and you can only do that by listening to yourself rather than to others.

> "Don't listen too much to your parents. Don't listen too much to your teachers. Listen to yourself."
>
> SHIMON PERES

THE POWER AND BEAUTY OF AUTHENTICITY

Authenticity has often been thought of as the opposite of artifice—with authenticity being something that is straightforward, sincere, and uncomplicated. That's a good start, but when I study leaders and people I admire for their authenticity, I see various traits. I've listed the most common nine here:

- **They know who they are and are always true to who they are.** The dictionary definition of authenticity says, "of undisputed origin." Authentic people demonstrate where they came from and are true to their roots. They have strong self-awareness, and they don't try to be something they are not because they don't need to be something else. They don't want to be something else because they have gotten over their own insecurities and are happy in their own skin.

- **They believe in integrity and honesty.** Always, always tell the truth. Trust is a fundamental part of authenticity—the only sure way to avoid being found to be fake is to always tell the truth. If people don't see your integrity, they will never be able to fully connect with you.

- **They practice what they preach.** Their words and actions are consistent with who they claim to be. They never pull away from acting on and standing up for what they believe in, even when it may not make them popular. Authenticity is built one day at a time, even one decision at a time, by consistently acting in accordance with who you claim to be. It is the consistent marrying of words and actions with the person you claim and want to be. But it isn't easy, and no one ever gets this perfectly correct.

- **They express who they are.** Because they know who they are and are comfortable being that person, they have no fear in revealing themselves. They share their true self. They show they are human and they reveal their real self, and by doing that they help people connect with them more easily.

- **They show and embrace vulnerability.** Vulnerability is perceived by most people as a weakness, but it is the exact opposite—it is courage and strength. As Brené Brown said during her second TED Talk, "Vulnerability is the birthplace of innovation, creativity and change." If you are going to be a player, someone who gets in the ring and exposes their ideas and crazy new thoughts, you have to realize that that is going to make you vulnerable. You have to become comfortable being vulnerable.

- **They sincerely connect.** Authentic people naturally attract people. Their sincerity, which comes from their authenticity, enables and accelerates personal connection and trust. Sincerity immediately allows people to accept a connection without pretense, with no false appearance or hidden agenda. Where sincerity exists, people assume best intent, they trust each other, watch each other's back, and genuinely care for each other. That builds the most secure environment for a team to operate within.

- **They tell it like it is.** They speak from the heart with passion, they have a committed point of view, and are open and willing to articulate their ideas without any game playing or hidden agendas.

- **They always speak with the same voice.** Some say that people need to be socially adept and adopt different styles when speaking with different people. There is a part of me that understands where they are coming from, but I don't buy it. I may adapt slightly when I spoke to my grandmother as compared to my children, but I always speak with the same voice, the same personality, the same

(continued)

soul. I never try to come across in a different way, and I don't do that at work either. As Einstein once said, "I speak to everyone in the same way, whether he is the garbage man or the president of the university."

- **They are predictable to those who know them.** Because authenticity and consistency are inextricably intertwined, people who know the authentic person instinctively know how they will react to a certain situation. Their reaction is easily predicted based on the consistency of previous interactions. The beauty of authenticity is this predictability, and this means that others aren't left second-guessing (and wasting time and energy) wondering and worrying about how the other person will react to news of a situation.

Authenticity is probably the top characteristic people want in their leader, and authenticity is, in my opinion, the single most important thing that has enabled me to enjoy my work. Being free to be who you are and true to your character has been, for me, the single biggest factor in personal happiness.

At the start of the book you read the story about the process I went through relatively recently that enabled me to become crystal clear about who I am and what I stand for. In this section, I also tell stories of people who demonstrated their authenticity and the value that brought. As we go through this section, which I believe is one of the most important in the book, I want you to really think about who you are. Please reflect and see if you are truly living up to your own description of yourself, or if you're being forced to modify who you are to fit into your environment. When I first did this with one hundred percent clarity, I realized I wasn't being entirely true to who I was. That caused a series of events that prompted me to leave Microsoft and write this book. This section is all about self-awareness and self-assessment. You will benefit most by being brutally honest with yourself.

Be True to Who You Are

In about 2008 one of our Motorola brand ambassadors, Wyclef Jean, came to our Libertyville campus north of Chicago. For those who don't know him, Wyclef is a three-time Grammy Award-winning rapper, musician, and actor who got his start as a rapper in the group the Fugees. He was born in Haiti and moved to the US at the age of nine—and in 2010, he filed for candidacy in Haiti's presidential election.

He and I were to do a chat show format discussion for roughly two thousand of our employees. We did this with our Brand Ambassadors so that our people could get to know the people who appeared in our advertising. Let me state right off the bat—I love Wyclef. He was genuine, authentic, charismatic, and very funny in all our interactions. We had met a few times before this meeting, and we always got on and had a good laugh, so I was really looking forward to the day.

It started off in a very telling fashion . . . we had some technical difficulties, and so he ran from the stage to the tech booth area and started trying to fix the problems himself. As he returned to the stage, he said, "You don't want to do this to me, you know I am a rapper, right?" He had the audience rolling in the aisles.

We had an amazing thirty minutes of chatting about almost everything—his career, the future of the music industry, where technology was going . . . he was smart, funny, and most wonderfully authentic.

We then broke to allow him to perform a few songs. He had brought his cousin Gerry (who is also an amazing person) to play bass guitar. Wyclef wouldn't let me leave the stage and made me play drums (despite me having no musical rhythm or ability). He sang his song "If I Was President," and made up the second line "I would make Jeremy vice president," and he just free-flowed for twenty minutes or so.

Then he started to get people to come and join in. He asked Steve Lalla (one of our senior product engineers) to shout out a request. Steve was not really a hip hop kind of guy. Every day he wore khakis, a blue shirt, shoes with tassels on the top, and he had a phone clipped to his belt. That was Steve. He was a very good guy, not born from the same mold as me, but he was a good bloke and true to who he was.

So Wyclef asked Steve for a request. Steve said, "The Gambler," which is a famous country and western song by Kenny Rogers. Wyclef agreed to Steve's request, but only if Steve came on stage and agreed to sing it with him. So Steve did.

So there I was, standing on stage, holding the mic for Steve Lalla (a khaki-trousered, blue-shirted, tasseled-shoe, country-loving kind of guy) while he sang a country and western song with one of the world's leading hip hop and rap stars. I would never have done what Steve did. I wouldn't. But here was Steve Lalla, knowing who he was, being comfortable with who he was, singing country with Wyclef Jean. Pure brilliance. Honest and true to who he was. And there was Wyclef, loving music and allowing people to be authentic to who they were—also pure brilliance.

As Katie Maslin has said: "When you show up being your real, imperfect, authentic self, you create a comfortable space for others to do the same. Walk boldly in your truth!"

I love that, "Walk boldly in your truth." Wyclef did, and Steve Lalla responded in his truth.

KEY LESSONS

You really must know who you are and then be true to yourself. Be comfortable with yourself, and when you have an opportunity that you never dreamed of, go for it without any hesitation, without worrying about what people may think. There were two heroes that day in my eyes. First, Wyclef was the authentic music-loving talent who showed his authentic self. He relaxed everyone and allowed all of us to find a space where we (and Steve especially) were comfortable being themselves. The generosity of Wyclef to Steve was amazing; he allowed him to be who he was, and Wyclef adapted to fit Steve. How many times could we do that for our people, and yet we fail because we always insist they adapt to us?

Second, Steve was my other hero that day. The image of Steve taking the lead with Wyclef following will stay with me until my dying day. Steve went for it, and he landed it.

Wyclef showed me the generosity of giving space for people to be themselves, and Steve showed me how to really GO FOR IT. Whenever you have the chance, GO FOR IT!

Walk boldly in your truth.

SO WHAT ARE YOU GOING TO DO ABOUT IT?

Write your thoughts here:

Have Confidants Who Hold You Accountable to Be the Authentic You

I was preparing for a speech to students in the London Business School, where I was going to be sharing lessons from my career. I wanted to share with them how important it is to have a philosophy for life and a manifesto describing what you stand for. (This was before I'd written my Personal Philosophy that I explained at the start of the book.) So, while searching for some inspiration on the topic, I came across this manifesto from Holstee, a company that supports mindful living through inspirational art and other curated resources. Their manifesto resonated strongly with me and spoke to me about what I value in life and gave me some rules that guide me. This is what it says:

THIS IS YOUR **LIFE.**
DO WHAT YOU LOVE,
AND DO IT OFTEN.
IF YOU DON'T LIKE SOMETHING, CHANGE IT.
IF YOU DON'T LIKE YOUR JOB, QUIT.
IF YOU DON'T HAVE ENOUGH TIME, STOP WATCHING TV.
IF YOU ARE LOOKING FOR THE LOVE OF YOUR LIFE, STOP;
THEY WILL BE WAITING FOR YOU WHEN YOU
START DOING THINGS YOU LOVE.
STOP OVER ANALYZING, ALL EMOTIONS ARE BEAUTIFUL.
LIFE IS SIMPLE. WHEN YOU EAT, APPRECIATE EVERY LAST BITE.
OPEN YOUR MIND, ARMS, AND HEART TO NEW THINGS
AND PEOPLE, WE ARE UNITED IN OUR DIFFERENCES.
ASK THE NEXT PERSON YOU SEE WHAT THEIR PASSION IS,
AND SHARE YOUR INSPIRING DREAM WITH THEM.
TRAVEL OFTEN; GETTING LOST WILL HELP YOU FIND YOURSELF.
SOME OPPORTUNITIES ONLY COME ONCE, SEIZE THEM.
LIFE IS ABOUT THE PEOPLE YOU MEET, AND
THE THINGS YOU CREATE WITH THEM
SO GO OUT AND START CREATING.
LIFE IS LIVE YOUR DREAM
SHORT. AND SHARE YOUR PASSION.

THE HOLSTEE MANIFESTO ©2009—HOLSTEE.COM/
MANIFESTO (reprinted with permission)

The students loved the freshness and spirit of the poster—I don't think it was what they were expecting from some senior exec someone had wheeled in to talk to them. This was also just before my elder daughter Alex's sixteenth birthday. She was growing into a young woman and was taking more and more control of her own life, and my influence on her was naturally declining. I realized this poster was a perfect gift for her. It was the most valuable—but not the most expensive—gift I gave her for her birthday.

So, this poster became very personal to me on multiple levels. In the following three or four years, I used this image and story many times in many presentations to many different groups, and it always generated a great reaction. It resonates with so many people. After a while, it started to become synonymous with me. Then one day shortly after telling this story for the umpteenth time to a new group, I walked into my office to find that a large wooden poster of that exact image was hanging on my wall. My Executive Assistant had found one online and bought it for my office.

In the next few weeks, lots of people came into my office, almost all would pause to read it, most would smile and internalize some part of it, some would comment, and some would take a photo of it on their phone. It inspired people on a fundamental level. It also helped people understand who I was and what I believed in.

One day, more than a year later, when I was going through some frustrating weeks at Microsoft, Steve Beinner walked into my office. Steve worked in my team, and he was my type of person. When I was living in Seattle before my family joined me in the States, he was one of the few people who had invited me out for dinner and a beer to stop me from dying of boredom at my hotel. We connected, and he became a good friend.

That day when he popped his head into my office he had just stopped by to see how things were going. I started to bitch about this and that and everything that was just so screwed up. This was unlike me—I am rarely a glass-half-empty person. So, after several minutes of listening to me whine and complain, he pointed at my poster on the wall behind me and said, "So are you going to live up to your own advice and quit?"

"What?" I said.

"Your poster, the one you always talk about. It says . . . 'If you don't like your job, quit,' that bit . . . are you going to live up to it?"

Crap! He was right. He called me out on it. If that poster was a true articulation of how I thought people should live their lives, which is what I had said probably more than fifty times in all those presentations, then didn't I have to live up to it? If I didn't, then I was just a fraud, someone who was all talk and no action. Was I just too timid to see those words through and walk the talk?

I decided two things based on that moment. First, I would stop bitching there and then—negativity is poisonous and kills the soul. Every time I bitched and moaned I was figuratively injecting my soul with poison and killing myself. I was livid with myself. Second, I had always wanted to be my own boss, and I knew I needed a different challenge. I loved Microsoft and its role in changing the world. I cared deeply about the retail team from all over the world. But I needed to find a new challenge and do what I really wanted to do, so I started working towards a plan for what I'd do post-Microsoft. Leaving was inevitable, but I needed time to build my plan for what was to come and for how I was to leave. I loved Microsoft and everything it has achieved and everything it will continue to do to advance the world for the better. I cared deeply about my team, and I wanted to ensure that they were all in a good spot for when I left.

KEY LESSONS

People always need someone to both confide in and to be called out by. Even though he was a couple of layers down in my organization, Steve was willing to call me out and call bullshit. Steve did that. He looked to me as an authentic leader, and when I wasn't living up to it, he had the confidence and trust to feel comfortable calling me out on it and holding me accountable to all that I had preached before.

This is one example of why you need trust among your team; they have to feel comfortable calling you out and telling you when you are being a fraud.

If you want others to hold you accountable to your most authentic self, make the environment you work in a reflection of your beliefs, principles, and philosophies. The Life manifesto on my office wall does that for me. Find what works for you. Your environment should act as an inspiration for you and for others, it should help them understand who you are and what you value, but most importantly, it doesn't leave any room for you to renege on your commitment because it is there in black and white on your wall. Thus, when you falter, when you fail to live up to those principles, people can easily see what is happening and call you out—and that is what we all need every now and again, when we don't do it for ourselves.

SO WHAT ARE YOU GOING TO DO ABOUT IT?

My suggestion: Does your environment help you stay true to yourself? If not, make it so.

Do you have confidants who will keep you true to yourself? If not, find someone and tell them of your expectations for yourself and for them in holding you to it.

Write your thoughts here:

Show Your Personality, Don't Suppress It

I commuted to London daily for about five years. I usually traveled on the 06:52 from Southampton Airport Parkway to London Waterloo and the journey lasted sixty-five minutes. South West Trains was one of the brands that I spent the longest time with each day. One thing consistently made some of my journey more enjoyable, and that was when Gerry was the train guard on our train. (Please note that this Gerry is not my wife.) All the regular commuters knew Gerry, and whenever we heard his voice over the loudspeaker, we would automatically smile.

Gerry had a fabulous disposition and brought a little bit of himself and a whole load of humanity to the journey. Let me give you a few examples.

One day when the train had been sitting an annoying few hundred yards outside Waterloo station for over ten minutes, there was obvious frustration and grumbling among the passengers. We heard the loudspeaker ping on and we all waited for the inevitable "we are sorry we are delayed; the circumstances are beyond our control, and we are trying to do all we can to complete our journey."

Instead we heard Gerry. Without any introduction, he started . . . "I wandered lonely as a cloud / That floats on high o'er vales and hills, / When all at once I saw a crowd, / A host, of golden daffodils . . ."

After reciting the entire "Daffodils" poem by Wordsworth, he closed by saying: "I felt it was getting a little tense in here, so I thought a poem might help." Then he was gone, that was it. Everyone laughed, and the atmosphere lightened. It was pure genius.

On another occasion, after a period of persistent delays, we (surprisingly) arrived at Waterloo on time. He spoke to us over the loudspeaker and said, "We are arriving at London Waterloo, bang on time, as per usual," delivering the last few words with a mischievous tone in his voice. Again the passengers left with smiles on their faces.

He always seemed to have the right words to cheer us up and lift our spirits.

KEY LESSONS

Gerry didn't follow the standard pre-prepared scripts. He was authentic to who he was, and that brightened our day. He was the best brand ambassador we ever engaged with on South West Trains because he allowed his personality to shine through.

When you speak, speak from the heart, be natural. Don't just deliver the words your company puts in your mouth, take their message and be true to the purpose, but bring a little of yourself and your personality too.

SO WHAT ARE YOU GOING TO DO ABOUT IT?

My suggestion: Embrace and celebrate the authentic people you encounter. Tell them they brighten your day.

Write your thoughts here:

Aim to Shine, Not Survive

Ask yourself the question . . . are you good at what you do?

If you are, then you will always be able to get a job, always be able to feed and clothe your family. And if you agree with that, then you have no reason on earth to play it safe at work. No one ever achieved greatness playing it safe—at least not in any organization that was worth its salt.

Hopefully by now you've learned the importance of being true to who you are—but it's just as important to be true to your potential—not just what you have achieved so far but what you can become. That means always trying to improve and become a better version of yourself.

Your purpose is not one of survival. I repeat, your purpose is not to survive. No, it is to create a long and exciting experience and deliver great value. Work hard; listen more; try new stuff; but never, never, never play it safe. When things get a little tough, playing it safe is the surest way to make things worse. Businesses are always changing: new managers arrive, the next inevitable re-org. In my experience, when there is a change, the good guys benefit ninety percent of the time. That's most of the time, but not all. There are also times when a company's fortunes take a dip, and there are times when your own fortunes may take a dip too. Your first reaction when that occurs shouldn't be complacency—it should be to fight and fight hard. Be yourself, be brave, be authentic, and if things don't improve and the experience is no longer exciting and fulfilling then (and only then) it may be time to move on.

I remember a point early on in my career when a person from Apple joined the company I was working for. His claim was that he was Apple's longest-surviving Chief Marketing Officer. That was his way of saying "Apple's best Chief Marketing Officer" because Steve Jobs' ruthlessness with marketing people was well known. I understood his sentiments, but despised the language he used.

Let me tell you: I don't think anyone who is any good should be defined by how long they survive. I don't want to endure. I would rather burn brightly and shine gloriously for a fraction of a second and then disappear like a shooting star than endure and endure but hardly get noticed.

Malcolm McLaren made a similar point when he said . . . "Art school taught me it was far better to be a flamboyant failure than any kind of benign success."

Seriously: "I was the longest-surviving Marketing Director at Apple!" Imagine when you are old and retired, you have your grand-child sitting on your knee, and you are telling them about the good old days. "Do you know, your Grandad was the longest-surviving Marketing Director at Apple?" If I were the grandchild, I hope I would say, "Well Grandad, that's crap, why did you embarrass your-self and play it safe?"

As François-Noël Gracchus Babeuf (and others) said, "I'd rather die on my feet, than live on my knees."

So SHINE and shine brightly!

KEY LESSONS

Don't just endure or play it safe. If you are, work out how you are going to stop that immediately . . . or, alternately, work out how you are going to justify that to your grandchild in years to come.

SO WHAT ARE YOU GOING TO DO ABOUT IT?

Write your thoughts here:

The Bottom Line

I firmly believe that you can only be truly happy when you know who you are and have found a place that enables (and ideally encourages) you to be the real you.

To be the real authentic you, you need to be very self-aware and know yourself intimately—that is harder than it sounds. A key step for me on that journey was writing my personal philosophy. I cannot believe I was over fifty before I wrote mine. If you don't have one, you need to start the process now and realize that it will and should evolve as you grow.

Once you know who you are, it is then a matter of being true to yourself every day and realizing that there are some people and some environments that don't allow you to do that. Don't change yourself to accommodate them, instead eradicate them from your life and find the places to work where you can be the real you.

Remember, if you know who you are—you will be willing to sing country with a world-renowned rapper. If you allow your personality to shine through, you will brighten the day for others. If you have confidants who will hold you accountable, then you have a valuable safety net for when you need a verbal slap.

Bottom line: Authenticity is both powerful and beautiful. Stop allowing people to make you something you're not. Just focus on being the best version of the authentic you that you can be.

Element 7:

PUT YOURSELF OUT THERE

"It's very hard to have ideas. It's very hard to put yourself out there. It's very hard to be vulnerable. But those people who do that are the dreamers, the thinkers, and the creators. They're the magic people of the world."

AMY POEHLER

"I will always believe in punk rock, because it's about creating something for yourself. Part of it was: 'Stop being a sap! Lift your head up and see what is really going on in the political, social, and religious situations, and try and see through all the smoke screens.'"

JOE STRUMMER

One of the most famous articles written about punk first appeared in the fanzine *Sideburns* in January 1977. It had an illustration featuring drawings of three guitar chords with a caption reading, "This is a chord, this is another, this is a third. Now form a band." The advent of punk in the late 1970s had an "anyone can do it" ethos. Punk songs often used just three chords, which made it possible for even very average musicians to become rock stars. Punk rock band members were far from accomplished musicians, but that didn't cause them any concern, they just put themselves out there and went for it.

As the story goes, in 1976 The Ramones performed in Britain, and while in the country they hung out with members of The Clash and the Sex Pistols. The Clash had been rehearsing for a while, but didn't feel they were good enough yet to perform at a live gig. Paul Simon mentioned this to Johnny Ramone, who allegedly replied, "We stink. You don't have to be good, just get out there and play." Later that day The Clash played their first gig, and the rest is history.

Fans of punk music put themselves out there in a similar manner, with colored mohawks, safety pin piercings, and extreme clothes—they didn't care what people thought, they didn't care about being judged. They were comfortable being who they were and doing what they believed in. For them to be authentic (see previous element), they needed to put themselves out there and pay no attention to the critique of others.

Putting yourself out there is the act of exposing your talent, your point of view, your beliefs, your ideas, your original thoughts to others and risking the uncertainty of their reaction.

To achieve success and deliver greatness in the professional world or in your life, you must put yourself out there. This is true no matter what field you're in—sports, business, arts, entertainment, or anything else—so why is it that so few of us actually follow this advice? I believe that the biggest single reason for unfulfilled talent is the fear of failure. People are too scared of criticism. When did we all become so sensitive? When did we start to worry so desperately about what others think? Whenever you try to do something differently or something entirely new, you put yourself out there, and that attracts attention and exposes you to both praise and criticism. To get anywhere in life, you need to accept and embrace that.

In my career, I have received both praise and criticism. For me, praise and recognition are addictive; they drive me on. Conversely, criticism used to hurt, but it hurts less so now. I have realized that you can't be a player who pushes themselves to do things they haven't done before without sometimes falling short. I now realize that I am a competitor, and competitors by their very definition strive for success and risk losing. But I like the mentality that if you are competing, you never lose, you either win or you learn. That helps you ignore the pain of criticism, and it helps equip you better to win next time.

> "You cannot let a fear of failure or a fear of comparison or a fear of judgment stop you from doing the things that will make you great. You cannot succeed without the risk of failure. You cannot have a voice without the risk of criticism. You cannot love without the risk of loss. You must take these risks."[1]
>
> CHARLIE DAY

Atychiphobia (the fear of failure) and FNE (the fear of negative evaluation) are probably the two most constraining and crippling diseases in businesses and businesspeople. Punks put themselves out there. The Ramones implored The Clash to get out there and perform. You need to do the same. We all screw up; we're all crap at certain times, but we still need to get out there and perform.

In this section, I recount the ways I and others have tried to conquer these constraining tendencies, as they exist in all of us to a greater or lesser extent. We'll look at times when some people chose to step outside their comfort zone, into the full glare of the spotlight, to do what was important while others stepped back into the shadows at their defining moments.

---

1 Peter Jacobs, "'It's Always Sunny' Star Charlie Day Pushes Students to Take Risks in Hysterical Commencement Speech," *Business Insider* (May 21, 2014), http://www.businessinsider.com/full-text-charlie-day-merrimack-college-commencement-speech-2014-5.

It's Not the Critic That Counts

For over ten years now, I've had a poster hanging in my office at home. It is one of my favorite photos, with my absolute favorite quote. The image is an iconic boxing photo taken from high above the ring looking down on Muhammad Ali, arms raised, turning away in victory as Cleveland Williams lies spread-eagled on the canvas. If ever there was an image that graphically displays the extremes of victor and conquered, it is this one.

The quote that is superimposed on the canvas next to the prostrate Williams is from Theodore Roosevelt's "Citizenship in a Republic" speech given on 23 April 1910 and is totally punk. I absolutely love it. Read and digest every word—and then we'll break it down, piece by piece.

> It is not the critic who counts; not the man who points out how the strong man stumbles, or where the doer of deeds could have done them better. The credit belongs to the man who is actually in the arena, whose face is marred by dust and sweat and blood; who strives valiantly; who errs, who comes short again and again, because there is no effort without error and shortcoming; but who does actually strive to do the deeds; who knows great enthusiasms, the great devotions; who spends himself in a worthy cause; who at the best knows in the end the triumph of high achievement, and who at the worst, if he fails, at least fails while daring greatly, so that his place shall never be with those cold and timid souls who neither know victory nor defeat.

"It is not the critic who counts; not the man who points out how the strong man stumbles, or where the doer of deeds could have done them better." The next time someone criticizes you for putting yourself out there, don't jump into action and start defending yourself. Pause for a moment and determine whether the critic is also in the ring striving valiantly, or if they are just a bystander sniping from the sidelines. If they are the latter, don't even waste your breath by responding as they don't deserve your attention. Their words are irrelevant. But if the person is in the arena, striving valiantly as you are, then welcome their opinion, study it, digest it—because they are a player, they are credible, and they have good insights that may help you.

"The credit belongs to the man who is actually in the arena." Life is not a spectator sport; it is not about watching the world go on around you. Life is about being a player, always competing, stepping forward, and striving to be the best that you can be. By just being a player and being in the arena, you will achieve more than most people ever dream of.

". . . who strives valiantly; who errs, who comes short again and again, because there is no effort without error and shortcoming." If everything were easy, everyone would achieve everything. Things that matter are often hard to achieve, which means that people who don't want them as badly as we do fail to accomplish them—or fail to even begin their pursuit of such goals. We should be grateful for all the barriers and walls that make us work hard for what we want.

". . . who spends himself in a worthy cause." You know my point of view on this issue from Element 1. I encourage everyone to work for a company with a worthy cause that makes the world a better place and is doing something you are passionate about.

". . . who at the worst, if he fails, at least fails while daring greatly." I love that phrase "daring greatly." May I dare greatly every day. Ask yourself: Have I dared greatly in my life so far? Did I dare greatly yesterday, or today? Will I dare greatly tomorrow? Steve Ballmer once bellowed at his whole worldwide sales team, "You have to ask yourself, are you going to be bold or cop out?" That is the challenge he laid before all of us, and that is the challenge we all have to answer. Some people are happy to go through life watching from the sidelines—that's their choice, I wish those people the very best. But if you have gotten this far through the book, then I know that isn't you. Dare greatly.

". . . his place shall never be with those cold and timid souls who neither know victory nor defeat." I love the dismissiveness of Roosevelt to those who aren't in the ring. There is no disgrace in defeat. If you fought valiantly while daring greatly there is no shame. The only disgrace is if you didn't step into the arena in the first place, whether that was through fear, embarrassment, or because you just couldn't be bothered. Remember, if you don't give up, you can never fail. If you don't give up, you can *never* fail, reaching your goal may just take you a little longer than first expected.

With the full context of this quote, I no longer look at the image of Ali and Williams as just a victorious champion and a defeated challenger. Instead, I see two heroes, two competitors, two people whose hard work captured the attention of the world. There is a common phrase, that the winner takes it all, but I disagree. They both strove valiantly and dared greatly, and they can hold their heads up high because they weren't timid souls but lived their dreams.

"To live is the rarest thing in the world. Most people exist, that is all."

OSCAR WILDE

Muhammad Ali certainly lived life to the fullest, and so did Cleveland Williams. But how many of the people on the periphery of the photograph can say that? How many of the people sitting outside the ring, being spectators, watching others dare greatly, were cold and timid souls who just existed?

Billy Idol, in his book *Dancing with Myself*, articulates this same point. "My fear was of mediocrity, of being just another cog in the relentless system that would eventually grind our spirits down to dust. I refused to be a prisoner in a gilded cage from which there was no escape. . . . I was determined to overcome my limitations, to stare my mediocrity in the face, to step up and dare to fail big, to go for the gold, live on the edge of uncertainty. At least I'd be alive to feel my own pain. . . . Dive rather than sink, and dare the current to take you!"[2]

Theodore Roosevelt, we toast you! As far as I am concerned his quote should reside on the wall of everyone who is a player, a competitor, and a warrior. These words are one of my daily reminders of how I want to live.

KEY LESSONS

Step forward, enter the ring, and be a participant.

Ignore the sideline critics.

Recognize that the path to success is usually riddled with obstacles, and these are what refine your skills and character with fire.

There is no disgrace in failing, only in not trying.

SO WHAT ARE YOU GOING TO DO ABOUT IT?

My suggestion: At your next all-person team meeting, take ten minutes to share your perspective on this great quote and explain how you want the principles to be visible in your organization.

Write your thoughts here:

---

2 Billy Idol, *Dancing with Myself* (New York: Simon & Schuster, 2014).

The Scariest Moment in My Life

By my second year of working at ITV Digital, the company was suffering multiple critical business issues that put its very existence at risk. Among other issues, our parent companies were suffering after the crash of 2000 and our encryption security system had been hacked, decimating our premium channel revenue in a few short months. With no apparent solution to these problems, the bankruptcy administrators were called in and took over management of the company while we tried to find a solution to the problems. We spent several weeks working with them to try to create a rescue package. We were renegotiating the cost of every contract, with some success, and we were cutting costs wherever we could. It was a difficult time. We had taken huge market share from Sky (see the "When Time Is Tight Great Things Happen" story on page 145) but it looked like we were doomed.

When the inevitable day arrived, the administrators came to the remaining directors around lunchtime and said that all the staff would be told later that afternoon that they needed to clear their desks and leave the building for the final time. ITV Digital was being closed down. Immediately I felt gutted—it was as though someone had died. I knew that when everyone found out later that day, they would be distraught. Many had worked there for far longer than I had and had put their whole being into making the company successful. I sat in my office alone thinking about the camaraderie, the vitality of the team, the challenger attitude, and how it was now going to end with these matter-of-fact administrators telling everyone to clear out their things in a manner that was almost certain to be cold and emotionless.

As the time approached, I kept thinking, *It cannot end like this.* It was going to end, I knew that, but we needed it to end in a way that was appropriate to the way we lived and worked together.

About five minutes before the meeting, I had an idea. I asked my PA to print off the words to a song, grab the portable microphone and speaker, and bring them to the second floor where the all-employee meeting was to take place with the administrators in one of the big offices—but to hide all the things outside the room.

We had a very brief meeting with the administrators, and I think (but I am not entirely sure) our CEO thanked everyone for their commitment and work. Then everyone was told that we no longer had jobs, and ITV Digital had effectively closed. It was a sombre, depressing affair. My sales and marketing team walked back to their desks totally despondent.

At this moment, I did what I think is the most uncomfortable thing I have ever done. For context, you need to understand that I do not have a musical bone in my body. I cannot sing a note; actually, it is worse than that—my singing is just painful. I picked up the portable speaker and microphone from outside the room and hurried into the middle of the second floor office where people had started to return to their desks in near silence. I saw a co-worker, Julia Luker (who was a senior manager in our customer service team), and for some reason I think I knew that she could sing. I said, "You can sing, can't you?" She nodded, and I said, "Okay, I need you, follow me."

We climbed onto a row of desks in the middle of the office. I turned my mic on and said something like . . . "Okay, ITV Digital, you've been an amazing team, done some fabulous work, and you can be very proud. We've been through too much together to go out in such a sombre way. We are going to go out with the vibrancy that we have shown over the past few years. We are going to go out with our heads held high and with a rousing rendition of the most appropriate song I can imagine, 'My Way' by Frank Sinatra."

The song sheets were being quickly handed out—I think we had between one hundred twenty and one hundred fifty people on our team. This was the moment of truth. If I had judged the crowd correctly, they would sing loudly and drown out my awful singing. If I had gotten it wrong, I would be left murdering a song in front of my close colleagues. I felt as exposed as a poker player going all-in on a pair of deuces—I had nothing to offer, and I was banking on their reaction to my appeal. The introduction finished, I started, and they followed, breaking out into a very passionate and loud rendition of "My Way." As soon as I had gotten it going, I ensured that my partner held the mic close to her mouth and well away from mine, but I needn't have worried as the team sang their hearts out and would have drowned me out anyway.

One of the senior administrators heard the commotion and came in to see what was going on and what all the noise was about. I saw him looking at me standing on the desk, and he just smiled at me and turned around and walked back out. He knew we had a young, lively team, and he understood we needed this moment.

As the song came to a finale everyone belted out, "WE DID IT OUR WAY!"

I concluded with, "Okay I expect to see everyone in The Mason's Arms pub in five minutes. Thank you, Battersea. Goodnight."

When I stood up on the desk, it was to do what I thought our team needed. We had to end in a way that fit with the way we had worked together. But I also thought it could be the most embarrassing moment of my life: standing in front of nearly one hundred fifty of the people I had led for the past two years, trying to sing when I can't sing a note. I could so easily have died a thousand deaths, and their lasting memory would have been that valiant but embarrassing stumble.

On most of the other occasions when I have put myself out there, I had confidence that I could pull it off. Generally, it was always doing something I knew how to do; but this time I knew that I could not do what I was about to attempt, and I could fall flat on my face. Fortunately, the crowd responded and hid my voice.

This moment was hugely important psychologically for many of us. I am not sure I realized it at the time, but instinctively I knew that how we left that building mattered greatly. With hindsight, I realize that if we had walked out to the cold, dull, monosyllabic words of the characterless administrators, we would have walked out as a defeated, broken bunch of individuals. Instead, the final recognition and appreciation of the team, crowned by communal singing, meant we left as a team with our heads held high and smiles on our faces. We had lost our battle to Sky—but we were going to choose our attitude and choose how we looked at things. As the saying goes, "I never lose. Either I win, or I learn," and I think that is how many of us accepted the news. We weren't going to be carried out of the arena as a defeated challenger—we were going to get to our feet and walk out, heads held high. We hadn't lost, we'd just learned something, and we'd be better the next time we stepped into the intensity of battle. And of course, we had failed while daring greatly, and so our place was "never with those cold and timid souls who know neither victory nor defeat."

There have been times when I have gotten the tone wrong and fallen flat, but I have been blessed with a gene that eradicates bad memories from my memory bank very quickly. In the pub that evening and in emails over the following few days, many people acknowledged the impromptu communal singing idea—people appreciated that their last memory in that building was a fun, positive, and happy one.

KEY LESSONS

There are times when your heart says to do something, to intervene in the course of what is taking place; when it does, trust it and go for it. You will not always get it right, but my experience is that the impact you have when you do get it right far outweighs the embarrassment when you don't.

The psychology of managing a defeat or a disappointment is a vitally important one. Learn how to do that for yourself and for your team. Embrace the "I never lose. Either I win, or I learn" mindset. If you don't learn how to manage defeat, you will always struggle to free yourself of the fear that prevents us from putting ourselves out there.

Put yourself out there, feel vulnerable; it stretches you in a good way. While it will not come off every time, you will cash out well up overall. You have to push yourself into uncomfortable situations. As Ray Manzarek said, "Growing up doesn't mean you leave the danger behind, it means that you jump into the danger, you confront the danger."[3]

Just like in the previous discussion on decision-making, don't try to get a perfect record; realize that putting yourself out there is a portfolio. Don't try to get it right one hundred percent of the time; try to get a high strike rate, of course, but what is more important is that you always go for it.

SO WHAT ARE YOU GOING TO DO ABOUT IT?

Write your thoughts here:

---

3 Ray Manzarek, in Legs McNeil and Gillian McCain, *Please Kill Me: The Uncensored Oral History of Punk* (New York: Grove Press, 1996), 251.

Be the First to Volunteer

At the start of this book, I introduced you to Dr. Michael Gervais, who had started to bring his sports psychology training into Microsoft. At the start of my team's first training session with Mike, he asked us whether we wanted to achieve great things and make a big difference in our lives? Were we really up for putting ourselves out there and going for it? We all were proud that we worked for such a great company as Microsoft and of course we all confirmed that we were.

Halfway through the morning, after we had done a few exercises and discussed our personal philosophies, one of his colleagues (Nicole Davis, a two-time women's Olympic volleyball silver medalist) asked which one of us wanted to volunteer to test their mental capabilities. Only one of us volunteered immediately.

Mike leaped in, asking in a very animated fashion, "Whoa, what just went on here? This morning you said you all wanted to achieve great things, make a big difference in people's lives, really put yourselves out there and go for it. Yet when you get the chance to do that and work with some of the best coaches in the world, you shrink back into your seats. Why didn't you volunteer?"

One of our team said, "Well, I thought we would all get the chance, and you learn more from not going first."

"Bullshit! No one ever said you were all going to get the chance. She asked: 'Which one of you would like to test your mental capability?'"

He continued his tirade. "Why didn't you volunteer? If we had asked for a volunteer at the Seahawks, we would have expected ninety-five percent of the players to volunteer and would've questioned the courage of the ones that didn't. In the military, it's counted as an honor to go first. We recently did a women's entrepreneurs event with over fifty people in the room, and every single one of them put their hands up immediately. You need to ask yourself why you've just been small and backed away from such an opportunity."

We thought that was it; he had stopped berating us. But he hadn't, he had just paused. Twenty seconds later he was back at it.

"When you put your head down on your pillow tonight, you should feel sick to your stomach. Today you were small."

That was it; it was over. There was a calm for about thirty seconds before . . . "When you go home and tell your spouse about this, they will tell you, 'It's all right darling, don't worry.' Well, when he or she says that to you, remember it isn't all right! You should feel sick."

He was right. This was a great lesson for all of us. We had the opportunity to work directly, one-on-one, with two of the world's best coaches, and most of the team was willing to pass that up because they weren't prepared to put themselves out there.

If we are all going to be the best we can be, we need to constantly be testing ourselves, putting ourselves out there, challenging ourselves, seeing how good we are. If we look at it from a physical perspective, we train by extending our muscles and our stamina beyond where we have pushed them before. The muscles are pushed, and then when they repair or heal, they are stronger than ever before. It is no different for our mental strength. Challenging ourselves in new ways and testing ourselves beyond what we have done before is what strengthens us and allows us to progress and improve.

I also think it shows an awful lot about people's leadership. Leaders lead. True leaders cannot help themselves when it comes to leading. They are willing to step forward at every opportunity. I know that all of us who endured Mike's tirade of abuse about being small committed that day to never back away again, and now we always step up and put ourselves out there by volunteering first.

KEY LESSONS

If you want to be the best you can be, then whenever there is an opportunity to improve yourself or challenge yourself, then you must step up.

Never, never hesitate when a personal improvement opportunity presents itself. Always volunteer to go first.

SO WHAT ARE YOU GOING TO DO ABOUT IT?

My suggestion: Assess your team on their willingness to volunteer to go first. Test this out at your next team meeting.

Write your thoughts here:

Never Shy Away from Accountability

In times of economic downturn, there are sometimes planned headcount reductions. As is normal, the HR department works with all the appropriate direct line managers to plan the communication with those affected employees on the chosen day, and then all the employees whose jobs have been eliminated get notified on that chosen date. Obviously, it is far from pleasant for the employees or managers.

During one of these group layoffs, various managers in my team communicated to about ten of our employees that their job was being eliminated. It was a difficult day for the entire team. The following day I found out that one of the managers, who spent about equal time working in our Paris and London offices, called one of his UK-based team members on the phone to tell him he was being made redundant. The manager had stayed in the Paris office on the communication day. I was appalled at how we handled this, and I know I went a little crazy. How dare someone not have the common decency to deliver such life-changing news to one of their team members face-to-face? Yes, the HR person was in the room, but for the manager to dial-in to deliver the traumatic news was totally unacceptable in my book. Just writing this now makes me angry again . . . I am still *livid*. He knew it was going to be a difficult conversation, and he simply didn't want to have to face it. He was so concerned for his own comfort levels that he forgot it's a thousand times harder to receive this news than it is to give it. Yes, making someone redundant isn't pleasant. It's not an easy conversation to have, but I felt it was inexcusable. How dare you chicken out and be so uncaring and fail to give the other person the dignity of being there in person?

To prevent any reoccurrence of this type of incident, our team adopted a phrase that became one of our guiding principles for our culture. I recounted the story to my managers and introduced the phrase: "That's why they pay us the medium bucks." This phrase was our shorthand for the fact that there are some jobs that are difficult or hard or unpleasant and that require our bravery and fortitude. That's why we are well paid, and we cannot just flinch from our responsibilities.

KEY LESSONS

Never avoid difficult conversations or circumstances. You just have to face them down. What defines a leader is where they stand in times of difficulty. If you want to be a player in the ring, you are going to have to take the odd hit, and you just cannot run and hide at the first sign of trouble.

SO WHAT ARE YOU GOING TO DO ABOUT IT?

Write your thoughts here:

If You Are Going to Be a Participant, You Risk Criticism— Get Used to It!

We have all received our share of criticism. Those in the public eye, such as celebrities, musicians, sports people, etc., have their criticism plastered all over the newswire, the press, and the Internet. Everyone in business gets criticism, but it is normally hidden in one-on-one meetings with your manager, or its visibility is at least limited within your company rather than in full view of your friends and family. I bore the brunt of extreme criticism in the press in 2003. I had recently joined Orange as Vice President of Brand Marketing, and with that role came the responsibility for all our communications. It was a high-profile job in UK marketing. Orange had launched several years before with some of the most iconic and visually beautiful advertising ever, like nothing anyone had seen before from a telecom. They had kept that style going for nearly ten years, but recently the adverts hadn't been having the same impact.

It was obvious that the biggest issue with the current advertising was that, while it was still beautiful and iconic (much of it shot by Academy Award-winning director Ridley Scott), the actual message had lost substance. Orange launched in 1994 with strong consumer benefits that no one else was offering, such as per-second billing, inclusive minutes, and free insurance. But now, although the ads remained beautiful, we were talking to consumers about video content that was becoming available on the phone—but no one had the bandwidth to effectively stream it with any kind of watchable quality.

So we resolved to go back to creating adverts that communicated what we called hard-center benefits for the consumer. We ran two campaigns around the same time: One was called Learn and one was called the Hard-Nosed Businessman. Orange Learn was a huge success, and to this day I still say that the adverts were in the Orange style. The Hard-Nosed Businessman, whilst also successful, was a departure from the Orange style.

I attracted some criticism from the marketing press for the Hard-Nosed Businessman, but it blew up into an absolute frenzy when Hans Snook (the original and ex-CEO of Orange) weighed in with comments like, "I think this is positively the worst advertising I have ever seen." The press picked this up and ran with it. I believe Hans was back in London doing a press tour to announce his opening of some colonic irrigation facilities. Normally, that wouldn't get much coverage, but as he was slating me and my work, he was headline news. All the journalists wanted to talk to Hans as they love to see a fight, and Hans seemed to be using the attention his criticism was getting to market his new venture.

Over the following three weeks, we kept getting more and more press attention. I think it was *Marketing Week* that came out and said I was taking the unprecedented step of holding a two-hour press conference to defend the adverts—no such meeting ever happened or was ever an idea, and I don't know where the idea came from. A couple of weeks later, one of my team shouted excitedly that I was named as #35 in "Marketing Week's Power 100," which was their ranking of the most powerful people in UK marketing. That cheered me up until I opened the magazine to read underneath my name, "but the brand marketing director has been under the cosh . . . [the campaign] has been much-criticized. The pressure is on."[4] Although I did beat David Beckham, who was at #100.

I wasn't prepared for it, and I didn't handle it very well, if the truth be known. Particularly because Hans' opinion was irrelevant. Within Orange, we all knew the statistics were showing that the campaign was having the success we intended. The opinions of the

---

4 Campaign, "POWER 100: This Year's Marketing A-list Is Marked by Challenges from Ryanair's Michael O'Leary and David Haines of Vodafone," *Campaign* (July 31, 2003), http://www.campaignlive.co.uk/article/power-100-years-marketing-a-list-marked-challenges-ryanairs-michael-oleary-david-haines-vodafone/186755.

people who mattered, our customers, and those running our company was all I should have been worried about.

KEY LESSONS

If you are going to put yourself out there, you will inevitably get criticism. You cannot please all the people, all the time. Criticism is inevitable, it may just be internally within your company, or it may make it into the press. When it happens, as it certainly will, don't allow it to dent your confidence or your willingness to pick yourself up, dust yourself off, and get back out there. Use positive self-talk, remind yourself of your strike rate, your batting average, the number of positive experiences. None of us go through life with a perfect record, and the more you can learn from each setback, the more equipped you will be to handle it the next time.

Especially ignore the sniping from people whose opinion is largely irrelevant.

SO WHAT ARE YOU GOING TO DO ABOUT IT?

Write your thoughts here:

Take Responsibility for Resolving Conflict

I remember Jim Wicks, head of design at Motorola, being disappointed about a situation where people were sniping from the periphery when a critical business decision was needing to be made. He burst out and interrupted the snipers and said, "Stop sitting on the sidelines, jump in and be part of the solution." He was spot on. I wrote the phrase down and committed it to memory. On several occasions I used this line and replicated Jim's leadership.

I love it when people who shouldn't be the leaders take responsibility and lead. They step off the sidelines and say I am going to sort this because it needs sorting. It might not be my job, but I am making it my job. Nowhere have I seen this form of putting yourself out there more evident than on the actual sidelines—of an American football game.

I was at the Seattle Seahawks game against the Atlanta Falcons in October 2016. Seattle had dominated the first half and was winning 17–3, but when the players came out for the third quarter, the whole momentum of the game changed. Seattle's success in recent years had all been based on having the meanest defense in the league. They were known as the Legion of Boom, and they just didn't give up many touchdowns. But in that third quarter, they were absolutely ripped apart and conceded three touchdowns. Atlanta was cutting through them like a knife through butter.

One of the touchdowns was simply embarrassing as there was some blatant miscommunication, which led to a blown coverage and a pathetically easy touchdown. Richard Sherman, a loud, aggressive, and in-your-face kind of player—and arguably the leader of the defense that day—came off in an absolute rage. He threw his helmet; was shouting and screaming at all his colleagues; had a bust up with five people, including the defensive coordinator; and all hell was breaking loose on the sideline. What happened next was, for me, the whole embodiment of the Seahawks culture. All the other members of the defense surrounded Sherman and started chanting, smiling, and bouncing; they were singing their happy song, trying to get Sherman refocused and back to being one of the team. (Go look for it on YouTube and see what I mean.)

The Seahawks coach, Pete Carroll, admitted that Sherman went over the top but added, "He got really emotional and he reacted really strongly. He was just being competitive and all that and he didn't want bad things to happen, so he responded. But what was fantastic was the way our guys took care of him." Carroll said of Sherman's teammates, not the coaches, ". . . our guys brought him back in. And they were best suited to make sure, to make sense and to get him right. And we got back. It took us a while."[5]

The players echoed that point of view. "We know each other, we understand each other, it's happened at practice several times," linebacker K. J. Wright said. "If it happens, correct it, fix it, move on. That's what we did. We moved on and we found a way to finish the game and then we fixed it the next day."[6]

"We don't really try and change anybody. We embrace who they are as a person and who they are as people. When you embrace who they are, you know kind of what to do to bring them back," teammate Bobby Wagner said. "[Stuff] happens. It's a very passionate game and [stuff] happens and it's our job as a team to get everybody back on to what we're trying to do."[7]

Sherman looked so at odds with the rest of his bouncing buddies, but that was the only way to get him back during that game. If they had all started shouting at him in retaliation with the same

---

5 Gregg Bell, "Pete Carroll after Regrouping from Richard Sherman's Sideline Screaming," *The Olympian*, Oct. 17, 2016, http://www.theolympian.com/sports/nfl/seattle-seahawks/seahawks-insider-blog/article108886797.html.

6 Tim Booth, "Seahawks' Richard Sherman: No Regrets for Sideline Outburst," Pro32, October 16, 2016, https://pro32.ap.org/progress-index/article/seahawks-richard-sherman-no-regrets-sideline-outburst.

7 Gregg Bell, "Pete Carroll after Regrouping from Richard Sherman's Sideline Screaming,"

venomous anger, then all hell would have broken loose, the situation would have deteriorated further, and I am sure they would have lost that game. But they somehow managed to regroup by the fourth quarter and win the game with a great defensive play by Richard Sherman in the dying seconds, preventing Atlanta from having a game-winning field goal attempt.

At work it should be the same for us; we need to be part of the solution. Typically, if there is a bust up, too often people step back and look for management to step in and sort things out. But everyone has a responsibility to do that. It's the whole concept of peer leadership.

SAME GAME, DIFFERENT CONFLICT, SAME APPROACH

My Executive Assistant, Livy, a big Seahawks fan, was also at this game with her son and two friends. She put herself out there by resolving a conflict of a different sort—but in a way not dissimilar to Sherman's teammates. Two guys in front of her group stayed standing up throughout the first few minutes of the game, blocking the view of Livy and her group. They couldn't see the game without standing up, and they didn't want to have to do that. One of Livy's friends confronted them and said, "Are you going to stand up all the way through?" To which one of the guys in front said, "I paid for these tickets, and I'll do what I want, lady." They proceeded to stand with total disregard for their fellow spectators.

Livy got angry and could feel herself boiling up for a confrontation. She was going to tap the guy's arm again and complain to him, but she knew that would be useless. He clearly had little regard for other people. So Livy tapped his arm and instead said, "Hey, this is going to be a great game, we're all sitting together, all cheering on the Seahawks, wouldn't it be better if we were friends, had fun, had a beer together and got along rather than fighting each other?"

The guy thought about it for a moment, then he agreed that she was probably right. They made a compromise: The two groups would stand during defense and sit during offensive plays. For the rest of the day they lived the ups and downs and the highs and lows of their beloved Seahawks

(continued)

together. They enjoyed supporting their team together and everything was fine, especially when the Seahawks won 26–24, thanks to a late field goal.

KEY LESSONS

People should take far more responsibility than has been formally given to them. Don't wait for permission: Take the lead and grab the responsibility to make things better even if it isn't in your job description—seize the initiative and be part of the solution.

The defensive team took the responsibility to bring Sherman back using a positive reconciliatory message rather than responding aggressively to his aggression, and Livy took the responsibility in the stands to use positive reconciliatory reasoning to find a good solution. Life isn't about picking fights when you cannot win either way; it's about finding the best way to get to your goal; it's about reconciliation in the face of hostility.

Resolving conflict requires you to know your colleagues, who they are, and what makes them tick, because then you can help them get back on track with the program.

SO WHAT ARE YOU GOING TO DO ABOUT IT?

My suggestion: Find the video of this game-time moment on YouTube and use this as a teaching moment for your team.

Write your thoughts here:

The Bottom Line

I love the "Citizenship in a Republic" speech. I've started playing an audio version of it to myself some mornings as a reminder of how I should embrace the possibility of every day.

There are many key lessons in this section, but it all ultimately boils down to whether you want to be a participant or a spectator. If you do want to be a participant, and I mean you really do want it, then you have to accept that there are consequences. Consequences like the always-volunteer-first mentality that Michael Gervais drilled into me. Consequences like always being the person to step forward and resolve conflicts. Consequences like being a visible, human presence when people are getting bad news or are in difficult circumstances. Consequences like leading the singing when you cannot sing a note. But the real consequence is that you are committing to a life of enjoyable successes and painful failures, and who knows what the ratio will be. But remember that quote, "I never lose. Either I win, or I learn."

I don't think you can avoid the pain of failure, however much you package it up in your own mind as a learning experience. For me, the most beneficial trait you can develop is selective amnesia. Jack Nicklaus, the legendary golfer, had it. There is a story of him telling an audience that he had never missed a putt from inside of three feet or three putted on the last hole of a tournament. During the open questions, a man in the audience asked Jack a question.

He stated that he saw Jack miss from inside three feet on the last hole of a tournament a few weeks ago, so how can he say he never has? As the story goes, Jack stared at the man with his piercing eyes and assured the man that he had never missed from inside of three feet on the last hole of a tournament. The questioner wasn't going to let it go and even stated he had it on film and offered to send it to him. But Nicklaus again denied it, "I have never missed from inside of three feet on the last hole of a tournament. Next question please." He had moved on to the next question and wasn't debating this anymore.

There are clearly two facts here. Jack Nicklaus has missed from inside of three feet on the last hole of a tournament. Jack does not remember it, or rather Jack does not allow himself to remember it, and as a result his confidence on those putts is sky high. Selective amnesia is so beautiful. It is an amazing ability to have, this power to ignore the painful or embarrassing defeats that can be so debilitating and instead recall only the joy of victory, which stimulates great effort and confidence.

Bottom line: Be the person in the arena. Accept victories and embrace defeat with equal humility and love the fact that your place will never be with those weak and timid souls who know neither victory nor defeat.

Element 8:

REJECT CONFORMITY

"Follow the path of the unsafe, independent thinker. Expose your ideas to the danger of controversy. Speak your mind and fear less the label of 'crackpot' than the stigma of conformity. And on issues that seem important to you, stand up and be counted at any cost."

THOMAS J. WATSON

"Conformity is the jailor of freedom, and the enemy of growth."

JOHN F. KENNEDY

"Undermine their pompous authority, reject their moral standards, make anarchy and disorder your trademarks. Cause as much chaos and disruption as possible but don't let them take you ALIVE."

SID VICIOUS

Punk was a movement that was born out of independent thinking, freedom to express yourself, and a desire to create a change. As a result, it was inevitable that punk would be nonconformist. However, it wasn't just its nonconformity, it was the *extent* to which it didn't conform that was shocking for many. It was as if punk had a visceral allergic reaction to conforming in any way. If there was something to rebel against, it did, and then the punks would look for anything else they took issue with.

Therefore, punk wasn't just nonconforming to the slow, cumbersomely long riffs that went nowhere and the dull music that preceded it, it was also nonconforming to authority, rebelling against society, and rebelling against corporations having dictatorial control by saying, "Screw this, I don't care what you think." More and more young people were disillusioned and looking for an escape from the boredom and constraints of society, and punks at that time were infuriated with what was going on in music, society, and fashion. They weren't prepared to accept the status quo, so instead they pressed the reset button like never before. They rebelled, and to make that statement loud and clear, they sought to cause offense at every opportunity.

Punks didn't just rip up the rulebook—they set it on fire and started afresh.

PUNK ROCK'S REFUSAL TO FOLLOW NORMS

Nothing about punk conformed to accepted norms. Let's take a fleeting glimpse to see the extent of this truth:

- Songs of the era almost always lasted between three and four minutes. Punk songs only lasted as long as the inspiration did and for as long as it took them to say what they had to say—rarely making it to the three-minute mark.

- What they had to say was utterly revolutionary and had never been said before in music: No one had chosen to sing about things like the royal family or dish out such abuse, not to mention the offensive language.

- Punk never sought a sophisticated and polished recording style and rejected it in favor of the raw energy and aggression of a fast-paced recording process.

- Album covers prior to punk were highly stylized and well produced, whereas punk rock album covers were hand-done and looked like they'd been knocked up in a few hours—which was often the case.

- The record industry said that to be successful you needed to garner good reviews from the music journalists, especially the highly influential *NME*, which slated the Sex Pistols in their early days. Instead, the handwritten and badly photocopied punk fanzines of the day were the viral voices that helped punk bands build their fame.

- Punks engaged with their fan base in the most nonconformist way imaginable. They would abuse their fans, swear at them, start fights at their gigs, and even spit at them. Curiously, the more offensive and alienating they were to their fans, the more people wanted to follow them.

- Punk style was equally unconventional: the ripped clothes loaded with zips, the safety pin piercings, the colorful hairstyles, and the extreme theatre-esque makeup.

Almost no rule in the music, fashion, or society rulebooks was left untouched by punk rock bands and their fans. Even the music industry's most sacrosanct rule—you have to be able to play a musical instrument to be a musician—no longer held true! Stunning, utterly stunning!

Nonconformity is about not blindly following the accepted rules, constraints, and guidelines. It's about challenging the status quo. It's about saying: These rules may have been okay for a previous time, but not anymore. Nonconformity is about challenging what has been established by declaring the establishment irrelevant where it provides no value.

Much of the establishment today is fast becoming irrelevant because the world is changing at breathtaking speed, and the establishment hasn't kept up. If there was ever a time in our existence when we should question conformity, it is now. We cannot blindly continue to abide by accepted norms and established principles that were created in a very different time for very different circumstances.

That's why many businesses could benefit from some good punk-esque nonconformity. It is all about being unaccepting of established norms. Today's corporate world is full of mediocrity, slowness, politics, false praise, and people too scared to say it as it is. More and more employees are disillusioned with lukewarm leadership that makes their jobs dull and boring and constrains their creativity, imposing limitations rather than empowering them. Therefore, and rightly so, our customers and work colleagues are crying out for the breath of fresh air that a bit of the punk culture would bring. Let's breathe some life into our workplace and our work by rejecting conformity and attacking the accepted norms that are pointless and futile and valueless.

In this section, I identify some of the occasions when the established norms made me want to cry. I offer examples of times when I am proud to have ignored the established corporate rulebook, and others when I am embarrassed I didn't stop the insanity sooner. I also gladly acknowledge a couple of brands that I admire greatly because of their nonconformist attitudes. As you go through these examples, I hope they inspire you to reconsider the world, challenge convention every step of the way, and call bullshit on those things that don't add value but eat up valuable time.

Although some punks rebelled against everything just to rebel, I am not suggesting that. It's not that convention is always wrong—it isn't—it's just that it's not always right, and we have become so immune to not questioning it that we don't anymore. We have to question the norms and reject conformity where it doesn't make sense. Ask yourself: What are you willing to blow to smithereens to liberate your team?

Don't Pander to the Corporate Facade

We were looking for a new PR agency shortly after I took over running the marketing of the Nintendo operation in the UK. We saw a few agencies, and I remember meeting a new agency called Cake that was still in the process of being formed. One of their founders, Mark Whelan, came to see me; the thinking they showed was good, and there was something very creative about them. I invited them back for the second round of pitches, and the work they showed was exceptional. The second time around I really liked Mark, whereas in the first meeting I wasn't so sure; I thought he may have been a little arrogant. Mark was one of those people who was different. I realized he wasn't conceited or arrogant; he was confident in his proposal and, therefore, not subservient. I wasn't used to an agency that wasn't pandering to you, and it was the first time I had met an agency person truly like this. In short, he was refreshingly different from what I was used to. (See my story "External Advice Should Be Strong and Honest," page 213.)

I wanted to hire Cake; I desperately wanted Mark working with us, and so did the whole of our team, including my CEO. Our discussions progressed, and Mark came down to Southampton, where I told him we wanted to appoint Cake if we could finalize a few things, including their fees. I said to him that we had a figure in mind that we wouldn't go above, and I didn't want to get into endless negotiations about their monthly retainer. I asked Mark to write down on a piece of paper the monthly retainer they wanted.

He wrote down £12,000 per month and pushed it face down across the table to me. I looked at it and crossed through his figure and wrote an alternative number down. I could see he was dreading seeing how much he had been cut by, but I knew he needed this account to get things started for their new agency, so he wasn't in a great negotiating position. I slid the paper back to him, and I said, "Tell me if that would work for you?" Mark looked at it, smiled, and said, "Yes, we can adjust it to that." I had written £16,000 per month.

Now why did I do that? A few reasons . . .

I wanted to pay a fair price. We had set our budget at £16,000, and some of the other agencies who had pitched had already indicated their fees, which had ranged between £16,000 and £18,000.

I honestly thought that they had low-balled it, and perhaps that was because they underestimated the workload. The last thing I wanted was for them to come back a few months later and say they needed to increase the monthly retainer, because that would have meant a whole load of process and angst as we would have had to engage our procurement team, and no procurement person takes kindly to renegotiating a contract three months in.

I wanted to have a buffer, so I could feel free to push for more work from them without constantly feeling like I was on a taximeter and without them constantly worrying about the viability of the account. I wanted our joint focus to be on coming up with cool marketing initiatives, and I didn't want our beautiful new relationship to get tainted with constantly haggling over fees.

So we had agreed on fees, and I had a contract ready to sign when my CEO gave me one last condition. He wanted to ensure that the perception in the industry press was that we had hired a strong, credible agency and not some low-rent start-up. I was instructed to check that they had suitable credentials as a big-city PR agency, by seeing their offices and meeting their entire team. That way we could be sure that there was sufficient infrastructure to fully service our business.

We all knew that Cake was a start-up, but one where all the founders had come from big-name agency backgrounds. It was bureaucracy again. I rang Mark and told him what I needed to do to meet my boss's latest requirements. He said that his new offices were swanky but were in the final throes of being refurbished, and he didn't really want to take me there in their current condition. He knew from my tone of voice that I didn't have a high bar in regard to what they needed to do to pass this final evaluation. He suggested that he show me a photo. I agreed—that was seeing them, wasn't it? Then he suggested that he bring his entire company to the offices of Leagas Delaney (our advertising agency), who was hosting our next "all agency" meeting. Sure, I agreed.

At the end of that next all agency meeting, Mark made a quick call from his mobile, and within a few minutes I had a string of people marching into this huge boardroom. The line swept in and circled the table. As each person passed by where I was standing, they would pause for five seconds, shake my hand, and Mark would introduce them and say what their role was at Cake. They would then carry on with their lap of the boardroom table and march out as quickly as they had arrived.

There were lots of people filing in, far more than I expected, and I soon realized far more than Mark expected. Mark started off well, and without missing a beat he would introduce the person and their role. However, by the time we reached about the fifteenth person, he didn't appear to be as familiar with the person or their role. By the time we reached the thirtieth person, he was almost clueless. I think we had about forty-five people come in and present themselves as Cake employees. I still don't know how many actually did work for Cake, but my guess in hindsight is that fifty percent of them were rent-a-crowd. Some were even carrying shopping bags; they must have been plucked off the street about five minutes before. I am sure Mark had never seen them before, and I presume he never saw many of them again.

I didn't care, and I certainly wasn't going to ask. My boss had asked me to check their building, and I had seen a beautiful photograph—well, artist's impression, actually. He asked me to check out the size of their team, and they did have a lot of people, at least on that day. I have never asked if my suspicions were true, and I never will, because I don't think I want to hear the answer. In fact, I think the chutzpah of the situation and the shenanigans actually endeared them more to me. They were my type of people. That was the type of attitude we needed for an agency who was going to help us manage a youth brand like Nintendo.

By increasing their fees and then allowing the validation shenanigans, I earned their trust; they knew that I was fair and would go to bat for them. Trust always goes both ways, and over the years they repaid that trust time and time again.

They were now my agency, and they would do me proud for nearly twenty years. They were absolutely fantastic for me. I was hiring them for their creativity, imagination, and hunger—I was not hiring them for their offices or the number of people they had or how low their fees were. In fact, the lack of beautiful offices and the limited number of people meant they were hungry, and I got the founders (Mike and Mark and Ben) working directly on my account rather than just overseeing far more junior people actually working on my business. They were committed to our business, and I like to think we helped make their name as an agency.

I DON'T CARE ABOUT CORPORATE FORMALITY EITHER

When Jim Thornton from Mother (see page 140) fell asleep in a meeting shortly after presenting some advertising scripts, I took it as a sign of the deep commitment shown over the previous forty-eight hours (and I mean forty-eight awake hours). He had reached his finish line, and he collapsed with fatigue. Others would have felt insulted; it would not have been the done thing. They would consider it rude and disrespectful, but for me it was the ultimate sign of respect. I felt honored—honored that someone would push themselves to the absolute physical limit to work on my behalf.

Another such example was when Mark Whelan arrived one morning to discuss the Pokémon launch plan. He started by saying: I think I've cracked it. Most senior marketing directors would have then expected a mood film, followed by demographic tables and a beautifully crafted PowerPoint deck. But this morning things were different. Mark reached into his pocket and pulled out a piece of paper the size of a bus ticket. He kept referring to his scribbles on this piece of paper and articulated a beautiful strategy for the launch of Pokémon. I subsequently found out that this piece of paper that contained such a beautiful plan was a triangular corner ripped off the free London morning paper, the *Metro*. I initially thought of this as a sign of last-minute planning, but that didn't worry me. Was it a work of pure genius? Hell yes! To me it didn't matter whether it was written on letterhead paper from Buckingham Palace or toilet paper; the content was genius, and I loved it. I so wish I had kept that piece of ripped-off newspaper; I would frame it and hang it in a place of honor in my office. I later found out that it wasn't last-minute planning. It was that Mark was a perfectionist, and all morning before we met he wasn't entirely satisfied with the proposal he was coming to give and kept wanting to make it better. So he worked on it during the one-hour train journey, and that was when he cracked it. So he presented the high-quality work written on the corner of a ripped newspaper rather than the less-perfect work beautifully documented in a bound document that he had in his bag. That was the right choice. Jim and Mark, unorthodox at times maybe, but legends in my mind.

KEY LESSONS

To be punk, we need to call bullshit or at least ignore some of those crap corporate facades that matter so much to some people but have always been irrelevant to me. Don't suffer the pointless requests you get for things that don't matter, and if you can't ignore them, gloss over them, tick the box, and allow a quick no-nonsense charade to play out.

Get over the show, get over your ego, and react based on the quality of work, not the superficial stuff that doesn't matter.

Trust is such a valuable asset to have with your business partners, and it is always a two-way street; be the first to demonstrate that, and you will make a huge statement during the embryonic days of partnering.

SO WHAT ARE YOU GOING TO DO ABOUT IT?

Write your thoughts here:

Put an End to Corporate Ass Kissing—Especially When It's Your Ass!

When I joined Orange, as is normal, I inherited a bunch of agencies. As is always the case when a new marketing leader comes in, all the agencies were, to some degree, worried and even paranoid about losing the account. Some rightly so, others not. I joined Orange on the back of my success at Nintendo with Pokémon and ITV Digital with Al and Monkey. While both of those marketing campaigns were huge successes, I was at that time a two-hit wonder with less than four years' experience in consumer marketing, having trained as an accountant.

I really liked some of the people at the advertising agency I inherited—their hearts were in the right place, and I genuinely felt they cared for the Orange brand. But they cared more for their retainer, and by so doing, they were far too accommodating to my point of view and far too focused on making me feel important. I could have said Wednesday was Monday, and I think they would have agreed. So many times, they hung on my every word and complimented me on my wisdom and insight. They arranged chauffeur-driven cars to pick me up and collect me and waved me off from their doorstep. I hated all of that. When I started talking to some other agencies, the ones I was attracted to were those who clearly stated their point of view—people who argued with my perspective, disagreed with me violently at times, and were not focused on stroking my ego but on doing great work.

I hate corporate ass kissing. I didn't need to pay the extortionate agency fees for people to tell me I was great, when I knew I wasn't. I was paying for creativity, innovation, great execution, and—above all else—honesty.

I am almost (but not quite) as proud of the honest, feisty, and pragmatic relationship I shared with all my agencies as I am with the great work we did together. Don't put up with corporate ass kissing, and tell the agencies that none will be tolerated. If I had my time again, I would state that loud and clear to every new agency within five minutes of meeting them. Maybe I could have saved them from themselves, if I had?

This principle works for good people you want to hire too. Chris Moss is considered a marketing guru in the UK, having been the marketing person behind the launch of both Virgin Atlantic and Orange. He was a freelance consultant when I was keen to get him to come and help us at ITV Digital. He agreed to meet me, but he did say he had been talking to Sky (our biggest competitor) for several weeks about working for them.

Chris came to meet me. I took him for a pint and a sandwich in the local pub, and we hit it off instantly. We talked about what we were trying to do, and it was evident how he could help us with his track record. I told him I wanted him to join, and before the day was out we had agreed on fees, we had a work plan, and he was on board.

Chris later told me why he chose ITV Digital over Sky. He said, "Sky was courting me for several weeks. They would take me out to sophisticated restaurants like the OXO Restaurant and the River Café and buy me expensive lunches, and our conversations would meander on and on. But you weren't interested in all that glamour. You took me to a local pub for a sandwich, and in that moment, I said to myself, 'I can work with this guy.'" A few hours later we had the whole thing settled. Chris always believed in trusting his gut, and he liked to see people who moved quickly.

Chris was an invaluable mentor and friend to me during my ITV Digital days and since. That was one of the cheapest but most productive lunches I ever had.

KEY LESSONS

Don't be seduced by the established VIP protocol that can exist with so many of your agencies and advisors. It clouds your judgment. So don't just ignore it, strip it away, and focus the relationship on the quality of their work.

For any firm or agency that works for you, stipulate the mandatory requirements of how you expect to be treated in the relationship. These should include words like honest, feisty, demanding, pushy, non-subservient, equal, etc. Also include a list of "do not under any circumstances do X." For example:

- Do not under any circumstances walk me to the door and wave me off—leave me at the elevator.

- Do not under any circumstances ask my PA what my favorite sandwiches are—I will gratefully eat whatever you provide.

- Do not under any circumstances say yes you agree with me when really you think I am talking crap.

Also, remember: A steak and a bottle of 1994 Chateau Mouton-Rothschild don't always beat a pie and a pint. Good people like to work with people who are down to earth, people of action, and people they connect with far more than the people with fancy trappings.

SO WHAT ARE YOU GOING TO DO ABOUT IT?

Write your thoughts here:

Don't Worry About the Optics . . . Sometimes Just Say No

One of the times when I wasn't very proud of myself was shortly after Mother had presented the Monkey scripts to us at ITV Digital (see page 140). We loved them, we were planning on making them, time was running tight, and we needed to go, go, go. Then my boss was concerned about the optics (how it would look to others) of us appointing a new agency without a pitch. I said I wasn't concerned, these things happen, but he wanted to be seen to be doing the right thing. I kept saying we didn't have time to do a pitch, we needed to get on and make the ads we all loved, but he was adamant that we needed to get other agencies to at least have exploratory discussions with us. So we came up with a brief document and asked three or four agencies to spend only one week thinking about it and come back with some initial thoughts. We weren't looking for a full creative presentation (like Mother had given us), just some initial ideas and thoughts.

So we put these three or four agencies through this process. We did clearly explain to them that we had received an idea we liked, so there was no deception at all. But quite honestly, we just didn't have time. We had fired our agency five weeks before our rebranding campaign was due to air. We had found a new agency and a great idea in less than a week, and yet here we were now with four weeks until the launch going through this loop for the optics of looking as though we did due diligence. It was crazy. It was madness, and I didn't feel at all good about it . . . but I didn't stop it, as I should have. As I said, we did tell the agencies that we had already received one idea that we liked, but we wanted to have some broader conversations before we finally decided.

The agencies came back a week later, and we had some decent conversations with a couple of the agencies. But I had fallen in love with the Monkey scripts, and the reality was that it was very unlikely that we would switch horses again. It was like when you are first truly in love—you don't have eyes for anyone else. I was smitten with the Monkey campaign, and I knew it was what I wanted to do; with hindsight, the other pitches were a waste of everyone's time.

The way we should have managed the optics was by doing exactly what we did—produce a great advertising campaign that drove brand love and gained significant market share. It also won campaign of the year. No one ever questions the process when you produce stunning work.

KEY LESSONS

Fight hard for what is right and don't go through a process for appearances. It's wrong and a waste of people's time to go through a process that is unlikely to pay dividends.

In today's fast-paced world, you just don't have time for worrying about the optics and managing perceptions by going half-heartedly through an accepted process.

SO WHAT ARE YOU GOING TO DO ABOUT IT?

Write your thoughts here:

. . . And Sometimes You Just Have to Say YES

Shortly after Motorola joined Product (RED) I was working late in the office when I got a phone call from Bobby Shriver, co-founder of Product (RED). Bobby was one of the Kennedy family, nephew of JFK and son of Eunice Kennedy Shriver and Sargent Shriver, who founded the Peace Corps. Bobby is a fabulous person, and his heart is absolutely in the right place, but he is also a little intense—in a nice way. I wouldn't change anything about him—his intensity is part of his charm.

Bobby rang me, and the conversation went something like this . . .

"Jeremy, Jeremy, this is Bobby."

"Hi."

"I am having dinner with Brett Ratner, and he wants to help us at (RED)."

"Great. What does he want to do?"

I quickly went to Brett Ratner's Wikipedia page to remind myself of his films. The list was longer and more impressive than I had imagined.

"Well, he is going to make some TV commercials for you free of charge, he is going to get all his famous friends on board, and he will make a series of TV commercials with them for you." Bobby listed a bunch of A-list names that we could never have imagined getting—and certainly not for free.

Brett Ratner clearly has a very impressive resume as a film director. He had recently just directed *X-Men: The Last Stand*, the TV series *Prison Break*, and the *Rush Hour* films. This was cool, but here I was thinking I was running the marketing for Motorola; I didn't even know we needed a TV advertising campaign, and here was Bobby having dinner with a director and planning with him to make a bunch of TV commercials for me. Now admittedly, he is a great director, and I am sure he had a whole bunch of great celebrity friends, but . . . well, it was a strange conversation.

"Okay Bobby, so how can I help you?"

"Well, he needs a quarter of a million dollars to make them, to cover all the expenses; you know, the studio costs and editing costs. He is going to shoot them next Tuesday, so you need to say yes now, so he can get going."

There I was thinking they were free, but to be fair, the costs were genuine costs.

"Do we have scripts?" I asked.

"Not yet, Jeremy. We only thought this up thirty minutes ago. We haven't even finished coffee yet."

"If you don't want to do this, I can offer it to one of the other (RED) partners," Bobby said, "But I need an answer now."

So here I was presented with something that would be either fabulous or awful. There was no process, no purchase order, no brief, probably no need, there was nothing. It was an idea that was barely thirty minutes old, hatched over dinner, but it sounded very exciting, and I was intoxicated by the potential.

At this type of moment, you have to take a deep breath, close your eyes, cross your fingers, and take a gamble. My grandfather (or Pop, as we called him) used to take me to football (soccer) games growing up and always used to tell me you cannot score if you don't take a shot. So, I impulsively said yes.

"Sure, Bobby. But I do need to send someone down to the shoot, just to help out with some of the product features and the specifics of our products."

I didn't go to my boss to get approval. I didn't even tell him until I found out he was in LA on the same Tuesday. I got him to pop into the studio, and he actually appeared in one commercial with Salma Hayek. That may have been my subconscious get-out-of-jail card, because if it had all gone horribly wrong, he was complicit now. He couldn't fire me for an ad campaign in which he appeared alongside Salma Hayek.

As it turned out, the commercials were pure genius. We had Chris Rock, Kanye West, Penelope Cruz, Salma Hayek, and more, the likes of which we would never have gotten in a million years on our own or for free. The commercials were brilliant. Kanye rapped . . . "To keep the H.I.V.s from becoming A.I.D.S. they need the A.R.V.s—A.S.A.P.! When you hit the S.T.O.R.E. buy R.E.D. Translation: buy this Moto (RED) phone, and it helps fight AIDS in Africa."

Chris Rock spoke very excitedly straight to the camera . . . "You can save a life by making a call. YOU! YOU—STUPID—YOU! You never did anything good in your life. Use (RED), nobody's dead."

With such compelling films it was then easy for me to find the money to book media to run them. They were the work of a genius and most importantly they drove sales.

SAY YES MORE

This story reminds me of the central idea of the book *Yes Man*. In it, the main character, Danny Wallace, gets chatting to an old man on the bus. Wallace believes he has received real enlightenment when he is told the secret to happiness is to "Say YES more." Just those three words. I do think there is a magical element to that advice. Just "Say yes more."

There are always so many reasons to say no. Sitting here I can think of twenty reasons why I should have said no to Bobby. I do think I was a little cavalier, crazy, maybe reckless, to say yes so quickly—but it worked out fabulously. What if I had said no and missed this opportunity? What would I have been . . . cautious, yellow-bellied, appropriate, and even more irresponsible for not capturing this amazing opportunity for the company? Which list of adjectives do you want associated with you?

The bottom line for me was that my bet was only $250,000. I know that is a lot of money in some regards, but it wasn't for us as a huge global company. If the ads hadn't worked out, we would have just used them in online marketing with a small media invest-ment. So my downside was small and relatively controlled . . . my upside was huge.

Even now when I look back at the option presented to me, surely you have to take that bet, don't you agree?

I also believe that this immediate decision showed Bobby what type of partner we were, and I believe that, as a result, we were always the first partner he thought of when a great opportunity arose. Again, it was a demonstration of trust that helped us to quickly form a very strong partnership that would serve us well.

KEY LESSONS

Sometimes you have to trust your gut, relinquish control, and place a few bets—just make sure you know what you are betting on. In my experience, I tend to bet on people and on ideas. In this story, I bet on Brett Ratner and his ability to attract high profile friends, and for that group of creative talent to produce a fabulous result. And I bet on the confidence I could feel emanating from Bobby. Bobby always delivered. I always trusted Bobby.

You can't win the lottery if you don't buy a ticket.

SO WHAT ARE YOU GOING TO DO ABOUT IT?

Write your thoughts here:

It's Okay to Ruffle a Few Feathers

One of the biggest challenges in the video games industry is managing the software inventory. Sixty-five percent of sales come in the first four weeks of a game, and it typically takes four weeks from manufacture for a game to hit the retail shelf, so you have to basically make your call on how many units you are going to sell before a title is launched. If you get it wrong, you end up having to significantly mark down the price of the excess stock to clear it. The cost of goods is quite low now because everyone uses discs, but back in the late '90s when we sold our software on cartridges, the cost was much higher, so the financial implication of clearing excess stock was hugely important.

The first game I became involved in after I joined Nintendo was *Killer Instinct*. The title had launched, and sales were well below expectations. We had made about a £2 million profit on the full-price sales, but we were looking at losing all of that through discounting the huge quantity we had remaining. So we were, at best, only going to break even on this product that was supposed to be one of our blockbuster titles that year.

It was imperative for us to work out deals and promotions and anything humanly possible to clear the quantities we had left for as much money as we could. Normally, the older a game becomes, the lower the price you can charge, so speed was critical—we needed to do some deals fast. We probably had about 400,000 units left in our warehouse at that time. All of our retailers had stock, and so there was no natural replenishment going on. Our sales team knew this was a hard sale to make and, in my opinion, were not applying enough attention to clearing it. They had moved on to the next new thing that was a far easier sale. As Commercial and Finance Director, the sales team did not report to me, and I was becoming increasingly frustrated at the lack of progress from them—but even more so by their apathy towards the problem.

I was sick of the I-can't-sell-it mentality. One evening our warehouse manager, Dave Hodder, came into my office and casually said something like, "Any chance of getting rid of some of the *Killer Instinct*? It's taking up a lot of space in the warehouse, and I am sick of seeing it every morning as I walk into the office. It's always there staring at me."

"Yeah, I know, I was only thinking . . . what did you just say?"

"Any chance of getting rid of some of the *Killer Instinct*?"

"No, the next bit."

"Oh, well, it's taking up a lot of space, and every morning I have to walk past it on my way to the office and quite honestly I am sick of seeing it now."

"Brilliant, Dave. Do you still have dummy boxes for *Killer Instinct*?"

"Yes, lots of those too."

"Okay, so how many *Killer Instinct* do we have left?"

"Just over 420,000 units."

"Okay can you bring up 420 dummy boxes please?"

Dave returned a few minutes later with a couple of guys carrying the 420 dummy boxes.

"Why do you want these?"

We went around to the sales team's office—they had all gone home for the day—and we built a huge pile of 420 dummy boxes of *Killer Instinct* in the corridor leading into their office, so that every day they too had to walk past *Killer Instinct* boxes stacked high.

Next morning, I went around to the Sales Director and told him that each one of those dummy boxes represented 1,000 actual units stored downstairs in the warehouse and they were a visual reminder to him and his team of the challenge that still lay ahead for us. Every 1,000 units they sold would result in one of the dummy boxes being removed.

This became their visual reminder of a key challenge we had to solve. They couldn't ignore our *Killer Instinct* problem anymore. It was staring them in the face every minute they were in the office.

It is the law of bumping into things. If something is there under your nose, you will frequently use it; apply that to your bike when you were a child, your daily tablets, or whatever. For me, if it was out and visible, you would use it. If it was put away and invisible, it was quickly forgotten.

This didn't win me many friends in the sales department, but life and work aren't popularity contests. I was annoyed at their lack of attention to the problem, and I wasn't going to avoid the issue. As Churchill said, "You have enemies? Good. That means you've stood up for something, sometime in your life."

KEY LESSONS

Make physical reminders. Use the art of symbolism to keep key priorities in mind and track progress.

I didn't win any popularity contests by building my dummy box mountain, but that wasn't my goal. Stand up for what you believe in. Don't care about keeping everyone happy—that isn't your job.

SO WHAT ARE YOU GOING TO DO ABOUT IT?

My suggestion: What is vitally important to you and your teams? Do you have a physical reminder of it in your office, so that everyone is constantly reminded of it? If not, get one.

Write your thoughts here:

Embrace the Unconventional—Encourage Customers to Stop Using the Company's Product

The week before I started working at Orange I went to the cinema, and I sat and watched the adverts before the film began. After the adverts came the trailers for the forthcoming releases, and the crowd started to get more excited as the film neared. Then when the trailers ended, there was one more advert; it was from Orange, which was greeted with booing from the audience. They booed because they didn't want another advert, they wanted the film. I was horrified. The only redeeming thing was that this advert was followed by a five-second film with a sweet message from Orange that communicated in a funny way a request for the audience to switch off their phones. That self-deprecating film received a good reaction.

During my first week at Orange, I asked about the cinema ads and, in particular, why ours was separated from the rest. I was told that we had bought the prime position, just before the film started as that is when the advertiser gets the most attention. These were called the Gold Spots because they were supposedly the most valuable position. I told the team that they may think that they are the most valuable, but I felt the position was the worst possible, based on the crowd reaction I saw and heard. We may have had the spot with the most attention, but we had interrupted their entertainment to try to flog something to them, and they were scathing in their reaction. My new colleagues had seen that reaction too, and we all recognized that by the time the crowd had been excited by the trailers, the last thing they wanted was another commercial. I felt the Gold Spots actually damaged our brand, and we were paying a lot of money to be booed. I said the only positive thing from all the advertising I saw was that people laughed when we entertainingly told them to "switch your phone off." The self-awareness of a mobile phone company telling the audience to turn their phones off was appreciated. I asked when we could move our advert to a new position and was horrified to hear that we had just signed a three-year agreement and even more horrified to hear the price premium we had paid for the most valuable position. I felt sick.

We put this issue to our advertising agency Mother. They came back a few weeks later and basically said that the strategy needs to be one of entertainment and not one of selling. There is nothing we can think of that is a good marketing or selling message that we can say at this time in the cinema experience. Consumers want to watch the film and be entertained. They, too, had seen that we received more brand value from the five-second "Please turn your phone off" message, so they suggested we combine the sixty-second advert and the five-second informational message and create a single sixty-five-second spot where we entertain the consumer, ask for the mobile phone to be turned off, and do that in a very self-deprecating way. That way consumers would at least give us credit for a little humility and for knowing our place in life.

Mother went on to present the proposed new Orange Gold Spots. The basic concept was that a group of fictional Orange executives on an Orange Film Funding Board would listen to an idea for a film being pitched to them by a big-name star. The Orange Film Funding Board would then painfully manipulate the concept of the film to promote Orange through various contrived product placement ideas, where the product was completely out of place. The payoff line was "Don't let a mobile phone ruin your film. Please switch it off." It was witty, entertaining, and full of humility.

Mother (our advertising agency) helped us secure some big names from Hollywood to appear in the adverts, including the late greats Patrick Swayze and Carrie Fisher, plus also Ewan McGregor, Spike Lee, Anjelica Huston, Snoop Dog, Ray Winstone, Jack Black, Juliette Lewis, The Muppets, Danny Glover, Rob Lowe, Dennis Hopper, Macaulay Culkin, and The A-Team. In the second season, we even managed to convince George Lucas to allow Darth Vader to appear. Most noticeably, we were able to negotiate a very low fee for these stars, as we positioned the spots as infomercials and not adverts.

I remember going to see the first screening of the commercials, sorry, infomercials, with a real audience; I was trembling as the advert approached. Were we still going to get booed? It was such a relief to hear the crowds laugh and appreciate both the humor and the humility. That campaign, with regularly updated infomercials, ran for over a decade and inspired other telecom companies around the world (including Cingular in America and Telstra in Australia) to copy the concept. It was recognized by the advertising industry with a prestigious Gold Lion award at Cannes.

As a side note, some months after the launch of these new Orange Gold Spots, I heard from one of the launch creatives for Orange that several years earlier they had tried to convince Orange management to sponsor the quiet zone carriages on trains (where mobile phones were not allowed to be used). That idea was very similar in concept to the Orange Gold Spots. A brand should know their place in society and having the confidence to sponsor places where you couldn't use the product showed that sense of humility.

So we decided there and then to create adverts that encouraged our consumers to stop using our product. Unconventional? Yes, but it was our only option.

With the Gold Spots, we were faced with a difficult situation, as we'd paid a lot of money for something but had misunderstood the dynamic at play. First, we had to acknowledge our mistake—which was easier for me as I had just joined the company. Then we had to abandon the norm and look for unconventional solutions. We wanted to deliver sales messages, but people were just not open to listening. So, we had to revert to brand films that didn't sell but rather entertained and even discouraged the use of our products. It wasn't a palatable pill to swallow, but it was one we needed to embrace. It wasn't what convention said we should do, but we had no choice unless we wanted to blindly continue with what we wanted rather than what consumers would accept.

The Orange Gold Spots proved to be incredibly powerful for Orange as a brand. They became loved by cinema audiences and reconfirmed Orange as a brand that had a point of view, a personality, and a sense of humility. That brand identity undoubtedly drove people to choose Orange. The Orange Gold Spot construct evolved slightly over the years, but the concept and payoff were basically the same for over a decade. It showed the value and longevity of a great idea.

KEY LESSONS

First of all, you have to quickly acknowledge when something is wrong and a bad decision has been made. Don't blindly continue just because you may be invested in that decision.

Realize the normal response isn't always right; sometimes you need to embrace the unconventional, which can give you an even stronger position than if you follow the norm.

Sometimes you just cannot sail against the wind, and you need to know when to change direction and make the most of a new course. Accept it, embrace it, and move on.

Don't allow your brand or your company to take itself too seriously. Know your place in the world.

SO WHAT ARE YOU GOING TO DO ABOUT IT?

Write your thoughts here:

Embrace the Unconventional—Close Your Doors on the Biggest Sales Day

I love REI, the American outdoor equipment company. I love them because of a stance they took when they rebelled against corporate America.

When I first moved to America, my favorite holiday was Thanksgiving. Thanksgiving didn't have the commercialism or stress associated with Christmas. It was simply families getting together for a two-day holiday, with a turkey dinner and some drinks.

The Friday after Thanksgiving, Black Friday, is when many retailers offer good-value one-day offers. It originally started as a way to clear old lines and ensure end-of-life items were cleared well before the Christmas holiday.

In recent years as retailers and brands have tried to maximize their Black Friday sales, we have seen more and more items attracting deep discounts, including many high-demand ongoing items. Black Friday is also no longer a single day. It has turned into a weekend, and online retailers named the following Monday: Cyber Monday. Then we saw retailers leaking their Black Friday promos a week or so in advance, so consumers could plan their hectic Black Friday dash around the shops. To get ahead of the game on Black Friday, some stores even open their doors on Thursday evening. So the beautiful, peaceful Thanksgiving is now overshadowed by the commercialism of Black Friday week (or two.) As one commentator put it, "Thanksgiving is now little more than a pre-game meal with Black Friday now the pivotal day of the week." So very sad.

Now Black Friday is also cropping up around the world, certainly in Europe and Australasia. It is the worst American export ever. I hate it. I hate it with a passion from a business point of view and from a family perspective. What Black Friday is from a business perspective is a day when brands discount the products that they would have probably otherwise sold at full price in the run up to Christmas—meaning we would all have made some profit on these sales. Instead, retailers and brands, not wanting to be left out, discount products heavily, many down to cost or below, because they cannot afford to lose market share. They take a huge amount of revenue and make very little profit, if any, which is not good for business.

What makes things worse is that, in the two weeks or so afterwards, consumers are slow to buy these products again, because (with the visibility that the Internet brings) they know what price they could have bought it at and don't want to feel like they missed out and got a bad deal, so they put off buying it. Black Friday and many other promo pricing initiatives only increase total demand a little, as many of the sales we see are just pulled forward. Hence why I hate Black Friday; it isn't good for retailers or brands trying to make a profit, and it ruins a restful family holiday.

So, after that rant about Black Friday, why do I love REI? Well, because they realized the adverse impact of it on this traditionally beautiful holiday, and they said, "We are not going to conform to this escalating practice." Instead, on Black Friday 2015, the busiest shopping day of the year, they closed all their stores. A *USA Today* article read . . .

> Outdoor gear and sporting goods retailer REI is canceling Black Friday this year. No promotions, no hourly sales, no doorbusters, no waiting in line.
>
> In an unprecedented move for the modern-day holiday shopping season, REI's 143 stores will be closed the day after Thanksgiving. The co-op business plans to launch a campaign Tuesday encouraging people to forgo shopping to spend time outside instead. With the hashtag #OptOutside, REI will ask people to share what they're doing on Black Friday on social media.
>
> REI is taking direct aim at the frenzied consumerism that dominates the holidays with a message to do the exact opposite of what Black Friday demands.

"Any retailer that hears this will be startled by the idea," says REI President and CEO Jerry Stritzke, who admits he was apprehensive about closing at first. "As a co-op . . . we define success a little differently. It's much broader than just money. How effectively do we get people outside?"[1]

Again in 2016 they followed suit and in a blog post stated . . .

Last year we started a movement for people to reconnect outdoors over the holidays. We closed on one of the most popular shopping days of the year, paid our 12,000+ employees to spend time outside, and invited America to join us. The response was overwhelmingly positive. More than 1.4 million people and 170 organizations chose to #OptOutside.[2]

This is the definition of punk. REI stood up to the establishment, said enough was enough, and called on the five percent of the world who change things to follow suit. I love that they also encouraged other companies to do the same. The temptation would have been to feel compelled to brand the initiative, to try to own it. It could so easily have been #OptOutsidewithREI. But thankfully it wasn't; they wanted to start a movement and welcomed everyone along for the journey. That's punk.

They undoubtedly won increased loyalty from their fans, they didn't trash the prices of their products, and they earned a huge amount of

---

1 Hadley Malcolm, "REI Closing on Black Friday for 1st Time in Push to #OptOut, *USA Today* (October 26, 2015), https://www.usatoday.com/story/money/2015/10/26/rei-closing-on-black-friday-for-first-time-in-its-history/74627872.

2 REI, "#OptOutside—Will You Go Out With Us?" REI website (undated post, accessed September 9, 2017), https://www.rei.com/blog/news/optoutside-will-you-go-out-with-us.

respect from so many people who want the essence of Thanksgiving back. The *Huffington Post* reported that Jerry Stritzke, REI's CEO, stated that "last year, REI saw a 100 percent increase in job applications in the 30 days after stores closed on Black Friday."[3] I am also sure they got many millions of dollars in extra sales. I know for one that they also got an extra $299, because I went into REI determined to buy something because of what they did. I emerged having spent $299 on a ski jacket. I would never have spent that money with them if it hadn't been for #OptOutside. I am sure I was not alone.

KEY LESSONS

Embrace the unconventional and do the unexpected when it is the right thing to do and is true to who you are. More and more these days, people buy into brands and what they stand for. REI stood up and showed they were different. Like-minded people were attracted to them, not because of what they sold but because of their point of view on the world. There was a morality to REI's actions that resonated with so many people who then rewarded them with their custom.

SO WHAT ARE YOU GOING TO DO ABOUT IT?

Write your thoughts here:

---

3 Alexander C. Kaufman, "REI Is Once Again Closing on Black Friday," *Huffington Post* (October 24, 2016), www.huffingtonpost.co.uk/entry/rei-black-friday_us_580e3581e4b000d0b157b3ff.

Being Overproduced and Perfectly Organized Kills the Lifeblood That Spontaneity Brings

When I moved to the corporate headquarters of Microsoft, part of the annual planning process in my group included the production of a five-hundred-line spreadsheet that all the senior leaders in our team had to complete. It stated where we were going to be every day for the next twelve months. This would enable our planning team to plan the year for us, build our *rhythm of the business* as we called it, and schedule all our standard and reoccurring meetings. At first, I suspected it was insane; within two years I knew it was.

Once the schedule was planned and locked, woe betide you if you suggested it needed to get changed. Here I was with a family of five, including three teenagers with their own lives to lead, running a constantly changing business in a world that is far from fixed, and I was asked to set in stone where I was going to be for the next twelve months. In my mind this was absurd. People need space for a little bit of spontaneity.

A new member joined our group, and he was given the finalized schedule for the following twelve months, including when he could schedule vacation. He went home and gave it to his seriously fabulous straight-talking wife, with the line, "This is the plan for where I am going to be every day for the next year and when we can take vacations." She looked at the schedule for about five seconds. "Good luck with that, I don't know where I am going to be next week with our four kids," and she threw it away with the disdain it deserved.

Another example of this craziness was in one of my company's January reviews. People were expected to prepare thoroughly; the meetings were intense, and they would become brutal if someone clearly didn't know their business. As a result, teams started to prepare well in advance of the meetings, agonizing over every word in the document and rehearsing their speech multiple times. It was a whole charade.

For the retail business, we started preparing in mid-November before we had even gone into the most critical six weeks of our year.

Our first few sessions were spent writing what we thought was going to happen in the key holiday sales season, before it had actually taken place. It was senseless. We had to rewrite our story most years as the reality often turned out to be very different from our predictions. Why would we waste our time doing this, when things would inevitably turn out different and we always had to rewrite everything?

I remember sitting in one room agonizing over every word, every punctuation mark, and whether a word hung on a line on its own. This was killing me. For fun, I calculated the estimated cost of the two-hour final grammatical scrub; it was nonsensical.

These are the types of things that Joey Ramone was referring to when he said, "Overproduced."

KEY LESSONS

Review your business and hunt down the areas that are clearly overproduced and then kill them. Bury them without a trace.

Fire the people who are creating that overengineering and redeploy that money by hiring some more rock-star salespeople.

SO WHAT ARE YOU GOING TO DO ABOUT IT?

Write your thoughts here:

The Tyranny of a Sales Forecast

One of the bullshit corporate dances that goes on almost everywhere that drives so many people insane is the one called the sales forecast. This happens after someone creates a product or service or some kind of proposition. It's new, has huge potential, and people are excited about the potential, but it is unproven. Someone has built the product on a business case that they can sell a certain quantity and sell it at a certain price. Let's say 200,000 units at $100 per unit. Someone asks the sales team if they can sell 200,000 units. Remember, these are the people whose bonus escalates greatly if they beat budget. These people, who are the most financially incentivized people in the company, are asked how many they can sell. Now there are some characters who masquerade as salespeople, and they have perfected what I call the hiss . . . the sucking in of air through their teeth while looking up to the ceiling and slowly shaking their head. "I just think that is too ambitious; twenty percent fewer is a do-able number, and I'll need some promotional funds to discount the final 40,000 units." The product group goes back to the finance team who now says the return on investment (ROI) just doesn't make sense. So the finance team says that to get back to a solid ROI, we'll need to cut the funds for the marketing campaign in half. The sales team is told their number has been accepted but the marketing has been cut. We then hear the second hiss. "Well, if the marketing is cut, we are not sure we can sign up for the 160,000 units anymore." And the cycle starts all over again.

Some salespeople become wealthy because they are often far better negotiators of internal budgets than of external sales deals.

What ultimately happens if you allow your sales team to become infested with conservative internal negotiators is that your product that has huge potential is launched with a whimper and never receives the campaign it deserves or the funds it needs to fulfill its potential. It is ultimately doomed to failure by the hiss from shallow, self-serving pathetic souls disguised as salespeople.

KEY LESSONS

Ensure you have bold sales teams who don't do their best negotiating during your budgeting cycle.

Engage sales teams early in the conceptual phase. Leaders need to step in and stop this pathetic dance early on. Don't allow this swirl to happen.

SO WHAT ARE YOU GOING TO DO ABOUT IT?

Write your thoughts here:

The Bottom Line

There is far too much bureaucracy and ass kissing, and too many processes that may be well intended but are overengineered and suck up valuable time and energy. There are too many platitudes and too many people obsessing over the process and the optics. There is just too much corporate crap going on. Too much conservative, play-it-safe job protectionism. Too much following the herd. Stop it! For goodness' sake, stop it!

Don't follow the fruitless path of conformity like a bunch of doomed lemmings. Stand up for what you believe in, place some big bets, focus on moving at speed rather than conforming to outdated cumbersome processes, and go with your instincts rather than follow the prescribed rules—because they are outdated and defunct. In the movie *Dead Poets Society*, Mr. Keating said, "There's a time for daring and there's a time for caution, and a wise man understands which is called for." I am fine with that, as long as the ratio is stacked heavily towards being daring.

Bottom line: Conformity and innovation rarely coexist. Decide which one you will pursue.

THE KEY REQUIREMENTS TO IMPLEMENTING A PUNK ROCK ATTITUDE IN BUSINESS

THE KEY REQUIREMENTS TO IMPLEMENTING A PUNK ROCK ATTITUDE IN BUSINESS

Let us pause for a moment and take stock.

We have looked at the eight elements of the punk rock movement that I firmly believe need applying in the modern business era. But this isn't quite the end of our story. There is a final section I need to share with you, if you are going to truly implement this Punk Rock attitude effectively.

This final section describes the foundational skills, characteristics, and requirements for someone to truly adopt a punk rock attitude in business and implement the lessons of the eight elements so much more effectively. The stronger your foundation, the more punk you can be. I have narrowed this list down to sixteen key requirements. As we go through these, rigorously assess yourself and your environment on each. Be brutally honest with yourself. Work out where you need to improve, develop, or change and how you are going to do it.

1. Humility: The X-factor

"People will walk through fire for a leader that's true and human."

PATRICK LENCIONI

Punk by its very nature is aggressive and in your face. In its most raw incarnation, it is likely to be too aggressive for most organizations because it can be intimidating. As John Lydon put it, "Nothing in rebellion is about gentle melodies."[1] But punk doesn't need to be aggressive if you apply a degree of care and humility. If people see that you are fundamentally a good person, whose heart is in the right place, whose motives are pure, who has charm and charisma, who isn't arrogant or conceited, who cares about people, and above all else is human and has humility, then you can apply all eight elements without worrying if you're going too far. That is why this characteristic tops my list. Let me share two stories that bring this skill to life.

I first met Drew Keith (a very senior member of Spencer Stuart in Europe) in 2011. During our conversation, I told him several of the stories I've included in this book: the Pokémon launch, twelve days to build a store, Bono and Product (RED).

The next time I caught up with Drew in November 2016, I knew I would be leaving Microsoft. I had contacted Drew to see if we could meet up, and he offered to meet me for dinner.

I arrived first, and Drew walked in a few moments later. He greeted me quite surprisingly, saying something along the lines of, "I remember all about putting Pikachu on the Nippon Airways plane, the twelve days it took you to build a store, but what have you done since we last met?"

We chatted about what we had both been doing in the intervening years. Drew is always great company. He then said to me, "I thought about you this summer."

---

1   John Lydon, *Anger Is an Energy: My Life Uncensored* (New York: HarperCollins, 2014).

"Why?" I inquired, puzzled.

"Well, I gave the graduation speech at my daughter's high school. I was going to talk about the particular attributes all the remarkable people I have met over the course of my career as a headhunter seem to share. But as I started to write down names, I was horrified to realize that in the ten years of doing this, I could only remember ten people. Only ten who were so remarkable, who truly distinguished themselves such that I remembered them."

It turns out (surprisingly) that I was one of those ten. He went on. "I thought about what made these ten people stand out, what differentiated them. I have seen thousands of intelligent, talented, creative, and ambitious people. What set these few apart? What I realized is that those few people had just one special thing in common: humility. Humility was the differentiator."

(Instantly, I told him he had a problem as my friends and family would disagree about that characteristic as far as I was concerned, so now he was down to just nine.)

But this is a fascinating insight from one of the most senior recruiters in the world. He must have seen somewhere between five thousand and ten thousand people, and he could only remember ten names. He did keep a list of truly exceptional talent that was a little longer—one hundred seventeen, to be precise—whose names he had written down after they truly impressed him in their interview. He studied his list of just over one hundred people, and he saw four characteristics. He saw intelligence, ambition, luck, and humility. But humility was the x-factor. Drew said to the graduating class, "It is my firm belief that this one ingredient is the most valuable of all. Knowing who you are, remembering where you came from, keeping your ambitions in check, respecting everyone with whom you interact, and knowing that good things will come to you simply by seeking every day in every way to do the right thing—this is how you can distinguish yourselves."

Those are valuable words from one of the world's most senior assessors of talent.

A few months earlier, Microsoft had invited Patrick Lencioni (the author of *The Five Dysfunctions of a Team*) to speak at an internal conference, and he had said the exact same thing. He said, "Humility is the x-factor in great leaders."

Let me give you another example. Shigeru Miyamoto is arguably the greatest video game designer, developer, and producer in history. He has worked for Nintendo since 1977. Miyamoto has helped create some of the greatest and most enduring franchises of all time, including *Super Mario Brothers*, *Donkey Kong*, *The Legend of Zelda*, and the Wii series of games.

Miyamoto is a very genuine and authentic human being. During my time working with Nintendo, he would occasionally agree to an interview with the British gaming press, and I would sit next to him in those meetings. It was like being in the presence of royalty. He commanded such respect from everyone who knew his work. Quite simply, he is a genius, but you could never be near him without also becoming aware of his deep sense of humility and care for humanity.

In 1998, Miyamoto was honored as the first person inducted into the Academy of Interactive Arts and Sciences' Hall of Fame. A conversation that occurred immediately after the ceremony and which was later recounted to me sums up Miyamoto in my eyes.

Miyamoto understood English to a limited extent, so when engaging with English speakers he would always be accompanied by a translator, and he would almost always default to his mother tongue. Just after the ceremony, a man and his son approached Miyamoto to congratulate him on the award.

"Mr. Miyamoto, many congratulations on the award. My twelve-year-old son is a big video games player—what tips do you have for him?"

The translator started to translate the question, but Miyamoto stopped him—he had understood. He then reached for a piece of paper and a pencil. He wrote something on the paper, folded it up, and passed it to the boy, rather than the father.

The boy opened the piece of paper and read the message. His eyes lit up, and then he looked up at Miyamoto and beamed a huge smile.

Miyamoto had written this simple message: "Play outside on sunny days." I absolutely believe that was his number one lesson about video games.

To me, this summed up this amazing gentleman. He never lost sight of the place his inventions should have in this world. He always showed a huge amount of humility and humanity. I think it takes someone special to encourage people not to use their products at every opportunity. It also shows a level of confidence and contentment with who you are and what you do.

I fully recognize that anybody who has been successful to some extent has an ego, myself included. However, I think the ability to keep a sense of humility is probably the single biggest lesson included in this book. The single biggest! So listen up: Humility is rare and magical and precious and an accelerator of success.

I have seen very few leaders who have mastered the art of being driven in business while doing it with humanity and humility. This is the holy grail for business leaders, for humility is the antidote to the abrasiveness of a punk attitude. It's not about toning down the punk; it's just that humility reassures people that the punk comes from a good place with good intentions.

Imagine two bosses who are equally demanding: Both require very high standards of performance from their team, and they continually push for better. One is arrogant—he or she gets branded a bully and resented by the team. The other has humility, and he or she is thanked by the team for pushing them to be better than they were. I have seen this to be true over and over again. Humility is the magic ingredient that shows your team and your colleagues that your motivations come from a good place.

KEY LESSONS

Humility is the x-factor that differentiates the truly great leaders. It allows you to be more demanding, because the push you give people will be received in a better way. Humility tones down the abrasiveness of the punk rock attitude without diluting the substance of Punk Rock Business and thereby enables it to be more accepted and therefore it becomes more powerful.

SO WHAT ARE YOU GOING TO DO ABOUT IT?

Write your thoughts here:

2. Attitude: The Perfume of Optimism

"The greatest discovery of all time is that a person can change his
future by merely changing his attitude."

OPRAH WINFREY

I believe in diversity. I love having a very diverse team, with just one
exception: attitude. I don't believe in any diversity whatsoever when
it comes to attitude. Attitude is contagious. Only hire people with
a great attitude. Only hang out with people with a great attitude.
Negativity sucks the lifeblood out of a team—it's poisonous. Avoid
it at all costs.

I visited our Italian subsidiary in one of my first few weeks after
joining Microsoft. I spent the day with the Italian retail team, which
was led by Silvano Columbo, a likeable and charismatic guy. There
was a palpable energy in the team and a great team spirit. I asked
our Xbox Category Manager, Evita Barra, what it was like working
for Silvano.

She said, "I love working for Silvano; he is magnificent, except for
when he sprays me with his cologne."

"Except for *when?*" Did I hear her correctly?

"When he sprays me with his cologne."

"Why does he do that?" I was totally confused. That must be
some kind of HR violation somewhere in the world.

Evita continued, "You see, if any of us are in his office, and we
become negative about something, he reaches into his desk drawer,
grabs a bottle of cologne, and squirts it at us while saying, 'Let me
spray you with the perfume of optimism and get rid of that terrible
smell of negativity.'"

Brilliant! I loved it.

Evita continued, "So you see, some days I have to go home to my
husband smelling of another man's aftershave."

Mauro, the guy who looked after our Microsoft Office business, spoke up: "And I have to go home to my wife smelling of another man's aftershave."

I've probably told this story a hundred times. For me, Silvano is the best optimism coach I have ever known. The beauty of his method is that he can call people out in a very nonthreatening way, so at the first sign of pessimism he steps in and stops it from escalating. It also allows anybody in the room to do the same thing in that same nonthreatening way. They can simply ask for the perfume or say, "watch out for the perfume" at the first sign of negativity, which enables the whole team to monitor each other for any wavering from an optimistic attitude.

Let me also be clear about one point. Optimism is not about blindly ignoring the pitfalls. There is no negativity in saying, "Let's spend some time thinking about what could go wrong and then ensure we have a plan to address each risk factor."

It is negative to say, "There is no way Paul will hit his numbers, and as a result we will miss our team goal." Whereas it is positive to say, "I am concerned that Paul will miss his sales quota as the numbers look challenging, and that could mean we could miss our team goal. So what are we going to do to help Paul close his gap or for others to over-deliver and compensate for any miss from Paul?"

The fundamental difference is that one point of view focuses on the problem; the other doesn't ignore the problem, it recognizes it, but focuses on the solution to the problem.

Also, optimism isn't blind optimism that ignores the fundamental issue. The solution to the problem may be that we need to replace Paul with a better salesperson. That's positive. Bitching never makes anything better on its own, so focus your energy on the fundamental question—how do we make things better?

As I have said before, punk rock at its heart is about making a positive change. For Punk Rock Business principles to get the most traction, they need to exist in a positive workplace environment. It is the beauty of the virtuous circle: A punk attitude needs a positive environment to thrive, and in turn a punk attitude helps create a positive environment. So don't allow the negative people and the naysayers to remain, dampen the movement, or infect the air with their terrible stench of negativity.

KEY LESSONS

Get rid of all negativity from your team. Either get people to change their negativity, or change the negative people.

Stop pessimism in its tracks and don't allow it to raise its ugly head, even for a moment—Silvano showed us how that can be done in a very positive, nonthreatening way.

When there is a problem, don't focus on the problem—that's negativity; instead, focus on the solution to the problem.

Quit bitching, start solving and resolving.

SO WHAT ARE YOU GOING TO DO ABOUT IT?

My suggestion: Always have a bottle of cologne or perfume in your drawer.

Look at your team today and identify the negative souls who are poisoning your team. You have twenty-four hours to address this issue with them.

Write your thoughts here:

3. Ingenuity: There Is Always Another Way . . . Always!

"A broken wing simply means, that you have to find another way to fly. Have a wonderful day people."

KERRY KATONA

At the height of the Monkey phenomenon (See "Champion Big Ideas through the Organization" on page 124), Fox, the cinema and television company, was launching the movie *Planet of the Apes*, and the London premiere was taking place in a week's time at the Odeon in Leicester Square. One member of my PR team, Marcus Agar, came up with the idea of trying to grab some of the huge attention that this movie was commanding. His idea was to put a building wrap (a huge poster that covered the entire building) on the four-story Capital Radio building that was next door to the Odeon, with Monkey dressed up in a *Planet of the Apes* costume. The tagline on the movie poster was "Control the Planet," so we adapted that to "Control the Remote."

We loved the image, and it was true to the cheeky tone that we had established for Monkey and our whole campaign. What made it even more fun was that the filmmaker was Fox, a sister company to our fierce competitor Sky and part of Rupert Murdoch's empire.

Murdoch was already very sensitive to Monkey; the campaign had already shifted market share from Sky, and it was now heavily in our favor. The building wrap went up on the morning of the premiere, and in less than an hour, we'd received a telephone call from Capital Radio.

Marcus came to see me, and he told me that Capital Radio had called and instructed us that they were going to have to take our building wrap down. The guys at Fox were "not very happy" and were demanding that it come down before Murdoch arrived for the premiere. Capital Radio had denied all knowledge of the content of the wrap to Fox (and I genuinely don't think they knew what we were putting up on the building), but Fox didn't care. Fox and Sky were allegedly threatening to never advertise again on Capital

Radio if they didn't pull it down. We politely told Capital Radio that we had a legally binding contract, so they couldn't do that, and we could sue them if they did. Capital Radio was in a big hole, and I did have sympathy for them. In the space of an hour, they were inundated with a series of phone calls: Fox and Sky were supposedly making all sorts of threats, and we were imploring them to honor the agreement they had made with us (and we threw in a couple of threats ourselves). In the end, Capital Radio apologized to us and said they just didn't have an option as Sky was such a large advertising spender with them, so the wrap was coming down.

We all felt despondent as it had been such a good idea and would have grabbed so much attention. We then came up with an idea. What if I rang our colleagues over at ITV News and got them to cover the removal of the building wrap as a news story? We made some hasty calls, and the news team loved the idea, but it would take an hour to get a news crew and camera operator over there. We rang Capital Radio and assured them that we wouldn't seek any compensation or remove advertising from them if they would just keep the wrap up for the next hour. They agreed as Sky had issued them a deadline to have it removed of four p.m.

So our crew got there to film the poster being removed, and that evening the story ran on the main ITV evening news. The news reporter showed the funny image coming down, stating that our friends at Sky had taken affront to it and were forcing Capital Radio to take it down before Rupert Murdoch arrived. An audience of several million people saw the controlling nature of Sky at its worst and the challenger brand of Monkey having a little fun at their expense. It was beautiful.

The beauty of the quick thinking was that we ended up gaining more coverage than we would have done if Sky hadn't acted in such a bullying way. We turned a potential disaster into an even bigger victory.

Phase two of our *Planet of the Apes* hijacking rolled into action a few hours later at the premiere. Monkey had now become a celebrity in his own right, despite him only being a puppet, just as Kermit the Frog is. As a result, Monkey had been invited to the premiere as a guest of a UK lifestyle magazine. We had made him a tuxedo, and he arrived with his puppeteer and both had their own tickets. The plan was to do a photo montage of Monkey's evening showing how he hung out with all the major A-list celebs. Monkey was a huge hit; many of the celebs wanted to have their photo taken with him, and he photo-bombed many others. He was hanging around on the red carpet and in the theatre entrance for about thirty minutes, having loads of photos taken with the stars. Then the inevitable happened. Someone from Sky or Fox took a disliking to Monkey being there and getting all the attention. Next thing we knew, Monkey and his puppeteer were being ejected by the bouncers.

"He has to go," a big, burly bouncer said.

"Why? He has done nothing wrong. He has his ticket."

"He has to go; he is not welcome."

"It's just some wool and stuffing. You cannot eject some old wool."

"Out . . . NOW!" The tone was now threatening.

So Monkey was ejected—I still don't know on what grounds, but he was thrown out. The story of his night was told a week later in the magazine. And once again the world saw the controlling nature of Sky. But Monkey's celebrity status was now in full swing.

Monkey was punk. He rebelled against the controlling nature of Murdoch and Sky, and he did it in a humorous way. He put himself out there. Well, I suppose we put him out there.

KEY LESSONS

A positive attitude sees a problem as a challenge and responds to it with ingenuity rather than despondency. There is always another way, another option; you just have to keep looking for it.

Often the problem is the key to the solution. Sky's bullying of

Capital Radio and roughing-up of Monkey was the seed of the solution. Monkey's rebellious and humorous antics were even more loved because of their stark contrast to Sky's actions.

Punk Rock Business is all about finding a better way of doing things. Ingenuity is vitally important to drive action, innovation, and smash the constraining bureaucracy.

Embrace the path of nonconformity.

SO WHAT ARE YOU GOING TO DO ABOUT IT?

Write your thoughts here:

4. Energy: The Driving Force

"Energy is contagious, positive and negative alike. I will forever be mindful of what and who I am allowing into my space."

ALEXANDRA ELLE

I couldn't stand working anywhere that doesn't have energy flowing through the corridors. And if there isn't energy flowing through the corridors, blame and fire the leaders, because that is their number one job.

There are only two types of people, energy givers and energy detractors, and I would argue there is no neutral ground in between.

Re-read the quote at the top of the page. "Energy is contagious, positive and negative alike. I will forever be mindful of what and who I am allowing into my space." Well said, Alex Elle! Don't allow anyone with negative energy to work in your team, in your department, in your division, or in your company. You don't deserve it and, more importantly, your people don't deserve to be subjected to that. You control which people they have to live with for eight plus hours per day, that's a huge responsibility.

Jack Welch, who turned around General Electric, gained a reputation as being one of the greatest hirers and evaluators of talent ever. He had five things he looked for in people: the 4Es and 1P, as he called it: Energy, Edge, Energize, Execute, and Passion. I will never know why he didn't name the fifth one Enthusiasm instead of Passion, that would have been so much neater, but I am sure he had a reason.

Anyway, my point is this: If the great Jack Welch used both the word energy and a derivative of that word (energize) in his list of five, then it must be fundamentally important.

ENERGY AND ENERGIZERS THE JACK WELCH WAY*

Welch defined Energy and Energizers as follows . . .

- **Energy**—Individuals with energy love to "go, go, go." These people possess boundless energy and get up every day ready to attack the job at hand. High-energy people move at ninety-five miles per hour in a fifty-five-mile-per-hour world.

- **Energizers**—These people know how to spark others to perform. They outline a vision and get people to carry it out. Energizers know how to get others excited about a cause or crusade. They are selfless in giving others the credit when things go right, but are quick to accept responsibility when things go awry.

Jack Welch said, "If you can't energize others, you can't be a leader." "Energy mobilizes people to action." It is as simple as that.

* Jeffrey Krames, *Jack Welch and the 4E's of Leadership* (New York: McGraw-Hill, 2005).

People use energy in two entirely different ways. Some bosses deploy negative energy as the driver, and others use positive energy as the motivator. Positive energy mobilizes me. If truth be told, I have had bosses who used negative energy to motivate me too, but that never works as well and only in the short term, because I will not put up with it for long. Bosses who use negative energy (and please note I didn't use the word leader) are taking the lazy option and deserve nothing good.

Let's get back to looking at things positively. If you run a large organization with many leaders, it is essential that you know which leaders energize their people. Who are the leaders who inspire their teams?

One day I told a strong-minded female colleague that a certain leader in our team (let's call him John) was leaving. It would soon be announced, but I wanted to give her a heads-up. She was visibly upset with tears in her eyes, and she said, "That is not good news. I will be very upset. I will really miss John, because I don't have many people like John in my life." That is one of the most touching endorsements of a leader I have ever heard, and I believe it was because John brought energy to her life.

You must find out which leaders have that impact on their people and then never let them go. It is one of the rarest and most precious skills.

ENERGY-GIVING LEADERS DO FOUR THINGS FABULOUSLY WELL

1. They create a compelling and believable vision. I love the phrase, "He has his head in the clouds, but his feet are firmly on the ground." A vision needs to be aspirational yet deliverable, and the ability to combine the two is what makes it all so compelling.

2. They demonstrate progress towards the goal. The most powerful motivator at work is when the team sees that their work is having an impact and progress towards an ambitious goal is evident.

3. They celebrate the rich contribution of the team when (and only when) it is deserved. They acknowledge the great work, applaud it, deeply understand it, and reward it. I have always hated the pithy two- or three-word emails: "good job," or "great presentation today," or "congrats." I hate "congrats" so much. If you are only going to say one word in response to my work, at least type the whole word! But seriously, all of those are pathetic superfluous pleasantries. Recognize the work with substantive comments that are specific. "I loved how you won supplier of the year; your communication during those supply issues made all the difference." "I loved the presentation, especially how you engaged the audience emotionally with all those stories—awesome! Tell me how I can help with the next phase." Take an extra ten seconds to type a sentence that shows you understood what was done.

4. They fully engage with people. Energy givers make people feel like they are getting someone's full attention. There is nothing more respectful than giving someone your full attention.

KEY LESSONS

Energy must be a constant companion to you and your team, every single day. Your number one job is to give energy and mobilize your people into action.

If you want to do great things you need energy, and lots of it. Energy will attract like-minded souls; it will create momentum, it will sustain the team when things get difficult, and it will enable them to push on when they get tired.

You need to understand where the source of the energy is coming from. It comes from the cause or the mission you pursue, it comes from the leaders who inspire, and it comes from the spirit among the team and all the experiences that are shared. It can come from the top, middle, or bottom of an organization. Success and energy are rarely far apart, so ensure everyone is creating energy.

Punk Rock Business isn't the easy path—it's a hard, exhilarating road that requires great energy but repays the effort with so much more in return.

SO WHAT ARE YOU GOING TO DO ABOUT IT?

My suggestion: Review your team and identify those who infuse others with energy and then realize their value.

Write your thoughts here:

5. Self-Belief: How Hard Can It Be?

"No matter what the problems that come up, you've got enough going on inside yourself and enough self-belief to win through."[2]

JOHN LYDON

I was having dinner with a senior sales leader within Fujitsu who was telling me about his son and how he was paying his way through college. He said his son was trading in limited edition sneakers from the likes of Adidas and Nike—and he was making something like $3,000 per month doing this.

I was intrigued. I learned that his son considers himself a small-time entrepreneur, but he is so much more than that: He is part of a complex economy of pre-owned sneakers where there are buyers, sellers, and market makers. Campless.com has even created the Kelly Blue Book equivalent (the definitive guide to the valuation) of sneakers.

Having looked into this market, the money that is changing hands is amazing. This is the training ground for tomorrow's Wall Street traders. Sneakers are being sold for thousands of dollars, and the total pre-owned sneaker market is thought to be over $1 billion. These kids can make very good money if they know the market and are good negotiators and traders.

My dinner companion continued by saying he went along to Starbucks to watch his son do a trade, and he came away in awe of his son's entrepreneurship. During our conversation, he recalled, "In our day, we worked in a bar for a few dollars per hour to pay our way through college—but not my son."

He then remarked that it was his son's attitude that made him different from when he was a student: Nothing fazed him. He was even supplementing his sneakers income stream with lots of other work, such as topiary hedge trimming.

2　John Lydon, *Anger Is an Energy: My Life Uncensored* (New York: HarperCollins Publishers, 2014), 89.

I was now confused. "What??"

"Yes, hedge trimming. We were at home the other day, and the phone rang, he answered it. I overheard the conversation, and he was clearly agreeing to do some work for a few hundred dollars. He ended the call, and I asked, 'What was that all about?' 'Oh, just some guy who wants their hedge trimming and all those shapes cut into it.'

"'But you have never done that,' I stated.

"'I know,' he said in a very unconcerned way.

"'Well, you don't know how to do it?'

"'No, I suppose not.' He shrugged his shoulders and responded with all the self-confidence in the world. 'But how hard can it be? I'll go on YouTube and learn. You can learn to do anything on YouTube.'"

That is it! The YouTube generation can learn anything at the drop of a hat.

If the senior sales manager's son were a stock, I'd invest in him.

However, let's go back to five beautiful words he used, "How hard can it be?" There is a beauty to the way self-confidence collides with naïveté. How energizing the innocence of youth is. Hold on to it, or rediscover it.

I told my team the story of this young entrepreneur, and it resonated greatly with them. In the months that followed, many would recite the phrase "How hard can it be?" when we were faced with a difficult challenge that we didn't know how to solve at that time. It became shorthand for, "I don't know how we will do it yet, but we'll work something out—we always do." It boosted our moral fortitude and even helped diminish the magnitude of the challenge in our eyes.

But let us delve into this a little deeper. How we look at a problem is vitally important. If we have a difficult problem to solve, we can allow fear of failure and perhaps our natural discomfort to make the problem seem insurmountable. The more fearful we are, the more insurmountable the challenge may appear, and we may have failed before we have even started, because of our mindset.

Why is self-belief so important to Punk Rock Business? Look, punk rockers were never self-conscious—they couldn't be. They had to have self-confidence to do what they did. Similarly, Punk Rock Business requires self-confidence and self-belief. How can you say it as it is, put yourself out there, create radically new ideas, and embrace nonconformity without it?

SELF-BELIEF IS A VITAL ATTRIBUTE

Self-belief is a vital attribute to success. The even more amazing thing is that it can be taught. There are techniques we can all use. The way you reinforce self-belief is through self-talk; remind yourself of when you have been faced with similar situations, how you overcame them, how you won through in the end, how you delivered. Go to Michael Gervais' website, www.findingmastery.net, and look at his videos on this subject.

You don't have to have the solution already to have self-belief; simply having confidence in your ability to work it out is enough. The sales manager's son couldn't give himself confidence by reminding himself of when he had previously trimmed a tree, but he could remind himself of when he was faced with something he had never tackled before and used YouTube to teach himself the skill.

KEY LESSONS

This sounds crazy to some but, to a huge extent, how you look at a problem determines how hard it is. A simple mental choice increases your chances of success greatly.

Not only do you need to learn the art of self-belief, you need to teach your team. It goes a huge way to getting them to deliver their best all the time.

Embrace the naïveté of *How hard can it be?* and train yourself how to more robustly adopt that mindset.

Embrace the uncertainty, explore the unknown, and trust in your ability to find the path to success, because it exists, and it is just waiting for you to find it.

SO WHAT ARE YOU GOING TO DO ABOUT IT?

Write your thoughts here:

6. Freedom to Excel: Never Ever, Ever Work for a Dickhead

"Shit happens sometimes, and every now and again in an audience there's one particular person that absolutely hates the ground you're standing on, and there's nowhere to go with that other than deal with it directly . . . But you have to meet the challenge."[3]

JOHN LYDON

Never ever, ever work for a dickhead . . . Enough said.

Well actually, I need to say more. This piece of advice, in itself, is worth the cost of whatever you paid for this book. Seriously: Never, never, never, never work for a dickhead or someone who is just being a dickhead to you. I have been blessed with working for many great bosses, but I have worked for some people who were or acted like dickheads too. They were almost always insecure, inept, paranoid people who tried to constrain me and others, and they made certain aspects of my life a misery. I put up with it for a while because I was able to compartmentalize it, but I would never do that again. No one has the right to make your work life miserable just because they are insecure. No one. It is outrageous.

First of all, when choosing a new job, realize that in reality you are choosing three things . . . the company, your role, and your boss. If your boss isn't someone you are inspired by, isn't someone who will make you better, isn't someone who will help advance your career, then say no. No exceptions. However, sometimes we are given a dickhead for a boss in the middle of our job, and in those circumstances, it's time to start looking for a new role (maybe within the same company) immediately. I am absolutely convinced that nothing good ever comes from working for a dickhead.

Now, having said that, you must ensure that you aren't a dickhead to work for either.

---

3 John Lydon, *Anger Is an Energy: My Life Uncensored* (New York: HarperCollins Publishers, 2014), 113.

There are two reasons for this . . .

First, no one has the right to make someone else's life a misery, and if you are being a dickhead to them, then you are undoubtedly doing that. So stop immediately. Go and see them tomorrow and work it out quickly.

Second, if you act like a dickhead, you will, at best, demotivate your team and, at worst, lose your best talent. The surest sign of a great leader is how they attract the great talent from within a company to move to their organization—and they retain the best talent, too. People in the company aren't stupid, and they know better than anyone who is inspiring, who gives the team space to flourish, and where it is fun to work. And the surest sign of a dickhead are those managers who frequently lose great talent in sideways moves.

Remember that old adage: People join good organizations but leave bad bosses.

Embracing a punk rock attitude in business is unconventional, and you need an environment where the benefits of that are encouraged rather than stifled. So this raises a huge question for you to answer. If you want to embrace many of the principles in this book in your working life, do you work in a company and for a boss where these principles could be adopted? Many can be adopted everywhere, but some organizations and some bosses are far more embracing of this approach to business. So, seek out the environments where you can really shine, and always remember that the greatest gift a boss can give a member of their team is the space to flourish. So if you aren't getting that, get out as fast as you can.

KEY LESSONS

It's this simple: Never ever, ever, ever work for a dickhead boss—it's never worth it.

SO WHAT ARE YOU GOING TO DO ABOUT IT?

Write your thoughts here:

7. Provide Great Context, Rather Than Seek to Control

"The best managers figure out how to get great outcomes by setting the appropriate context, rather than by trying to control their people."

NETFLIX CULTURE DOCUMENT

Punk is all about freedom, freedom to be who you are and to do what you like. Adapting that concept to a business environment is not as difficult as it may first appear, but it requires you to be willing to let go a little and not be a control freak.

There are two ways to manage your team: by controlling what they do or by providing them with good context and then giving them the freedom to translate that context into appropriate decisions. When I first read the Netflix quote at the top of this section, it instantly had an impact on me and made me question how I had been managing. An hour after reading it, I happened to be on a call with our Australian team.

Four weeks earlier, we had introduced a new product in a new category in North America. Sales had been a little below par, and so we were now more cautious about the product, and we were looking carefully at which new markets we would roll it out in. We had locked on just four new markets where we would launch next. We called these our wave two markets. There was far more scrutiny on these plans now, and quite honestly the product's performance in these new markets over the next two months would determine whether we continued developing products in this space or whether our participation in this category would just be a fleeting visit.

Australia had been cut from the wave two markets, much to the disappointment of our Australian team. I had previously dismissed a business proposal from them as their low forecasts suggested we would lose millions of dollars in the first year if we launched there. It was clear that their desire to launch was driven by the fact that this was the new bright shiny thing and that they wanted to chase revenue rather than profitability.

So, in response to the original proposal being rejected, they submitted a new business forecast. In my mind, their new business forecast and proposal were works of fiction: double the market share that they had previously forecast and with all promotional activities removed. It currently delivered a small profit, but now it was the logic that didn't stack up. I asked them how confident they were in the numbers, and they assured me that they were "rock solid," despite them being so different from their previous proposal a few weeks before. It was clear that the forecasts were whatever numbers they needed to plug into the model to make it look viable and stack up.

I was just about to question the validity and their commercial common sense, and ask "What did they take me for?" when my newfound context-setting mindset kicked in.

"Okay, I understand your plan. So just before we agree to that, let me explain a little more about where we are with this business. As you know, sales have been slow. We are questioning whether we can be successful in this space with this product. Our CFO is very likely to cut the funding for this project if we don't show that we can be successful in the next four markets we launch. If you want to get added to that list, then you need to understand that your performance against the numbers you sign up for is going to be reviewed at the very highest level of the company, and the future of our participation in this category will be on your shoulders as well as the other four countries."

The Australian team quickly jumped in. "Well, we didn't realize that context. That paints a very different light." They used the *context* word.

"But your numbers are rock solid, right?" I questioned.

"Er, we couldn't absolutely guarantee them. Mmmm, perhaps they are a little optimistic. Perhaps wait and see how the next four countries do after all." My context-setting explanation elicited a far more circumspect response.

So, these rock-solid numbers had suddenly become a little optimistic. A far more logical and commercially responsible point of view was now coming from the mouths of our Australian team. Twenty minutes earlier I had been disappointed with the Australians for submitting such fictitious numbers, but I wasn't anymore. I wasn't angry with them, I was livid with myself. Why hadn't I set the right context before and allowed the good quality Australian team to make a more sensible proposal? The power of setting great context was now very evident to me.

Why is context so much better than control? It comes down to three fundamental reasons. First, you attract and retain better people. Second, you have greater alignment in the team and more people can make better decisions. Finally, you move far faster.

Good people like to work in places where they are managed through context rather than control, because they can make a bigger contribution in a context-based environment. They are more informed, feel more trusted, understand the decisions of others better and can make better decisions themselves.

By its very definition, when you provide more context, more people fully understand the whole plan, so they make better decisions because they have greater knowledge of the complete strategy.

In contrast, control environments are all about top-down decision-making, often with multiple approval levels, cumbersome processes, and the inevitable slowness that this all brings. In places where a context-based mentality rules the roost, there is greater clarity of strategy, delegation of decision-making, simpler processes, and therefore much greater speed.

Netflix challenges its managers . . . "When one of your talented people does something dumb, don't blame them. Instead, ask yourself what context you failed to set."

Managing by setting context isn't simple. It requires good leaders to provide great context, which means investing time to provide clarity of strategy, assumptions, goals, plans, roles, and decision-making authority. It then requires a spirit of transparency from everyone.

Managing by setting context is far more aligned to the punk attitude. If you are encouraging people to be authentic, dare greatly, and go for it—then by definition you have to give them a reasonable amount of freedom. Control restricts freedom. Setting context gives freedom.

It is punk to explain the circumstances and let things happen as they will, leaving some room for an element of uncertainty rather than just a predictable outcome.

Clearly there are some critical issues or emergencies where a command-and-control approach is more appropriate, so there is always a balance. But you do have to choose: Are you fundamentally going to be a context-setting leader or a controlling boss? This is a critical choice you have to make.

KEY LESSONS

Context setting beats command and control nine times out of ten. It allows all the bright, intelligent people you have hired to make the best decisions possible, and if they are making good decisions, then you need to be involved far less.

Controlling managers come from the school of "I know best," whereas context-setting managers come from the school of "creating great and empowered teams." If you set good context, then the right decision is usually obvious for all to see.

Context setting allows creativity to be applied by those who are close to the frontline operation, and these are the people who have the best view of the action. Don't eliminate that source of input by being too controlling.

Understand that setting context requires you to invest the time in it, but you save all that time and more downstream by having far fewer interventions to correct things.

SO WHAT ARE YOU GOING TO DO ABOUT IT?

My suggestion: Assess your current modus operandi and decide which approach you truly believe in: context setting or command and control?

Write your thoughts here:

8. Empower Others: There Is Nothing So Powerful as Empowering Others

"The important thing is to encourage people to do things for themselves, think for themselves and stand up for what their rights are."[4]

MICK JONES

Punk rock developed for many reasons but a critical one was because it was so empowering. Punk gave the youth of the day the freedom and empowerment to be who they wanted to be and to change what they wanted to change. That was a key attraction. On the *Teen Ink* website, Frannie R. from San Diego in her article "How and Why Punk Rock Developed" sums it up perfectly:

> Punk rock is not a bad thing. For a lot of teens, it did represent rebellion, kind of a slap in the face to all those 'normal' people out there. But for a lot of people . . . It represented the freedom to dress how you liked, to listen to what you liked, to speak out about things you were passionate about. It gave kids and adults the power to show what you believed in, rather than having it all sit inside you, getting old, and stronger and turning you into a cynical, bitter person. It's empowerment."[5]

Empowerment is a fundamental part of punk rock. It's all about giving people the opportunity to speak out, act, and do what they want. Empowering employees to solve their problems and find the

---

4 Mick Jones, quoted in Steve Walsh, "The Very Angry Clash," in *Let Fury Have the Hour: Joe Strummer, Punk, and the Movement that Shook the World,* ed. Antonino D'Ambrosio (New York: Nation Books, 2012), 24.

5 Frannie R., "How and Why Punk Rock Developed," *Teen Ink* website (accessed September 4, 2017), http://www.teenink.com/nonfiction/academic/article/470239/How-and-Why-Punk-Rock-Developed/.

most appropriate solutions to a particular situation is so effective. I learned the power of this vividly one Christmas.

John Murr, my amazing HR partner, suggested that I give all my team members a gift card at our Christmas party in 2014. I asked, "Why?" I thought we paid them well—plus, we were putting on a free party for them and their spouses. I didn't understand why we needed to give them a gift card on top of that. I wasn't being a scrooge, but I just didn't understand why it was necessary.

He told me that a sales team that operated very close to my sales team was being given a $300 gift card at their Christmas party, and he didn't want our people feeling left out. This other team was experiencing very challenging times; they had missed all their bonus targets as the product wasn't living up to expectations, and it was a gift to try to keep their morale up.

I said I still didn't want to, but John kept coming back to it. I would have preferred to give them an actual gift—wouldn't that be far more personal than just a chunk of money?

In the end, I succumbed—but with conditions.

The evening arrived, and an hour or so into the party I was handed a microphone.

"I want to thank you all for coming out this evening and celebrating the holidays with us. It is great for so many of us to be joined by our spouses, who are the unsung heroes of Microsoft. We all work hard and put in long hours, often travelling around the world, being away from home, and it is our spouses who hold the fort and cover for us and allow us to do the amazing work that we are doing. I therefore want to recognize all the spouses this evening on behalf of Microsoft and thank you for all that you do to support your partner and thereby support us at Microsoft. So, I have a gift for every person in my team. When you leave this evening, you will be offered a bag that has an envelope in it. In that envelope is a gift card. Please take one with Microsoft's best wishes and thanks, but you can only take one if you promise to do two things. You must promise to spend the money on your spouse or your children over the Christmas holiday and thank them on behalf of Microsoft for all the sacrifices they make during the year. Second, you have to send me a photograph of what you spent it on, so that I can see how you put that money to good use. The best three photos that I receive will win another gift card to do it again."

I got a great reaction that evening when they realized they had received $300 and an even better reaction after the holiday break. I received photographs of families out scuba diving, at restaurants, spa breaks, and a host of other treats. It was evident how well this idea had been received, but for one of the most powerful incarnations of it, I had to wait three years.

Three years later at four thirty p.m. on a Friday afternoon, Scott Nielson, a guy who worked in my group, knocked at my office door and asked if he could have five minutes. He came in, and I sensed that he was a little emotional.

He started, "I just want to thank you, and it is long overdue. Three years ago, I don't know if you remember, but you gave us a gift card for Christmas under the strict condition that we spend it on our spouse or our family. Well, I took one of those gift cards. That Christmas break my wife and kids were on vacation in Hawaii with my parents. My parents are quite wealthy, so there is nothing I can ever buy them that they really need or want. But because you had given us the rule that I had to spend it on the family, I paid for us to all go on a snorkeling trip. We had an amazing day, and it was so great for me to see my parents swimming around and having fun with their grandchildren. We had money left over from the gift card, so we bought the video memento of the day as well."

Scott then told me how his dad had passed away about ten months ago.

He continued, "A few weeks ago I was talking to my son about some of our best experiences and memories, and he asked me what mine was. I thought about it and then told him it was when we went snorkeling with his grandparents and what a fabulous day that was." Scott told me that his son agreed, and they got out that video and watched it, remembering the day and remembering their father/grandfather.

Scott continued, "So I just wanted to come and say a belated thank you. Twenty-five years from now, I don't know where you will be, or what you will be doing, but I want you to know that you can look back and know that you made a difference, and what you did meant an awful lot to me."

This was a very nice thing to say to me, but totally undeserved.

All I did was arrange for Microsoft to give people a small amount of money, I acknowledged the importance of their families, and created an environment for them to do something good for the people they love. I empowered, and they delivered, yet I got a huge amount of undeserved credit. Effectively, I just said, "I am giving you the task of being creative, go do something fun for your family." I delegated everything to the individual; they were the ones who were creative, they were the ones who executed, yet I got the credit. It was crazy! That's the power of empowerment.

Just do this for your team if you can; it has a huge impact.

The gift was very symbolic, and $300 for each family with the challenge I set was so much more impactful than giving a $300 gift card that no one would remember spending.

What I also realized through this process was that I found out many people in the team had so much more creativity than they had shown in their work and so much more than I had given them credit for. I saw new depths in many of them, and from then on, I looked to encourage those people to apply that same creativity in their work. I now knew they had it in them, and it was my job to extract that regularly from them.

KEY LESSONS

People want to be empowered, and if you empower people and give them the opportunity and the responsibility to respond to your challenge, more often than not, they will amaze you. When they are empowered, they will feel increased responsibility, accountability, and ownership of the task. They realize that they are being entrusted with a key task, and they don't want to disappoint. In this story, they didn't want to disappoint their family, and I am sure that their family held them accountable to deliver a great experience.

SO WHAT ARE YOU GOING TO DO ABOUT IT?

My suggestion: Give this gift and set the challenge to your team the next time you have an opportunity to do so.

Write your thoughts here:

9. Sell, Sell, Sell: We Can All Sell, We Learned at an Early Age, Don't Stop Now

"Everyone lives by selling something."

ROBERT LOUIS STEVENSON

Late one evening in 2006, I was in my office in Motorola's Libertyville campus engrossed in a difficult conversation with one of my team members. My phone rang, and I saw that it was my wife calling. Not wanting to be distracted from this critical moment, I pressed ignore. Twenty seconds later she rang again. Again I pressed ignore, I just couldn't take the call at that time. Twenty seconds later it rang again—now I was quite worried; she would never ring three times like that if it wasn't an emergency. I explained the situation to my colleague and asked to be excused for a moment.

"Hello. Is everything okay?" I said, somewhat worriedly.

"Hi, Dad."

It was Francesca, my youngest daughter, who was five at the time.

"Hi, Darling, what are you doing using Mom's phone?"

"I had to talk to you."

"I cannot talk now Fran; can we chat when I get home?"

"When will that be?"

"Well, not for a while, probably about eight thirty p.m."

"I'll be asleep by then, so we'll have to talk now on the phone," she said assertively.

"I cannot, Fran, I need to go back to my meeting."

"Well, I need to talk to you, Daddy." I hate it when the kids add Daddy on to any sentence to make you feel guilty.

"Well, just quickly, tell me what do you need to talk to me about?"

"Okay. Well, you know how we cannot have a dog because you are allergic to dogs?"

"Yes, that's right."

"Well there are now hypoallergenic dogs. Lauren at school has one."

"What's a hypoallergenic dog?" I asked dismissively.

"It's one that they have bred specially so that people with allergies aren't allergic to them. So we can now have a dog—isn't that good news?"

"Fran . . ."

"Isn't it, Daddy?"

"Fran, can we talk about this tomorrow?"

"No, I need to talk to you tonight about it."

"Fran . . . where's your mother?"

"Anyway Daddy, what we need to talk about is which type of hypoallergenic dog we are going to get." (See that presumptive close?)

"Fran, I cannot do this now."

"So Daddy, I have been researching on your computer all the different breeds of hypoallergenic dogs, and we need to decide which one we like best."

"Fran, I really need to go."

"Daddy, I really need to talk to you about this, and if you're not going to get home before I go to bed, we need to do it on the phone now."

"Fran . . . Fran . . . Fran!"

"Daddy, the first one is . . . "

"Okay. Hang on, I have an idea. You print off a sheet about each of the dogs you have researched on the computer, give each one a score out of ten, and then leave the pile of them on my desk. And when I get home, I will do the same. Then when you get up in the morning you can compare your scores with my scores and see if we like the same ones."

So she agreed to do that, and I was allowed to get back to my meeting. Anything just to get back. She knew I would never hang up on her, and she kept exploiting that fact.

The next evening, I was again home late, and she was in bed. My wife was out and a high school girl who lived across the road had been babysitting.

As I walked her back across the street, I asked if Fran had mentioned how she had forced me to score these hypoallergenic dogs. She said, "Yes. She told me all about it. She says she has narrowed it down to two breeds." Then, holding her thumb and index finger slightly apart to demonstrate a small distance, she added . . . "And that she has worn you down, and you are this close to giving in, and she is sure you will give in by the weekend."

I was staggered. Here she was selling me on a dog, having destroyed the only real objection we had ever put in her way, and then going for the close by pressuring me to agree.

The next day, we spoke. I was going to throw up new objections.

"What happens to the dog when we go on holiday?"

"That's what kennels are for Daddy."

"Who will take him for walks?"

"We will, we promise." She had by now brought in reinforcements: her two big sisters.

"Well, I don't want to have to pick up dog poo. I am just not doing that."

"You won't have to; I am going to do that."

"But you won't."

"Yes, I will. You will never have to pick up poo, I promise."

"So, can we Daddy? Can we? Please can we? Alex wants one, Maddie wants one, Mommy wants one."

"I can assure you, your mother doesn't want one."

"Well, that still means three of our family do and only two don't."

That weekend I sat in a dog enclosure at our local pet store with a really cute cockerpoo—a cross between a cocker spaniel and a poodle. I had to sit there with the dog for five minutes to ensure I wasn't allergic. Sadly, I wasn't. An hour later, Charlie came home with us. Fran had won. She had launched a masterful sales campaign and succeeded. Here she was demonstrating the refined and honed selling skills she had developed over her full five years: leveraging the relationship, providing a complete analysis of the market, expert handling of objections, working on key influencers to gain their support for her argument, even disputing my sole decision-making authority, and pushing for the close.

This story is a simple everyday example of having something to sell—and if you analyze your days, you will see that you are regularly selling. Whether it is to win a new job, gain support for your work, secure a place on a project team, convince your hairdresser to squeeze you in when there are no appointments left, or get the credit card company to waive that late payment fee—we all need to sell regularly! The skills of selling are critical tools that go hand in hand with success. As Robert Louis Stevenson said, "Everyone lives by selling something."

The sad truth of the matter is that so many people think they are bad salespeople or don't know how to sell. You do! We all do! We learned how to sell at an early age. Francesca was an expert by the time she was five; I bet you were too. The problem is that many people don't realize that they can sell, so they assume they cannot. Or more likely they don't like to sell to people they don't know for fear of being told no, because it hurts when we are told no. So recognize that, or whatever it is that is holding you back, and tackle it.

Now having said that, I will state that selling is an art. It isn't hard, but it is an art, so it needs to be practiced and refined.

KEY LESSONS

Every one of us is selling something or needs to sell something regularly. Every one of us can sell—we learned it naturally, and we learned it at an early age—we just may not feel comfortable selling to people we don't know for fear of rejection. Get over it!

Selling is not a slimy, sleazy activity to be avoided but a powerful skill that propels your cause, your product, your career, or you. Selling is an art. Practice it; make it feel natural and unforced.

A footnote to this story is that about eight years later, when Francesca was thirteen, she and I were out one evening walking the dog together. Charlie did a poo. I passed Fran the bag and said, "Come on you do it, that was one of the conditions when we got the dog, you said you'd pick them all up."

She just looked at me incredulously. "And you believed a five-year-old? Seriously?"

So now she was questioning my judgment from all those years ago . . . and rightly so.

SO WHAT ARE YOU GOING TO DO ABOUT IT?

Write your thoughts here:

10. The Art of Business Summarization: Tell Your Story in 30 Seconds or Less

"If you can't say it simply, you don't understand it well enough."

attrib ALBERT EINSTEIN

The Art of Business Summarization is born from the suppression of the irrelevant so that the relevant can shine through. That was a key lesson I learned from Mitch Koch, my first boss at Microsoft.

The stripping away of everything that is superfluous and unnecessary was a key tenet of punk rock. Punk songs often had no more than three chords, no long introductions, the lyrics were straight to the point, and most songs lasted less than three minutes. In the same way, anything that clutters the crisp articulation of the business situation should be brutally cut as it distracts from what is really important.

There are plenty of things I am not good at—but this is one area where I do believe I have a skill. When I was about to leave Microsoft, one of my colleagues recounted our first-ever interaction. She said she had come to a business review and embarked on a ten-minute monologue about a particular issue and what they were going to do about it. When she concluded, I then responded by saying, "So what you are saying is that X is happening because of Y and so you are going to do Z to overcome it. Is that right?" It took less than fifteen seconds.

She told me she immediately asked herself why she hadn't said it so succinctly and simply, and she resolved there and then to improve that skill.

I regularly did this succinct paraphrasing of my team's long-winded summaries for four reasons:

1. I wanted them to see how the art of business summarization helped synthesize and simplify a problem and the action plan, so that they would work at that skill.

2. I wanted them to be more focused on the real crux of the issue, and I did that by trying to strip away the parts of their story that I felt were less relevant.

3. Starting my response with "So what you are saying is . . ." was my way of endorsing their plan (after all, all I was doing was repeating parts of their plan), albeit just the critical parts as I saw it.

4. It was my way of testing my grasp of the situation. Often, my teams would modify my simplified summary as I had stripped away something vitally important that I hadn't grasped initially. By doing this, it helped me validate my understanding.

TELL YOUR STORY IN 30 SECONDS OR LESS

One of the absolute most important skills people need to develop in business these days is the ability to succinctly articulate the status of their business, its performance, the issues and opportunities, their plan, and the critical success factors for their business, their project, or whatever it is that they are doing.

Businesses are complicated. It is a skill and an art to be able to synthesize all the information into a concise expression of the story. As the statement earlier says, less is more. It is all about stripping out the unnecessary detail and side stories and focusing solely on the really important stuff. I believe you have to be able to deliver a comprehensive but succinct story in thirty seconds on any subject in your business. Your people need it, your customers need it, and your boss should demand it.

I have always said that people who cannot succinctly express their business situation cause me concern. I fear that they don't really understand what's going on, and if they don't, then how can they really know what they need to do?

I love a quote that has been attributed to Mark Twain (among other people), "I didn't have time to write a short letter, so I wrote a long one instead." He is right; there is an art to stripping away the irrelevant facts, data, and dialogue so that the critical issues get the sole focus they deserve. Focusing on the critical issues brings clarity; and clarity, in turn, puts focus on the necessary actions. The reason I say this is because there is an art to finding the fine dividing line between stripping away too much or too little. As Einstein purportedly said, "Everything should be made as simple as possible, but no simpler."

The art of business summarization is a talent that allows Punk Rock Business to be more effectively implemented. It gives people confidence in you because they see your deep understanding of a situation and, as such, they trust you more and are more willing to let you lead. It also helps greatly when driving speed and action (see Element 4 "Drive Speed and Action" on page 139) because too much time these days is spent looking backwards at what has gone on, assessing the facts, and trying to understand the past, with far too little time spent trying to create a better future. State the past and identify the insights quickly. By so doing, you allow more time to be invested in planning for a better future.

Why do people spend more time looking at the past, rather than planning the future? I don't really know, but I suspect that too many people feel comfortable in the precision that comes from facts and data. They would prefer to stay in that space rather than move quickly into the far more complicated and uncertain but valuable area of planning for the future and working out how to improve things. It is far easier to be assured that your point of view of the past is accurate than it is to express your point of view of the future and be open for criticism and debate.

KEY LESSONS

There is no clearer way for people to demonstrate their deep understanding of a situation than by their simple explanation of it. The art of business summarization brings focus to the key issues and the key elements of the plans that people need to execute.

Continually strive as a team to master the art of business summarization as it helps provide alignment and clarity across the team and that, in turn, brings speed. If you want to move at the speed that punk demands, you have to get good at articulating things quickly and succinctly.

SO WHAT ARE YOU GOING TO DO ABOUT IT?

Write your thoughts here:

11. Storytelling: Practice the Art

"He who wants to persuade should put his trust not in the right argument, but in the right word. The power of sound has always been greater than the power of sense."

JOSEPH CONRAD

Storytelling helps bring your message to life. It is the style to go with the substance of your message. It can be the emotion that makes the rational argument far more compelling.

The art of business summarization is all about bringing focus to the key salient points, but that needs to be complemented with the art of storytelling. Storytelling brings emotion and soul to the basic facts.

If you are going to be successful, then like it or not you are going to have to be a good communicator. For me, the best communicators I have seen are great storytellers. Learning the art of storytelling takes time, effort, and practice, but it is such a valuable skill to acquire and hone.

However, if you have nothing interesting to say, then you are totally screwed. One of my colleagues was once promoted to a very senior role in the company in a new department, and he had to give a presentation to the top one hundred fifty people in this huge company within a couple of weeks of assuming the role. Clearly, he didn't have an in-depth view of his new area, but he was a great presenter, and he constructed and delivered a great presentation that had everyone fully engaged and laughing. One of his closest friends found him afterwards and said, "What a great presentation and so typical of you: fabulously delivered, very engaging, but absolutely no substance." Brutal, but true.

So, let's assume you have something worthwhile to communicate—that's an important starting point. But you may still be screwed if you cannot communicate it in a compelling and engaging way. In today's media heavy, noisy, cluttered, and always-on world, where attention spans are shorter than ever before, you need to be able to grab people's attention and make them not just hear your words but feel them too and remember them. You must ensure that you leave them with a lasting impression.

Today, you need the capability to be a great orator and the flexibility to deliver that in a one-on-one conversation or on stage in front of thousands of people. Today, you must be an articulate writer, whether in a fifty-page white paper or a 140-character tweet.

The power of effective communication is not about what the communicator says; it is (and always has been) solely about what the recipient hears and feels and the response it stimulates. Writing, speaking, and presenting in a manner that inspires a response in others is damn hard. It doesn't come easy to most of us. So you have to study, learn, practice, review. Study, learn, practice, review. Study, learn, practice, review. And storytelling is, in my mind, at the heart of all good communication. Storytelling is hugely powerful.

When we were launching Orange Phone Trainers (see story "The Key Reasons Why Orange Phone Trainers Succeeded" on page 113), we needed to sell the concept of the Phone Trainer to all 1,852 people who were currently our store salespeople and whose role we were now changing. I went to every single training session to explain the concept, because if they didn't buy into the concept and deliver on our promise, the idea would never have landed.

We weren't just making them the heroes of the story, we were looking to them to deliver a fabulous experience for our customers. We were spending millions of pounds communicating to the British public the experience we would now be delivering in the places formerly known as Orange Shops. We were raising the bar and setting high expectations for what would now be occurring.

We had a good story about why we were making this change—we had the insight, the context, and the consumer need, but we needed to appeal to them emotionally as well as rationally. We were betting on them, and we needed them to know that. To do that, I wanted to show them how we were making them the heroes in our

TV advertising campaign that we were developing. They needed to know, and more importantly they needed to feel, how much confidence we had in them and how important they were in our eyes.

I desperately wanted to show them the TV campaign as it would bring this concept to life for them, but we hadn't even shot the commercials yet. So, I had nothing to show. All we had were the scripts. Someone suggested I put the scripts up on a PowerPoint slide and read them out, but how dull would that have been? They needed to be acted out. Someone else suggested that I take along one of the agency creatives to do that. But I wanted to show the employees how invested I was personally in the initiative, so I made one of those suggestions I immediately regretted—I would act them out myself: After all, the creatives had done it fabulously well when they had presented them to us.

The following day I got the creatives to present the scripts to me again. This time I studied intently how they did it, where they put their vocal inflections, and how they moved. I then imitated them and soon became comfortable doing it. They effectively gave me a crash course in acting.

One week later I was on the campaign trail. I was telling the store staff the story of our next marketing campaign and how they were going to be the stars of that story. I was explaining the context and rationale for the change, all with solid logic—then inspiring them by way of the funny and engaging adverts that made them the heroes—all acted out by yours truly.

The more I presented, the more comfortable and confident I became and the better reaction I received. I even had to act them out to our Orange France colleagues where every line had to be translated by my French counterpart.

FIVE KEY STEPS TO BEING A GREAT PRESENTER

The first two points relate to the content of your story and the final three are all about how you execute the delivery of it:

1. **Have something worth saying.** It is vitally important that the content in your presentation has substance. Is it interesting? Is it beneficial to the audience? Will it stimulate a reaction from them? Be certain of this. Check it out with a sample of the audience weeks in advance. Realize that it takes time and hard work to prepare a substantive presentation. As Mark Twain may (or may not) have said, "It usually takes me more than three weeks to prepare a good impromptu speech."

2. **Say it in a memorable and engaging way.** I usually end up with far too much content in my presentations a week or so before I give them, and that is when I really start cutting the content down, which I find hard to do. For every single story or slide, I ask myself: Am I excited to see the reaction of the audience to it? So it isn't just a question of whether it is an important message, it is as much a question of whether I am delivering it in a way that will result in a visible reaction, laugh, gasp, surprise, whatever. If I am not genuinely excited, because I don't think it will stimulate a reaction, then I usually cut it.

3. **Get well trained.** You can be trained to be a better presenter. Find a good trainer and hire them. If your company will not pay, then pay for the trainer yourself—it is a very worthwhile investment. If you cannot afford it, then there are loads of great books on the subject—or you can even just go on YouTube. I would also tell you to take acting classes . . . seriously, I mean it. Nothing helps you get outside your comfort zone more than learning to act.

4. **Stick to your style.** I screwed up often in my early years and still do sometimes. It always happens when I deviate from my natural style. My natural presentation style has these elements: lots of slides with very few words on them, most with photos, images, or simple charts. I look at the slides as nothing more than a visual accompaniment to what I am saying. The presentation itself is a story that I tell, committed to memory, with my slides being my cue card to each story or key point. No teleprompter notes,

(continued)

because whenever I use those, I drift into reading exactly what's there, and I lose all sense of speaking naturally. I typically go through about two hundred slides in forty minutes, and despite the maths of twelve seconds per slide, it doesn't feel rushed or like a blur of flashing images. That's my style. It may not be yours, but find yours and stick to it. Every time I've been disappointed in recent years, it's been when I succumbed to using a teleprompter or someone constrained me on the number of slides I could use. Find your style and stick to it.

5. **Practice.** "I found a book entitled *How to Succeed at Anything*. It only had a single page inside, and on that page was just one word. PRACTICE." —Anonymous

This is the bottom line—you need to be able to command an audience, to hold their attention, and to inspire them. For that, you need to be able to create a good story that has both substance and style, so that it has the potential to be memorable and excite people. Then once you have that, it is all about the delivery. This is where you end up relying on the training you have undertaken, the familiarity you have with your own style, and the hours of practice you have put in. If you have done each of those, then you should be confident in your ability to do a fine job.

KEY LESSONS

Communicating and storytelling are inextricably linked, and they are skills that need to be practiced and honed, so create a plan to become a better communicator by being a master storyteller, both verbally and through the written word. It will take time, but it is one of the most critical talents you can harness.

SO WHAT ARE YOU GOING TO DO ABOUT IT?

Write your thoughts here:

12. Be Inquisitive and Learn

*"I don't think much of a man who is not wiser today
than he was yesterday."*

ABRAHAM LINCOLN

You may believe that learning is not a very punk thing to do; after all, the punk bands didn't even learn to play their instruments. However, bear with me and I'll explain over the next few pages.

When I was eighteen, I was leaving high school, and I didn't want to go and do a degree at university. I was sick of exams and studying. I remember distinctly one of my (not so close) school friends saying on his final day at school that he "had a thirst for learning and couldn't wait for university." I thought that summed up why he was full of crap! I was worn out and fed up with learning, and I had no interest in books. (I know this is ironic given I am now an author, but things change!) I liked, no I *needed* to be active and be with people. Books were the opposite of that: When reading, you are stationary and alone.

Looking back now, if there was one thing I would do differently in my career, if I had my time over again, it would be to read more books and be far more disciplined and dedicated to learning. I learned from experience, I learned from my mistakes, I learned from working with really smart people, but I didn't learn enough from reading, certainly in my early career.

Reading, whether you like it or not—and I don't really—is still a great source for learning new things and testing your previously held beliefs. I think many of the greatest minds in the world are pathological readers.

What I learned from the CEOs at Microsoft is that they all have a passion for knowledge and an insatiable appetite for learning. I joined Microsoft several years after Bill Gates had handed over the CEO role to Steve Ballmer, but Bill's *Think Weeks* were legendary.

Bill's Think Weeks were twice yearly affairs where he would go off into isolation, away from work, family, and friends, and spend a week reading papers submitted by employees from across the company. He would read and think about the future of Microsoft and the future of technology; he would strategize and think through big challenging problems. He would sometimes work eighteen- or even twenty-four-hour days, often going through over one hundred papers in the week. He didn't just read them; he commented on them and circulated his thoughts across the company. It was considered a great honor for your paper to be chosen for Bill's Think Week, and people would wait with great anticipation for the thoughts and musings of Bill to come out of his cocoon of solitude. Think Week spawned many of the greatest ideas to come out of Microsoft at that time. One of the 1995 Think Weeks inspired Bill to write a paper entitled, "The Internet Tidal Wave," which led Microsoft to develop its Internet browser and usurp Netscape as market leader.

Steve Ballmer's learning style was very different from Bill's. He had an amazing mental capacity for understanding all the businesses in Microsoft in immense detail. He seemed to be able to absorb knowledge and data in an osmosis kind of way and then in an instant, compute the solution to a problem we had been agonizing over. His breadth and depth of understanding of our businesses was so impressive.

When Satya became Microsoft's third CEO, he introduced the concept of a growth mindset and demanded that we all embrace it. He implored us to be "always learning and insatiably curious," and I do believe that it was this inquisitive pushing that has boosted Microsoft's fortunes in recent years. Satya didn't see how people could be creative and innovate if they weren't curious and interested in the future. I was listening to Satya speak one day, and he said that he was "defined by his curiosity and thirst for learning." I thought that was really cool, then I remembered my school friend using that same phrase "thirst for learning."

Thirty years on I had an entirely different reaction to that phrase "a thirst for learning." Satya and my old school friend were so right, and the eighteen-year-old me was the one who was full of crap.

However, in my mind, there are two types of learning: one where you learn something and simply replicate it, and a second type where you are curious about something, study the subject, and innovate to make things better. I have less interest in the first, but I am excited by the second, as that is where new things come from.

This type of watch, study, and innovate process is exactly what the early UK punks did and was at the heart of the movement they created. There was a group of Sex Pistols fans who followed the group in the early days, and they helped popularize punk in the UK. They became known as the Bromley Contingent, as that is the part of London many of them came from. However, this group of fans wasn't satisfied with purely watching and enjoying the music. The Bromley Contingent included Siouxsie Sioux and Steven Severin (of Siouxsie and the Banshees), Billy Idol, Pamela Rooke (aka Jordan, an English model/actress famed for her work with Vivienne Westwood), plus others who would make their own marks on the punk scene. They watched what was going on, and what they saw inspired them to innovate and create something new in that embryonic genre.

That's the type of learning we need today. The world is changing so rapidly with the digital revolution that learning how we did things in the past is often of little value. Curiosity combined with innovation is more powerful than knowledge and experience. It is summed up in the following phrase (which appears to be a paraphrase of Alvin Toffler's own words and of Toffler quoting psychologist Herbert Gerjuoy's words in *Future Shock*), "The illiterate of the twenty-first century will not be those who cannot read and write but those who cannot learn, unlearn, and relearn." Today what matters is not the extent of our know-how, it's the speed of our learn-how.

Each year we brought approximately one thousand of our worldwide retail sales team members to a sales event. I was trying to make this very point about learning to my team, talking about how the world was changing greatly in the digital revolution and we all needed to invest time in our own personal development if we were to stay relevant and effective in the new world. I flashed up a slide that (jokingly) announced my retirement date in four years' time. I said I had realized that what had worked in the past was no longer relevant in the future, and we all needed to learn, unlearn, and relearn. I said, "I have come to the realization that I will be of no use to anyone in four years' time . . . " I hadn't finished my sentence when Neil Thompson (who was one of my direct reports) shouted out and heckled from the audience, "Four weeks more like!"

Everyone laughed, including me.

I replied with a smile, "What I was going on to say was . . . I have come to the realization that I will be of no use to anyone in four years' time (not four weeks as Neil thinks) unless I dedicate time to keeping up with how millennials and Gen Z are living their lives."

I added with a cheeky tone, "I am so looking forward to doing Neil's annual review."

But the postscript to this story is that I did dedicate two hours per week to learning and personal development. It helped me keep up with developments and stay somewhat in touch with the exploding technological world that is second nature to the millennials.

KEY LESSONS

Probably the biggest lesson I learned from my time at Microsoft was the fundamental importance of learning, the value of being curious, and the need to dedicate time to read and think. This isn't natural for many of us who are in a rush, but it is vitally important. We must all dedicate time to learning for the good of our business and for the good of our careers.

Don't just learn and replicate, rather study and innovate.

Today isn't about the extent of our know-how, it is all about the speed of our learn-how.

SO WHAT ARE YOU GOING TO DO ABOUT IT?

Write your thoughts here:

13. Relationships: These Are Always at the Heart of Business

"All things being equal, people will do business with, and refer business to, those people they know, like and trust."

BOB BURG

Relationships are fundamentally important in business. They are an accelerator in so many ways that stretch across the eight elements of punk rock, and that's what makes them crucial. Too often, businesses treat their customers, suppliers, and agencies as just someone they do business with, but the reality is that they can be so much more if you invest the time in those relationships. Customers, suppliers, and agencies need to be considered valued partners, and I have always wanted to be perceived by our suppliers, customers, and agencies as their best partner. We may not have always been their biggest partner, but I always wanted to be their closest or favorite partner.

This was brought home to me most tellingly in May 2014 when we were planning the launch of Xbox in China. We had invited many of the leading Chinese retailers to come to Seattle for full disclosure and planning meetings. Our Chinese sales team had a very strong relationship with Mr. Lan, who was our most senior contact at JD.com, a huge online retailer driving unbelievable growth for themselves and for Microsoft. Mr. Lan and I had met a few times, and we had chatted about golf, as we are both keen golfers. I extended an invitation to him to play at my golf club during his trip to Seattle. We played at Sahalee Country Club, which had hosted a major championship (the US PGA Championship in 1998, which was won by Vijay Singh). Mr. Lan really appreciated the hospitality, and we had four hours together where we cemented our business partnership and even built a friendship despite some inevitable language barriers.

A few months later I was travelling to Shanghai on a very brief trip to meet with our team there. I received an email from our China team leader asking me if I could find time to play golf with Mr. Lan, who had heard I was coming to China and wanted to return the hospitality I had shown. I sent an email back saying there just wasn't time in my schedule; in addition, Mr. Lan and JD.com were based in Beijing, and I was only visiting Shanghai, so we would have to play golf on my next trip.

The following morning I received a call, not an email, insisting that we needed to find time in my schedule to play golf. Those are the types of calls I normally like, but I explained we just couldn't do it, there was far too much that I needed to accomplish during that short trip.

Then I was educated. "No Jeremy, you need to play golf. It would be a great dishonor if you didn't allow him to reciprocate and entertain you the next time you were in his country. He will fly to Shanghai, but you must play golf with Mr. Lan." There was an assertiveness in his voice that told me I had no choice. I relented, and we had a fabulous morning at an amazing golf course. Our partnership went from strength to strength. In the space of three years, they went from our 279th largest partner to one of our top ten. Obviously, it wasn't all due to those golf games, but they helped cement a special relationship that always ensured our teams paid special attention to our mutual business.

My Chinese team taught me an important proverb that is so true:

你不会和一个从未吃过饭的人做生意，也不会和一个从未喝过酒的人做朋友

This means "You will not do business with someone until you have shared a meal, and you will not be friends with someone until you have shared a drink." Having seen the expenses that my teams from China have claimed over the years, I know they go the extra mile to live up to that proverb. I never worried about the relationships we had with our Chinese retailers, but sometimes I worried that my team members were giving their livers for the company.

KEY LESSONS

Relationships make you go the extra mile to find opportunities to grow together. They make you think of that partner first rather than their competitor when an opportunity arises. They sustain your partnership if you encounter a problem. They are fundamentally important to everything you do. Sustain them.

SO WHAT ARE YOU GOING TO DO ABOUT IT?

My suggestion: Look at the list of your top partners and ask yourself how deep those relationships go at every level. If they are not really strong, then what are you going to do about it? Draw up a relationship map for each of your partners and identify and assess the key relationships. Look at the gaps that exist, prioritize where you need to improve, and get your account manager to build a plan.

Write your thoughts here:

14. Friends: Co-workers Aren't Enough, Colleagues Aren't Enough, You Need True Friends

"Friends are the people who make your problems their problems, just so you don't have to go through them alone."

UNKNOWN

One of the most undervalued elements of your working life, and one of the greatest pleasures I have been lucky enough to experience during my career, is the joy that comes from working with people who become great friends.

If you are going to spend your working life trying to do great things, pushing yourself and others, putting yourself out there, and being nonconformist, then being surrounded by friends, rather than people who are just colleagues or co-workers, makes everything better.

When you work with friends, the journey is so much more enjoyable and the successes so much sweeter. However, probably the greatest value that friends bring is when difficulties and challenges arise.

This was very evident when we were representing Motorola in Las Vegas for the Consumer Electronics Show (CES) in January 2008. We were holding a hugely important press conference. I was going to unveil a new product (the MotoZine) that we had high hopes for, and we desperately needed it to be successful as the world was moving away from the stylish feature phones like RAZR (that had been the core of our recent success) and towards new smartphones.

We had been planning this press event for over two months; we had built a strong presentation and a number of really compelling videos to bring the MotoZine to life. Then, just before the press conference, the team got together, and we knew it all came down to the next hour. So as the lights came up and the walk-on music started, the whole team was understandably a little nervous.

I walked on stage in front of about eight huge TV screens to present our new products to a room full of the industry's press and analysts. At that moment, the TV monitors that were going to show the videos and slides started to go black, one after another. I looked to the back of the room, and my teleprompter also went black. I was living my worst nightmare. I bumbled through a few words trying to remember what I was supposed to say, but not only had the teleprompter and the screens gone blank—so had my mind.

Two good friends of mine (Jim Wicks and Melissa Gardner) who had been lead members of the presentation team were chatting at the back of the room, initially oblivious to the nightmare that was unfolding.

I managed to find a little composure and suggested that we should wait a few moments while we resolve the technical problems. I joked at that point that it was times like this that I wish I had said yes to hiring some Vegas dancing girls to come on stage to fill the gap—I did get a laugh, but I was dying a thousand deaths inside!

At this point, my friends realized the situation and sprang into action. Jim Wicks began to walk towards the stage contemplating whether he should imitate one of those dancing girls to give me time to recover my poise. Melissa Gardner ran behind the stage and started checking to see if any of the five hundred or so cables had come unplugged!

As it happened, a couple of technicians from our crew casually stepped forward and turned the screens back on. A few then went off again, but the technicians kept turning them back on, and we had enough to continue.

I started again, far more flustered than I had been originally. My mouth had dried up horrendously, and I was just trying to get through the first ninety seconds to the point when my first video would be played. I introduced that first video, and then I had two minutes to regain my poise and drink enough water to be able to speak properly.

The video was very well received, and that gave me confidence, so we pulled through. Ultimately, we were pleased with the event, the press responded positively, and their focus was on the exciting new phone and not the technical problems, but the technical issues had come so close to screwing it all up.

It subsequently transpired that a journalist from the online blog site *Gizmodo* had thought it would be funny to use an infrared remote to turn off the screens during our press conference, and he repeated the juvenile prank on the show floor the following day. He then posted the video of everyone's concerned responses, and he received a bad reaction from most people. It was known as Gizmodogate, and the journalist in question was banned for life from CES.

I have a firm belief that we all need friends at work, not just colleagues or co-workers—friends, people we hang out with outside of work because we like to spend time with them and people we know we can count on. We spend too much time at work not to have true friends that we can enjoy the experience with. We work in a pressurized environment and those are the places when you most need a support network of true friends. I know this is true instinctively from my career, but research supports this claim. Christine M. Riordan, a professor of management at the University of Kentucky whose research focuses on labor-force diversity issues, leadership effectiveness, and career success, has studied this thoroughly. She stated in an article, "We all need friends at work," after studying research that people are far happier when they have friends among their co-workers and as a result "their job is more fun, enjoyable, worthwhile, and satisfying."[6] Her article cited a Gallop poll[7] that suggested close work friendships boost employee satisfaction by fifty percent and "People with a best friend at work are seven times more likely to engage fully in their work."

---

6 Christine M. Riordan, "We All Need Friends at Work," *Harvard Business Review* (July 3, 2013), https://hbr.org/2013/07/we-all-need-friends-at-work.

7 Gallup, "State of the American Workplace," *Gallup News* (February 2017), http://www.gallup.com/services/178514/state-american-workplace.aspx.

Riordan identifies that friends create for each other a strong support network that helps both professionally and personally that has wide ranging benefits. "Whether rooting for each other on promotions, consoling each other about mistakes, giving advice, or providing support for personal situations, comradeship at work can boost an employee's spirit and provide needed assistance."[8]

KEY LESSONS

The moral of the story is that when you are in need, co-workers may help, colleagues will support, but friends jump into action, even when that may be personally embarrassing (Jim dancing) or they haven't got a clue what they are doing (Melissa the electrician). True friends don't sit on the sidelines when a friend is in need—they spring into action, because your problem is their problem.

And of course . . . always tape over the infrared ports on the TV screens when doing an important presentation.

SO WHAT ARE YOU GOING TO DO ABOUT IT?

Write your thoughts here:

---

8 Christine M. Riordan, "We All Need Friends at Work."

15. The Five Roles of the Mature Leader

"Leaders don't create followers, they create more leaders."

TOM PETERS

At Motorola we had hired a very senior leadership guru to come and conduct a two-day leadership training session with our senior team. During that event, I learned a really powerful leadership framework—the only surprise was that it didn't come from the guru, but from Ray Roman, my colleague who ran the sales function.

Ray was asked to talk for five minutes on his leadership principles. He started by holding up the book *King, Warrior, Magician, Lover: Rediscovering the Archetypes of the Mature Masculine* (HarperSanFrancisco, 1990) by Robert L. Moore. Now I haven't ever read that book, but it identified the four roles a mature man needs to play in his life. Ray went on to say that he had created a similar framework to assess the archetypes of the mature leader, and he had identified five: warrior, wizard, creator, simplifier, and muse. He said leaders need to be multifaceted and able to play different roles in different circumstances. For him, every leader needed to be able to play all five roles well at different times every single day. The framework really resonated with me, and in the years since then I have documented what I remember of Ray's descriptions of each archetype and added my own words and descriptions to the framework. I've documented the archetypes and my current articulation of each here.

These are the five archetypes:

1. **The Warrior**—A person who is swift into action, who will fight valiantly and fearlessly, who does not shy away from battles and conflicts. They do this because they have a natural competitive desire to deliver the business performance and always meet their goals, which thereby enables them to claim victory.

2. **The Wizard**—A person who is an expert in their field, whose capabilities astound their colleagues, whose understanding and grasp of the business situation sometimes appears almost magical. They can make the exceedingly difficult appear amazingly effortless.

3. **The Creator**—A person who is innovative and when faced with a difficult problem is excited to search for (and usually finds) a new way to achieve the goals. They question, they ideate, they test, they refine, they love using the phrase . . . "What if we . . . ?" They never tire of searching for the solution.

4. **The Simplifier**—Commerce these days is complex, multidimensional, and can be just downright complicated. The simplifier can focus in on what really matters; they strip away the irrelevant so that the relevant can be clearly seen. They turn difficult tasks into much easier ones by simply reframing them, providing focus, and breaking them down into manageable pieces.

5. **The Muse**—A person who inspires trust, who inspires collaboration, and who inspires great performances. A person who is a confidant, a leader, and a collaborator. A person who applauds others rather than seeking recognition for themselves. A person who is highly regarded by their colleagues and partners for their market insight, their drive, their direction, and selfless teamwork ethic.

I believe these are the roles that I need to play as a multifaceted leader, and they are what I want my team members to embody too. The words matter. We don't want salespeople who will try hard to hit their target. No. We want warriors who are swift into action, who will fight valiantly and fearlessly, not shying away from the battles and the conflicts. The words are emotive, deliberately so. I could have written that I want people with the five following characteristics: determination, knowledgeable, solution-oriented, orderly, and encouraging—that's the same five things, right? No! There is a huge gap between someone who is determined and a warrior; an ocean between someone who is knowledgeable and a wizard.

I use this list in three ways. First, I use this framework to assess myself at the end of each day. I ask: Have I been a warrior when challenges arose, was I the wizard I would have expected, did I help in the creation process, did I simplify things for my teams, and did I help energize and inspire the people I worked alongside? If I cannot immediately see that I played at least four of those five roles in my day's work, then I feel disappointed, and I commit to doing better tomorrow.

Second, I regularly share this material with my team and any new recruits to my team, as it sets expectations with them of the type of leader I want to be, but in so doing it also outlines the breadth and extent of the leader I want them to be. As you will see from the quote at the top of the story, leaders don't need followers, they need to create more leaders. So, by showing them the type of leader I aspire to be, they see the traits I admire, and they see my expectations of the leaders in my team. I know many have adopted this framework or a slightly modified one for themselves.

Finally, I use this framework when I interview potential new recruits to our team. I try to assess how strong they will be in each of these areas. Do they have that hunger and determination to really be a warrior? Do they have the expertise to be considered a wizard? Do they have that creative gene? Are they able to make the complex understandable? Will they enhance the team spirit and inspire the team to greatness? What I have found is that if someone doesn't clearly tick at least four of these boxes, then I am just not excited about hiring them; and if that is the case, I always say no.

KEY LESSONS

Be clear about the leadership roles that you expect yourself to play and create a daily list that you regularly review yourself against. Use as much or as little from my list as you like.

A key role you have as a leader is to create more leaders, so invest the time with your team to help develop that skill with them and be intentional about the types of leaders you want your people to be.

SO WHAT ARE YOU GOING TO DO ABOUT IT?

Write your thoughts here:

16. Demand Excellence

"The way you get a better world is, you don't put up
with substandard anything."

JOE STRUMMER

During my time at Motorola, I went on vacation to Cancun, Mexico, with my family over the New Year's holiday. The president of the Mexico operation of one of our business partners who sold our phones knew I was visiting. He had insisted that his regional sales lead would collect me and my family from the airport and be available if I needed any assistance during my stay.

I asked the regional sales lead for recommendations for local golf courses; as he was a keen golfer he offered to join me, and we arranged a game for the morning of December 31st.

When I arrived at the golf course a few days later, he warned me that he needed to join one conference call in an hour or so and that it would interrupt the round of golf. He was very kind in asking my permission, and he was very apologetic, but I assured him I didn't mind, I understood.

After about the fifth hole, he dialed into the call, and it was comical seeing him try to swing the club with a phone trapped between his shoulder and his ear. I gestured to him to take a few holes out and just stay in our golf buggy. I didn't mind playing a few holes on my own.

The call was, naturally, in Spanish, so I didn't understand anything he was saying. But it was evident that it started in quite a tense tone, but changed to a great deal of relief and pleasure towards the end of the call.

After he finished the call, he again apologized profusely.

"Everything okay?" I inquired.

"Yes, it is now. You see, yesterday was our end of quarter. Our region has beaten its sales quota for the last eighteen quarters, but yesterday at 5:30 p.m., we found that one of our big sales hadn't come in on time and we were 217 phones short. It was horrifying, but we were determined that we weren't going to let our winning streak end."

This was a big business, and I estimated that this region's quarterly sales must have been in the hundreds of thousands. So to be within 217 phones of the goal was agony.

"What did you do?" I asked.

"Yesterday evening the whole team went down to the district where all the bars are with a bunch of phones; we went around and sold them to the people in all the bars and restaurants. But we needed to get them activated by midnight for them to be registered, so we were having to do that for the people too. We had about five hours to sell and activate 217 phones."

"Did you succeed?"

"That's what that call was about; we needed to ensure that all the phones we had sold had actually registered on the network. And yes, we beat the target by seven phones. So we retained our winning streak."

The attitude of the team was inspiring to me, and over the next two hours, I learned more and more about their sales culture and how they set a high performance bar, which they then lived up to.

There was never any question of them allowing themselves to miss their goal. Once they signed up to a target, there was no doubt they would hit the number (perhaps there was a question of *how*), but they always found a way.

Throughout this book, you have read stories about my colleagues who didn't settle for average but strove for greatness. Their unwavering commitment to deliver excellence is like a common thread that runs through all the pages. From the very first story, you saw how Guto, with a store to build in twelve days, didn't settle for average; he wanted to build a stunning retail experience, and he did—the store won North American Retail Store of the Year. Nick Moore didn't want just one Phone Trainer in each store, he wanted to change the whole environment. The customer rep in the Orange call center didn't go home and put her feet up, she went and searched for the returned phone with the distraught mother's baby photos. Bobby and Bono set out to help eradicate AIDS in Africa.

Do you know what the most beautiful thing is about all of these people and many of the other people in this book who did amazing things? They didn't allow themselves to be realistic. Guto didn't ask whether it was realistic to build a store in twelve days—if he had, he wouldn't have started. The call center customer rep didn't allow the realistic chances of finding that returned phone stop her from searching. If people only attempted what was realistic, nothing great would ever be achieved. As Will Smith said, "Being realistic is the most common path to mediocrity."

All of these people set high performance bars for their organization, their team, and most importantly for themselves. They demand excellence and are unaccepting of mediocrity. For them, good enough is never good enough. There is probably nothing more important when striving for success than to hold yourself accountable to a high performance bar and demand excellence of yourself.

One key reason I joined Microsoft was because of the performance bar it set for itself. I was inspired to read that one of their values was "taking on big challenges and seeing them through." I wanted to be part of that.

While organizations and leaders should demand excellence from their teams and are vital in setting that performance bar, it is one hundred times more important to fill your teams with people who self-impose this demand for excellence on themselves. There are some people who perpetually deliver excellence and whose attitude is summed up in a quote attributed to Vince Lombardi: "Every job is a self-portrait of the person who did it. Autograph your work with excellence." You don't have to work with people for long to recognize whether they have that valuable gene.

I always tell my teams: With high performance comes high expectations. Every time we deliver, we show we can be trusted to deliver, and inevitably more will be expected of us. Don't be disappointed by that, embrace it. We get a new bar against which we can measure ourselves and show people how good we are and what we can achieve. We had a statement that was shorthand for the excellence we held ourselves to. "There is no room for average in tech; there is no room for average when you are changing the world; there is no room for average in our team."

Always demand excellence.

KEY LESSONS

Demand excellence in everything you do. If you start to accept mediocrity or try to pass off average as being good or seek to excuse or explain away substandard performance, all you are doing is redefining who you are and what you want to be known for.

Demanding excellence is great, but recruiting people to your team who self-impose that requirement is so much more important. Search them out and attract them to your team.

In everything you do, don't you dare be realistic, at least not immediately and not until you've allowed yourself to dream of how magical it would be to deliver excellence.

SO WHAT ARE YOU GOING TO DO ABOUT IT?

Write your thoughts here:

THE FINAL WORD

"All you need is one guy to stand up and say 'F*** this,' and everyone goes: 'Voice of a generation—thank you. I've been thinking that, I never had the guts to say it.'"

HENRY ROLLINS, BLACK FLAG

Punk Is an Attitude

For me, punk was never about the music or clothes or piercings or colored mohawks: Punk was and is and forever will be an attitude. A beautiful, authentic, pure, and dynamic attitude.

Many of the lead protagonists of punk knew that.

Mike Watt, who has been described as a "seminal post-punk bass player" said, "Punk was not really a style of music, it was more like a state of mind." But Joe Strummer nailed it with his response to the question: "Is punk rock something you grow out of?" He replied . . . "Never. You see, punk rock is like the Mafia. Once you're made, you're made. Punk rock is not the clothes or the music. Punk rock is an attitude, the 'don't-give-me-any-bullshit-because-I-can-see-right-through-to-the-heart-of-the-situation' attitude. Because I'm wise to the tricks of the world. We're sick of all the bullshit. Give us some truth. That's the energy of punk rock."[9]

9 Mark Anderson, "Afterword: The Virus That Cures: The Revolutionary Alchemy & Eternal Relevance of Punk," in *Beyond the Music: How Punks Are Saving the World with DIY Ethics, Skills, and Values,* ed. Joe Biel (Portland: Cantankerous Titles, 2012), 183.

That is why punk rock is so applicable to business. As I hope you have seen throughout this book, Punk Rock Business has nothing to do with the music but everything to do with the attitude that spawned it and made it indelibly etched in our minds.

That attitude can be seen as the red thread through all eight elements and the sixteen characteristics we have covered. Let me show you.

1. Have a cause: Punk attitude is about seeing that something is wrong, being angry about it, but having the passion and drive to want to do something about it. Punk has a point of view. Punk wants a better world and seeks a positive change.

2. Create a movement: Punk attitude is about joining forces with like-minded people and setting about changing the world or just their world. Punks don't sit on the sidelines smoking pot—they are out there fighting on the dance floor for what's right.

3. Create new and radically different ideas: Punk attitude is optimistic, it's believing in better, it's about taking responsibility for making things better, and most of all it's about creating things that are new and better than before.

4. Drive speed and action: Punk attitude is all about going for it. Decide, act, move! Next!

5. Say it as it is: Punk attitude means that your words are always pure, stripped down, and no bullshit. It's no-nonsense. Nothing false and nothing superfluous.

6. Be authentic: Punk attitude is about people who allow themselves the freedom to be who they are. That's almost the only rule of being punk: to be yourself and be comfortable being who you are.

7. Put yourself out there: Punk attitude, because it requires you to stand up for what you believe in, means that you inevitably will be exposing yourself to both praise and criticism. Punk attitude doesn't allow the fear of criticism to constrain the potential you have.

8. Reject conformity: Punk attitude is about being unaccepting of the crap that goes on every day that is pointless and futile and bland. Punk attitude questions and punk attitude is intolerant of bureaucracy.

Bottom line: Punk is an attitude. An uncompromising, unrelenting, unquestioning, unwavering attitude about everything we do at work or in our personal lives. It is about optimism, believing in the impossible, believing there is always a way, believing in the power of the human endeavor, and above all else believing in yourself. It is about taking accountability and making things happen—making things better.

—

THE DIFFERENCE BETWEEN NORMAL CORPORATE LIFE AND PUNK ROCK BUSINESS

You've read the book. You know what is required, and you're surely equipped with enough of the skills to start being more punk. And I sincerely hope that you have started to embark on the journey of implementing some of it already. If not, what's stopping you?

As we wrap this up, there is one thing I want to check with all of you. Realize how fundamentally different Punk Rock Business is compared to normal corporate life. Look at the following list and realize the magnitude of the difference. The attributes of normal corporate life are in the left-hand column and those where we embrace a punk rock attitude in business are in the right. Compare them: Which column do you want to be associated with?

Normal Corporate Life	PUNK ROCK BUSINESS
Settling	STRIVING
Dullness	VIBRANCY
Improvement	DISRUPTION
Conservative	RADICAL
Play it safe	PLAY IT LOUD
Best decision we can make	BEST DECISION WE CAN MAKE—NOW!
Avoiding risks	PLACING BIG BETS
Duck below the parapet	STAND UP AND BE COUNTED
Modest plans	SCARY EXCITING IDEAS
Good	WHOA! (IT'S THE NEW WOW!)
Extent of know-how	SPEED OF LEARN-HOW
In perfect control	WHO CARES ABOUT CONTROL
Honor the processes	LOVE THE IDEAS
Evolution	REVOLUTION
Indifference	UNBRIDLED PASSION
Believe that things will get better	ENSURE THINGS GET BETTER
Seeking permission	SEIZING THE INITIATIVE
Controlling your minions	EMPOWERING YOUR ROCK-STAR TEAM
Job security	PROJECT EXCITEMENT
Apathy	GIVE A SHIT

There really is no choice for anyone with passion, vibrancy, and soul.

Punk doesn't have to be aggressive. Punk doesn't have to be threatening to people, but it does threaten the norm. It's about changing the status quo by rebelling against the accepted norms. It is one person saying, "It doesn't have to be this way," and then a group of likeminded people saying, "Yes, let's change things . . . for the better."

Punk is the Fight against Apathy and Complacency: That's the revolution we called for right at the start of the book. So go on and do these three things . . .

Go and be part of the movement to strip away the bureaucracy from business today: Don't allow it to clog up your working life. Your time is too precious to do that.

Go and fulfill your full potential and accelerate your career: If anything in this book helps accelerate your career and enables you to achieve more of your potential, then I will be delighted. I hope you feel more equipped to just go for it and try to be everything you can be. Have confidence and trust in yourself.

Go and enjoy your life more: Working had better be fun, because we spend too much of our lives doing it for it to be dull and boring. Many of the lessons also apply to other parts of your life, so apply them there too. Ensure you are doing things that really matter to you and make a difference to others. Make sure you are doing them with other exciting people who energize you and who you want to be around. But most of all be true to yourself, the genuine you. As Iggy Pop said, "They say that death kills you, but death doesn't kill you, boredom and indifference does."

Go and embrace the punk rock attitude.

Let's Go . . . !

"I don't think punk ever really dies, because punk rock attitude can never die."

BILLY IDOL

P.S. Let me know what happens. jeremy@punkrockbusiness.com

INDEX

ABOUT THE AUTHOR

This Is Me

This book is not about me. It is not an autobiography. But I do tell lessons from my career to highlight the attributes of a punk rock attitude in business. Some of you may want to understand the chronology of my career, so that you can place the stories on some imaginary timeline in your head. And maybe you want to know a bit more about me as a person. If so, read these four pages. If you don't care about these things, move on ahead.

My Career

TARMAC (1983–1991)

I trained as an accountant at Tarmac, a building conglomerate in the industrial Black Country of England. Ready-mixed concrete was exciting to me back then. This is where I learned the flow of money, the critical skill of understanding the dynamics between sales, costs, and cash flow that always determines your success. I worked with honest and good people who talked straight and wouldn't put up with any arrogance.

ANC (1991–1995)

ANC was a franchised express parcel delivery service that was subsequently sold to FedEx. I joined the finance team, and my first piece of work showed that their pricing strategy was counterproductive. The Managing Director sent me home while he considered my report. The next morning, to my surprise, I arrived to hear that the Managing Director had fired the Commercial Director and appointed me in his place. That was the start of my real business career.

NINTENDO (1995–2000)

A headhunter was trying to find a Commercial Director for the video games industry. He would never have found me at ANC through his normal searches; however, I knew a friend of his, and he introduced me. So, good fortune gave me my first foray into the world of consumer tech, which would become my home from then on. I loved the brands and products I now worked with: GameBoy, Mario, Donkey Kong, GoldenEye for N64, Zelda, Tetris, and—the ultimate—Pokémon. The last of these I suffered serious addiction to, but I have been clean for over fifteen years now.

ONDIGITAL/ITV DIGITAL (2000–2002)

The story at ITV Digital was all about how we used a knitted monkey, imaginatively called Monkey, and a larger-than-life stand-up comedian with a gruff accent to rebrand the company and transform our sales. The campaign gained huge attention and notoriety, and demonstrated the power of marketing in a way I had never seen before. Our success was ultimately destroyed by a number of things, including some dark forces.

ORANGE (2002–2004)

The task at Orange was all about helping it to rediscover its mojo. It had lost its substance and points of differentiation. We created Orange Wednesdays (a membership benefit with all the UK cinemas) and Orange Phone Trainers to once again make us stand out from the rest.

MOTOROLA (2005–2009)

I have been lucky and blessed to join companies at just the right time, none more so than Motorola. A few weeks after I arrived, we unveiled the iconic RAZR that would generate a fortune for Motorola and establish it as one of the coolest brands on the planet at that time. As they say, "It's better to be lucky than good."

MICROSOFT (2009–2017)

It was a privilege to work for Microsoft, one of the enduring all-time-great companies that changed the world for the better. When I first joined, there were moments when I thought I had joined a cult. But then I realized that, although it was huge, it still had a true sense of family and its employees cared deeply. It was fascinating because of its complexity and breadth. We operated in all four corners of the world; we competed in the video games arena against PlayStation, in computers against Apple, and in productivity software against Google and free competitors.

MY NEXT CHAPTER (2017+)

I have been working as CEO with a start-up in the football, entertainment, and digital world, and I finished writing my first book—this one. I hope the start-up will grow, the book will be appreciated, and they will fill my working life for the next few years.

My Life

Location: I was raised in Sutton Coldfield, one of the nice parts of Birmingham, England (there are nice parts). I lived in the far-from-glamorous towns of Cannock and Hednesford before moving to Southampton and working in London. Motorola took me to the Chicago suburbs. Microsoft initially took me home to the UK where we settled in Ascot (walking distance to the Queen's horse racecourse and an hour's commute to London). Microsoft then took me back to America, where we made our home in Bellevue (near Seattle). We now split our time between Chicago and Ascot.

Family: I was blessed with amazing grandparents and fabulous parents. I became friends with a beautiful young lady named Geraldine (Gerry) whom I was fortunate enough to convince to be my wife. We have three amazing daughters, Alex, Maddie, and Francesca, who inspire me with their talents and humanity. They know who I really am, and they ensure that I stay grounded.

Interests: I love sports. I played football and cricket at a decent level. Technically, I played football semi-professionally—if you count receiving £5 per game being paid. I am still an avid golfer. I go to a vibrant and exciting church. I am involved with a children's orphanage in Kenya.

Education: I went to an English comprehensive school and achieved good grades but didn't study for a degree as I wanted to get on with my career. Shortsighted, perhaps.

Little-known facts: I survived cancer. I was DNA tested as part of a murder investigation. I stole toilet paper from Buckingham Palace. I own a BAFTA. I made a citizen's arrest when someone tried to steal my neighbor's car. One of my ancestors is supposedly Abraham Lincoln. I was named one of the Top 100 most influential people in the movies by *Total Film* magazine, between Tom Cruise and Matt Damon. (It was in alphabetical order.) I had to inject my future mother-in-law's tortoise with antibiotics daily for three months because it had a cold and couldn't hibernate. (My wife and I were still dating at that time and obviously I was still trying to impress.) I lifted a car off a woman (not singlehandedly) who was having a cardiac arrest.

It's been far from dull.